WARFARE AT SEA, 1500–1650

Maritime conflicts and the transformation of Europe

Jan Glete

First published 2000
by Routledge
2 Park Square, Milton Park, Abingdon, Oxon, OX14 4RN
Simultaneously published in the USA and Canada by Routledge
270 Madison Ave, New York NY 10016

Routledge is an imprint of the Taylor & Francis Group

Transferred to Digital Printing 2005

© 2000 Jan Glete

Typeset in Bembo by J&L Composition Ltd, Filey, North Yorkshire

British Library Cataloguing in Publication Data
A catalogue record for this book is available from the British Library

Library of Congress Cataloging in Publication Data

A catalogue record for this book has been requested

ISBN 0–415–21454–8 (hbk)
ISBN 0–415–21455–6 (pbk)

CONTENTS

CONTENTS

PREFACE

The initiator of this book is Professor Jeremy Black who asked me to write it as a part of the Warfare and History series. Professor Black has also patiently read the drafts of the manuscript and tried to improve it in style and content. I am very thankful both for his initiative and all his help. The responsibility for the idea that the book should be a broad survey of warfare at sea combined with an attempt to put these conflicts in a transformation of Europe perspective is mine. My favourite theme in this process is the interaction between warfare, entrepreneurial innovators and the increased capability of Europeans to sail and fight at sea. Before further studies of that subject can be undertaken it is, however, necessary to survey the conflicts at sea in this period and sketch an outline of their connections with political, economic and social change.

I have attempted to carry out the historian's basic responsibility of setting the record straight by reading studies from several countries and looking at the same problem from more than one perspective. The text is brief on most subjects and every chapter could easily have been expanded into a book of its own. An obvious limitation is that I have made no effort to explain why non-Europeans (except in the Mediterranean) made so few attempts to use force at sea in order to project power and make economic gains. The explanations for that are part of greater problems than I have been able to discuss in this work.

This book has been written with a grant from the Faculty of Humanities, Stockholm University, for studies in early modern state formation and military development. I intend to present other results from this research in a forthcoming book. In the last stage of the writing I have also received a grant from The Bank of Sweden Tercentenary Foundation for research on the early modern Swedish navy as an organisation.

My wife Yeo Sang Kum and our daughter Jihi are thanked for being present in my life.

A note on displacement

The approximate size of warships and fleets in this book is illustrated by calculations of their displacement, measured in tonnes (metric tons). The displacement is the weight of the ship, in this case at full load. They have been calculated by the author who has followed principles outlined in J. Glete, *Navies and nations* (Stockholm, 1993) pp. 74–76, 527–530. Like most quantifications in early modern history, such calculations are approximate and often uncertain, but they make comparisons easier. Displacement should not be confused with contemporary estimates of size which were measurements of the cargo-carrying capacity and not (as often supposed by modern authors) of displacement.

A note on dates

Up to 1582 all Europe used the Julian calendar. From then, the Catholic countries and the Dutch used the Gregorian calendar. Other Protestant countries, including England, Denmark-Norway and Sweden, continued to use the Julian calendar. From 1582 dates in this book are given according to the Gregorian calendar, except for events in the Baltic which are given in the Julian calendar. Dates during the Anglo-Spanish war of 1585–1603 are given in both calendars.

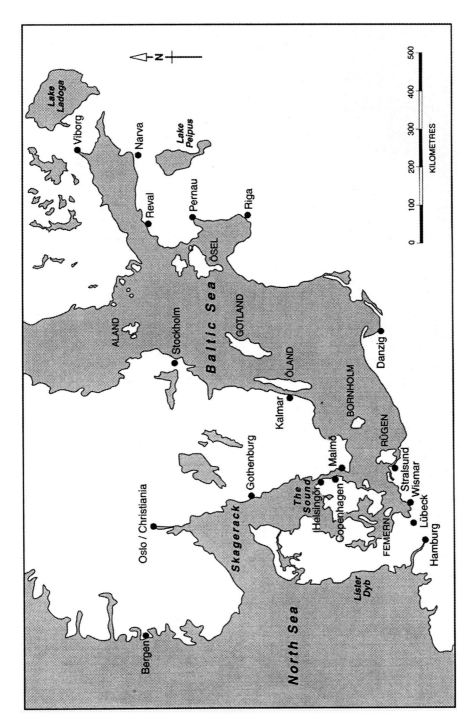

Map 1 The Baltic region

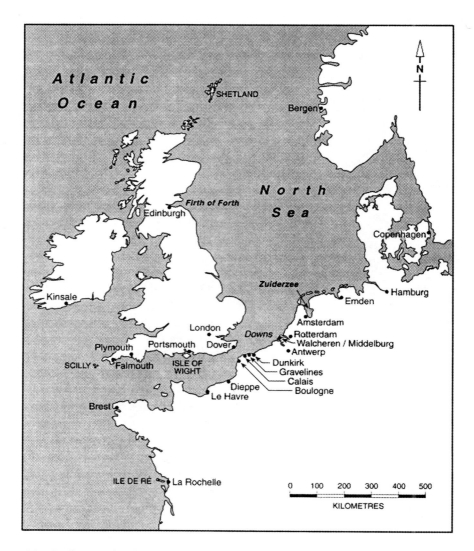

Map 2 The North Sea region

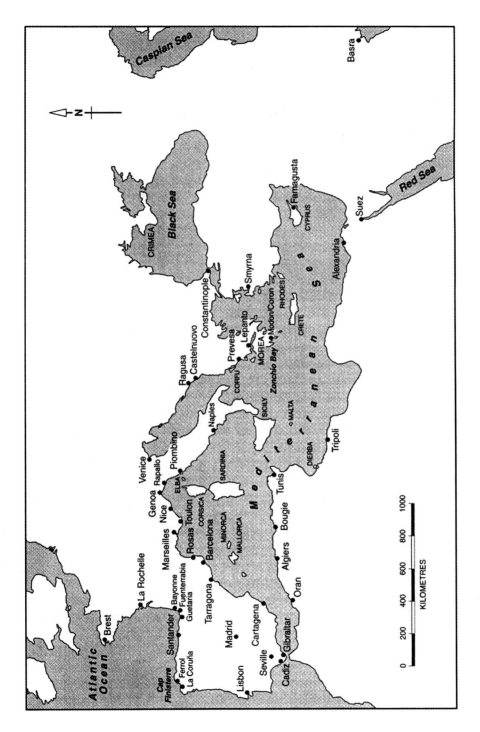

Map 3 The Mediterranean and Southern Europe

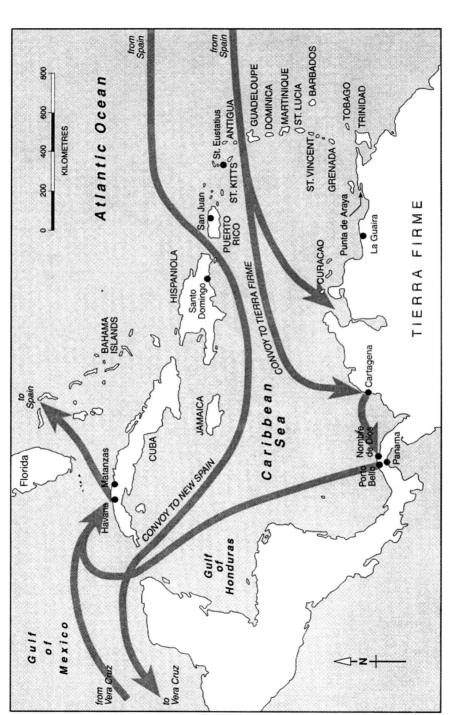

Map 4 The Caribbean and the Spanish convoy system

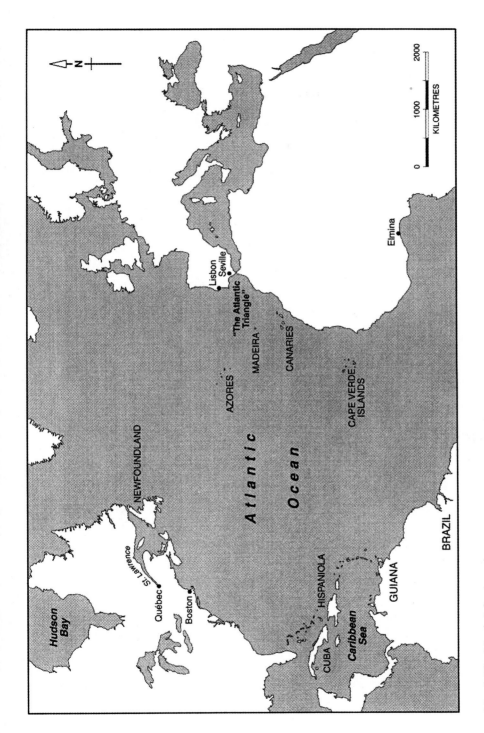

Map 5 The North Atlantic region

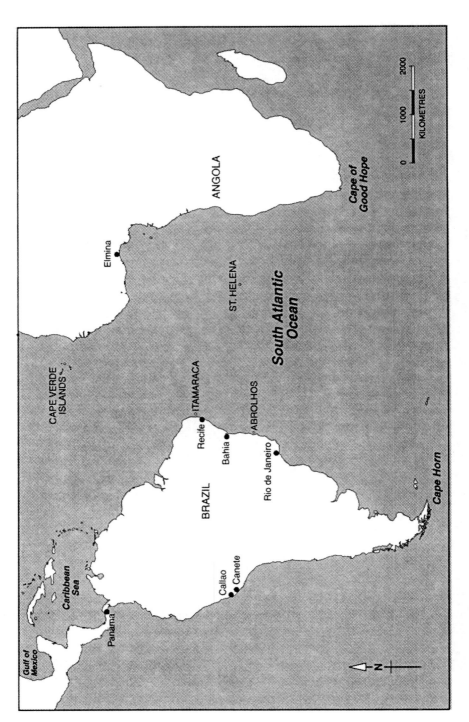

Map 6 The South Atlantic region

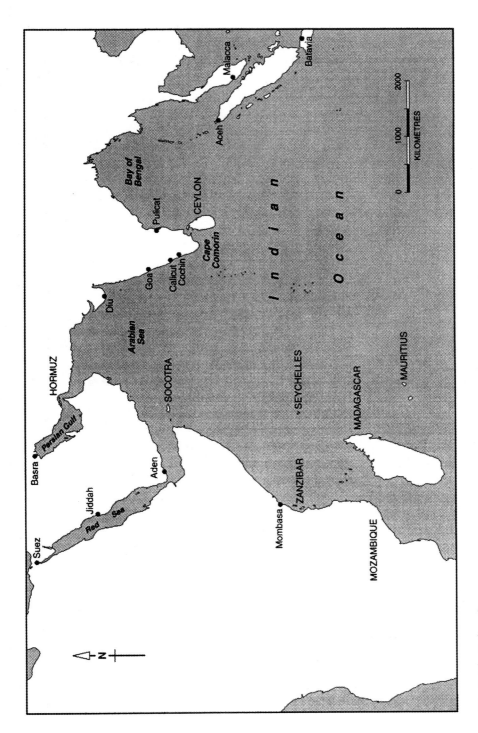

Map 7 The Indian Ocean

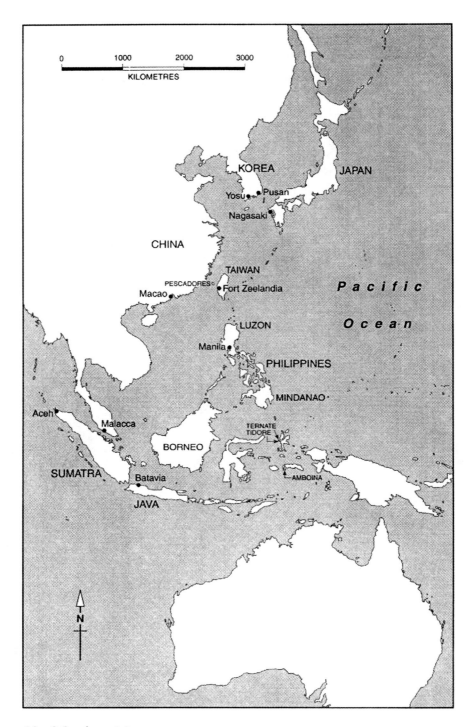

Map 8 Southeast Asia

1

WARFARE AT SEA IN EUROPEAN HISTORY

The transformation of warfare at sea

This book focuses on maritime conflicts as a part of the transformation of Europe from the end of the fifteenth century to the mid-seventeenth century. The main lines of this transformation are well known. From a maritime perspective some parts of the process are especially important. Long-distance trade increased and the role of capitalist entrepreneurs in society became more important in large parts of Europe. In the Mediterranean, the Spanish and the Ottoman empires became dominant during the first half of the sixteenth century. In the last decades of that century and the early decades of the seventeenth century the economic and political power of north-western Europe rapidly rose while the Mediterranean stagnated. The importance of the territorially integrated states in Europe rose and they began to develop permanent organisations for enforcing a state monopoly of violence on land as well as at sea. Finally, Europe developed an ability to influence economy and politics on a world-wide scale by its superior competence in warfare at sea. Warfare itself was also transformed. At sea, the institutional, organisational and technical frameworks for war and violence changed decisively between 1500 and 1650.

This book will emphasise change but some basic features of conflicts at sea remained unchanged. Warfare at sea is essentially a contest about the *maritime lines of communication*. These lines are used for trade, for power projection into territories close to the sea and as a source of wealth extracted by violence or through protection from violence. Consequently, wars at sea are fought in the interest of those who use the sea for trade, for the projection of military power and for resource extraction: plunder and taxes. Wars are also fought by those who feel threatened if competing groups are given free access to the sea for such activities. For the defender against seaborne invasion the sea is a forward area for naval operations which aim at delaying and preventing threats against his territory. Wars may have their immediate cause in accidental diplomatic breakdowns, domestic power politics or the vanity of rulers but once started they are shaped by the practical possibilities of inflicting damage on the enemy and giving protection to friends.

1

Up to the late fifteenth century European warfare at sea had a stable character within an institutional framework which was typical for the high and late medieval period (thirteenth to fifteenth centuries). Wars were usually regional and the radius of power projection was limited to Europe and the Mediterranean. Violence was used both by temporarily organised naval forces and by private groups. Permanent navies controlled by states were rare. Territorial powers had only a limited role in warfare at sea which was dominated by independent city states and mercantile interests in loosely integrated territorial states. Warfare at sea was often financed and organised by groups with a direct economic interest in protection or coercion at sea, not by states.

This was natural in a period when violence was not the monopoly of sovereigns and when sovereignty over a territory was often divided between central, regional and local power-holders. Wars were waged through social institutions rather than with organisations created by states. Many regions and cities were connected by dynastic bonds or commercial networks which crossed national boundaries. Groups with a strong interest in maritime trade normally had access to concentrated capital, the necessary hardware for war (ships), and a superior know-how in maritime matters. This often gave them a decisive advantage in conflicts over maritime lines of communication.

Medieval Europe was divided into two spheres with different types of maritime war. In the Mediterranean, oared galleys and chains of fortified coastal bases constituted a well-established system of warfare where the control of trade routes and territories close to the sea was well co-ordinated. Oared ships were the only specialised warships in Europe. In the Atlantic and Baltic sailing ships dominated in war, but they were primarily used as means of transportation for troops. Only occasionally did sailing fleets fight at sea. Sailing ship technology had not reached a stage where ships could be easily manoeuvred in combat or safely used close to a lee shore, essential requirements for a warship. Sailing ships used in warfare at sea were seldom owned by states and there were few permanent navies. Tactically, fighting at sea was carried out with infantry weapons and the crews of a fleet could easily be used in amphibious warfare. There were differences between combats at sea and on land but a general training for war might qualify a man for both types of combat. Finally, and most important, the European way of war at sea did not fundamentally differ from that of the civilisations in the Indian Ocean area and the eastern seaboard of Asia.[1]

A century and half later the institutions for warfare at sea had radically changed. From the mid-seventeenth century the European naval scene was dominated by the development of large sailing battle fleets, bureaucratically organised officer corps and warfare supported by taxes and customs duties raised by territorial states. The navies had become permanent and complex organisations: they were the policy instruments of centralised states and the ships, guns and dockyards represented huge investments in capital and specialised know-how. Sailing warships with heavy guns were now the dominant weapon system at sea and oared warships had their main use as specialised forces for amphibious and coastal warfare. Amphibious warfare was still strategically important, but, to be successful, it now required careful planning and co-operation between two separate, specialised and hierarchical organisations: an army and a navy. Private use of force at sea became strictly regulated by the states. European battle fleets could increasingly be deployed overseas, a unique capacity which enabled the Europeans to control the sea lines of communication around the world. This control was the power base of the economic and military penetration which later, and for a long time, made Europe the centre of the world.[2]

The extension of the sea lines of communication was also a dynamic factor in the global economic development which contributed to the creation of the modern industrial world. Growing seaborne trade and European expansion around the world created a network of contacts and an international economy where the flow of merchandise became essential for the dynamic development of production and consumption. This network was created by new combinations of commercial skill and the ability to wage war and protect long-distance trade at sea. By 1650 the centre of this dynamic maritime network was situated in north-western Europe. This region also became the centre for the new large sailing battle fleets. Southern Europe and the Mediterranean, which up to the sixteenth century had been the economically most sophisticated part of Europe and the pioneering area for overseas expansion, had rapidly declined in importance.[3]

The main purpose of this book is to give the reader a broad survey of the role of various types of armed conflict at sea in the transformation of Europe. Trade, state formation and the rise and decline of various centres of economic and political power are related to technical, strategical, tactical and organisational changes of warfare at sea. Naval operations, battles and seaborne trade based on armed force are therefore placed in their political and economic contexts. Conversely, the changing abilities of states to sail and fight at sea were important for the political and economic transformation of Europe and these developments are highlighted. No attempt has been made to formulate any macro-level thesis about the role and importance of sea power in this age. On the other hand, micro-level details such as the names of many admirals and the – often unknown – exact strength of the contending fleets are usually avoided. Essentially, it is a study of a number of historical meso-levels, where certain important historical questions are related to events on the maritime scene, including major naval operations and battles.

Primarily the book is based on existing studies of warfare, economy, political power and socio-economic structures. As will soon be obvious to the reader, many essential studies of warfare at sea in this period remain to be done. The sources are uneven and fragmentary but if the proper questions are asked they may give the historian much information about the growing endurance and sailing capabilities of warships, the development of gunnery, the transformation of naval tactics, the changing skills and social status of seamen and sea officers, the importance of logistics and the connections between political and economic power and warfare at sea. The purpose of this book is partly to introduce readers to questions and methods of research which may be useful for future studies about warfare at sea and its connection with state formation, economy, social structures and technology. Such studies, which have been rare for this period, will without doubt modify some conclusions in this book or make them entirely obsolete.

The changes in technology, tactics and strategy in warfare at sea were connected with a similar transformation of warfare on land and with the general transformation of the relations between state and society in Europe. Much of what has been written about war, military organisations and state formation in this period is almost exclusively based on studies about warfare on land, usually also only about parts of Europe. This study not only attempts to take the reader to sea. It also attempts to cover all parts of the world where Europeans fought at sea.

A disjointed historiography

A survey of warfare at sea must be based on studies of the subject which already exist.[4] For the post-1650 period most navies and the wars they fought are treated in a substantial literature specially devoted to these subjects. Much of it is old; some navies and wars have been studied in greater details than others, and administration, economy and the development of naval capabilities are often inadequately treated. However, the basic facts about combats at sea are usually available and naval history from different countries has a striking thematic similarity – naval policy and administration, battles and wars, warships and dockyards, officers and men. Recent scholarship has also asked new analytical questions which have made it possible to reassess old problems and formulate some new ones.[5]

The historiography of warfare at sea from 1500 to 1650 is different. Scholarly studies centred around the critical problems in naval warfare in this period are rare. The sources are fewer and often unfamiliar to naval historians who are used to the archives of the bureaucratic navies of the post-1650 period. Historians who are familiar with the period and its sources are seldom interested in warfare at sea except major events like the battle of Lepanto and the Armada campaign. Other wars, such as those in the Baltic and the worldwide Dutch-Iberian contest during the first half of the seventeenth century are relatively anonymous. On the other hand historians have done much research on questions related to warfare at sea in this period but it is thematically centred on maritime trade and global expansion, war and foreign policy or state formation and the governance of states.[6]

Somewhat paradoxically it might be argued that the structure and change of maritime violence in our period have been obscured by the fact that they are parts of important processes which have attracted the attention of historians who often have had little special interest in the details of events at sea, naval technology and naval administration. The importance of the maritime dimension in history is often underlined by historians, but the historiography of warfare at sea from 1500 to 1650 is more disjointed than in later periods. As an historical phenomenon, it can be related to at least five major changes in this period, changes that all are well-known from textbooks on early modern history. Each of them raises at least one question of importance for a study of warfare at sea:

1 The formation and integration of territorial states

The development of states with extensive bureaucracies, permanent armies and navies and centralised political control over territories fundamentally changed the relations between state and society. Compact and integrated territorial states grew in strength and claimed an increasingly effective monopoly on the use of violence on land and at sea. At the same time the transnational power of composite empires and the church as well as the localised power of feudal and mercantile groups was reduced. Their ability to use violence independently of the centralised territorial state declined decisively.[7]

This raises the question why some of the new strong territorial rulers were interested in creating permanent navies. Did they use them for power projection, empire building and defence against invasions, or were they primarily interested in protecting and attacking trade? Did they develop an organisation with the necessary skills to handle modern naval technology in order to motivate increased taxes and a royal monopoly on violence, that is, was the navy primarily a part of their ambition to create a strong domestic power base? And why were not all territorial rulers with a coast equally interested in creating a permanent navy?

State formation may be described as the result of political interest aggregation behind increased resource extraction from the society and the creation of permanent organisations, among them navies. Which of the groups taking part in this process were especially interested in navies and in what ways were navies developed and adjusted to the national base of political interest aggregation? Were there mechanisms of governance in navies which reflected the fact that various interest groups wished to keep control over at least part of the naval efforts?[8]

2 The rise and decline of maritime political and economic empires

The early modern period saw the rise and decline of several maritime empires within Europe, that is political and commercial spheres of influence connected by sea lines of communication. Some of these, like the Spanish, Ottoman, Danish and Swedish empires, were primarily political, while others, like the Hanseatic network of trade in Northern Europe and the Dutch control of large parts of seventeenth-century Europe's maritime trade, were economic or informal empires. The Venetian empire was a mix of both. In what way were the changing fortunes of these empires connected with early modern changes in naval technology and naval organisation? Were the nations which were successful in developing trade empires only economically successful or was their rise a result of an efficient naval and maritime policy also?

3 The expansion and restructuring of interregional seaborne trade
During the sixteenth and seventeenth centuries, inter-European seaborne trade increased in volume and complexity. Larger volumes of more diversified types of products were traded over longer distances. This opened new areas for more sophisticated production and consumption and formed a prerequisite for later economic development. An important change was the decline of Southern Europe and the Mediterranean area and the dynamic rise of Western and Northern Europe which became the economic centre of Europe. Were these changes connected with maritime warfare and new conditions for protection and coercion of long-distance trade? Was the efficient use of modern types of violence at sea a necessary skill for the rise of new entrepreneurs in long-distance trade?

4 The European expansion overseas
The most dramatic and well-known development in the maritime sphere is the expansion of European activities from the coastal waters around Europe to most parts of the world. Africa, Asia and America were connected with Europe and with each other through a maritime network of trade controlled by the Europeans and the European powers began to compete and wage war with each other far from Europe. In what way was this European expansion connected with new forms of and ambitions for warfare at sea?

5 Technical transformation of warfare at sea
The development of efficient guns and the versatile sailing gun-carrying ship are normally regarded as outstanding examples of European innovative capability in this period. It has been given a prominent place in the history of technology and often also in text-books on general history. Should these developments be regarded as more or less autonomous changes which triggered off the political and economic developments or should the political and economic changes be regarded as factors of demand which moulded technology? Was technology for war at sea primarily developed within the private sphere of the societies or as an integrated part of the skills of the new centralised states?

Are these questions asked and answered in the existing literature? To a large extent the answer must be no. The division of existing historical scholarship into various subjects and traditions is inadequate for this period of change. It may be better suited to the medieval period when the institutions for warfare were more integrated with the society and to the period when permanent navies controlled by states dominated the scene. Historians who write about medieval knights and seafarers are usually aware that they are studying men who were both economic actors and warriors. The modern period with its fully established specialisation between organised navies and non-belligerent merchants may be studied by specialised historians. Specialisation is less suited to a period of transition. Political history, economic history, the history of technology and even archaeology must be interconnected and these scholarly traditions must be developed to ask questions related to the use of violence, questions which usually have been asked by military and naval historians as well as historians of international relations.

Some early modern European navies have been studied as organisations, but little has been done to integrate naval history with the development of state formation and with the role of war as a driving force in that process. War and conflicts at sea have been studied very unevenly and comparative studies of different navies and different regions are scarce. Privateers and pirates have been extensively studied, but the role of private entrepreneurs in naval warfare and the supply of naval stores have been neglected. The possible interaction between state formation, warfare at sea and the changing pattern of maritime empires has received scant attention beyond general remarks. Historical sociology has had considerable difficulties in understanding the maritime sphere and its role in European state formation. Economic history based on main-stream economic theory does not regard the use of violence for protection and coercion of competitors as an economic activity to be analysed in terms of efficiency and profitability. Consequently its role in the creation of new markets and new networks of trade has not been studied as an economic phenomenon.

European maritime activities overseas have been better covered by historians, but much remains to be done in a comparative perspective. Naval technology have been intensely studied in a few countries – primarily English sailing warships and sixteenth-century Venetian galleys – but many archives are unexplored and questions about the interaction between technical, economic and political development are often not asked. Nautical archaeology has in the last decades of the twentieth century become an important part of the history of maritime technology in this period, but co-operation between archaeologists and historians excavating archives could be improved. Early modern warfare at sea is both a challenging and exciting field for new questions, new empirical research and new interpretations. There is a wide scope for historical debate: historians with different scholarly and national backgrounds may come up with rather different explanations.

There are also interesting and challenging differences in historiographical traditions between the Atlantic and Mediterranean spheres. In Western and Northern Europe, naval history is primarily the history of naval policy, the development of an officer corps and naval administration, warships and shipbuilding and the role of navies in the rise of the nation. It is an organisation-centred type of history, often to such a degree that the connections between naval operations and the policy of the state, trade and warfare on land is pushed into the background. In this type of history, naval operations and their outcome are often analysed as results of the quality of the naval organisation: its officers, men and administrators, ships, guns and dockyards. The naval organisation is often looked upon as the embodiment of sea power, a concept which in the Atlantic hemisphere sometimes has reached almost mythical proportions. Dynamic change and expansion are often emphasised, especially in the dominant Anglo-Saxon literature on maritime and naval history. The period from the 1580s dominates this literature.

In the Mediterranean early modern naval and maritime historiography is different. Chronologically, the period up to 1580, the era of large scale galley warfare, dominates. Thematically, there is little about state navies as organisations, their administration or the policies that created them. Instead, we find structural, more or less non-chronological studies, which in theme and scope often cross national boundaries. Naval warfare and the armed forces are thematically subordinated to the general economic and political development. Stagnation rather than dynamic change is emphasised. Naval operations are analysed as if they were directly connected with the policy of the states without the intermediate link which the naval organisation provides: its bureaucracy, ships, officers and men, its dependence on long-term policy decisions and investments in hardware and know-how. The Atlantic concept that navies may have a dynamic and inertia of their own and that they embody the sea power of the nation is seldom to be found in the Mediterranean area. Fernand Braudel's *magnum opus* about the sixteenth-century Mediterranean is typical of this type of history. It is a study of structures and events but in spite of Braudel giving much scope to warfare at sea he does not treat navies as parts of the structure. The same approach to history has dominated in analysis of Spain's and Portugal's naval activities even outside the Mediterranean area.[9]

To cross this historiographical borderline could be fruitful. For our period it has mainly been done by Anglo-Saxon scholars who have studied the Mediterranean navies and Spain with a mixture of Atlantic-style organisational and policy history and Mediterranean structuralism. John F. Guilmartin has made a study of sixteenth-century Mediterranean galley warfare in which he underlined that it cannot be analysed within a 'sea power' framework in the sense that Alfred Mahan interpreted the term in his trend-setting studies in the late nineteenth century. I. A. A. Thompson has studied Spanish naval and military administration, with its unusual development path from state bureaucracy to armed forces predominantly run by private entrepreneurs, while Carla Rahn Phillips has made a micro-study of one of these entrepreneurs within a broad framework of Spanish naval history. Colin Imber and Palmira Brummett have made brief but pioneering studies of the organisation of the sixteenth-century Ottoman navy, while Idris Bostan has made a study of the seventeenth-century naval dockyard in Constantinople as an industrial enterprise. José

Alcala-Zamora has crossed the border-line from the other direction and made a partly Mediterranean-style study of Spain's effort to create a maritime power position in Northern Europe in the 1620s and 1630s, a last attempt to turn the tide of economic and political power dislocation from south to north.[10]

Wars, states and societies in historical explanations

How have historians explained the interconnections between warfare at sea and the transformation of European societies and states in this period? With few exceptions, scholarly historians have avoided the question.[11] The same cannot be said about historians interested in warfare in general and warfare on land in particular. War and the development of the modern state has also been an important subject for historical sociologists and we will return to them in Chapter 4. In this section we will first concentrate on the historical debate about an interesting but surprisingly elusive phenomenon, called the Military Revolution, and some other attempts among historians to explain the role of war in the transformation process. After that we will look at some of the few attempts that have been made to evaluate the role of warfare at sea in the transformation of European politics and economy.

Since the 1970s attempts by historians to provide generalised explanations about the connections between the development of armed forces and the transformation of early modern Europe has been centred on the Anglo-Saxon Military Revolution debate. At least originally it was centred on possible inter-connections between the transformation of the armed forces, states and society in early modern Europe. During the debate, various *prime movers* behind this transformation have been identified. Michael Roberts who originally formulated the phrase the Military Revolution in 1955, argued that it was changes in *military tactics* which transformed state and society. Central to this assertion were the reforms in tactics introduced by Maurice of Nassau in the Dutch army in the 1590s and developed by Gustav II Adolf in his reforms of the Swedish army up to about 1630. The new type of army (Roberts said nothing about navies) required well-drilled and disciplined soldiers and a large number of professional officers to train the men and lead more articulated formations. As it was the training and the group cohesion that was the strength of the new type of army it had to become permanent. A better disciplined army might in its turn be used for more ambitious strategies which in its turn required more soldiers. Larger armies put greater strain on societies and required more sophisticated administrators, thus creating a connection between the changes in tactics and military organisation and the growth of the states. To Roberts it was this change in society and state that was the important end result; the military revolution was to him a great divide between medieval society and the modern world.[12]

The debate about the Military Revolution was initiated by Geoffrey Parker in the 1970s. He accepted Roberts' idea that the early modern period saw a major rise in the size of armies, but instead of the emphasis on infantry drill as the key element and 1590–1630 as the decisive period of change Parker put the emphasis on the development of modern fortifications, *trace italienne*, designed to resist heavy artillery. They changed strategy and army composition, forced army size upwards and presented the European states with the challenge of how these increased armies should be maintained. This development took a long time to spread to various parts of Europe and Parker's military revolution is a process extending from the early sixteenth century to around 1700. Parker also brought the growth of the navies into the picture and behind both the new types of fortifications and the growing navies he found the development of artillery. In Parker's explanation, *technical change* is the prime mover behind the transformation process. He explicitly refrained from presenting any general ideas about the impact of war on society or of the reciprocal relations between a state and its military system. Instead, his aim was to trace how the European military and naval innovations were initiated and then follow how they spread over the world as instruments for European power projection up to about 1800.[13]

Roberts and Parker both argued that it was the military innovations which had political effects. In the early 1990s, Jeremy Black raised some fundamental questions about the interaction between political and military factors. He saw much of the earlier writings on military revolution and state formation as typical for a period (say the 1950s to the 1970s) when historians and sociologists were mainly interested in the development of armed forces as instruments for rulers with absolutist ambitions. More recent scholarship has put more emphasis on co-operation between rulers and the elite and this consensus rather than coercion of internal enemies was the base for the growth of armed forces. Black could not detect any great change in 'Roberts' century' (1560–1660) and suggested that there had been two early modern periods of radical changes which may deserve to be called military revolutions. He singled out the periods 1470–1530 (firearms, fortification) and 1660–1720 (massive increases in the size of permanent armies and navies, flintlock muskets with bayonets replacing matchlock muskets and pikes, line-ahead tactics in navies) as the most dynamic before the great changes during 1792–1815. Fundamental to Black's explanation is that he sees *political changes* – compromises and co-operation between rulers and social elites – as the prime mover behind major transformation in the military sphere.[14]

Many historians have not accepted that there were causal links between the military development and the transformation of the early modern European society. This attitude is reflected in surveys of the theme 'European war and society in the early modern period', a subject that became popular among historians from the 1980s. J. R. Hale and M. S. Anderson wrote two parts of the *Fontana History of European War and Society* series. Both authors largely refrained from discussing the military revolution or any other concept of interconnection between military transformation and state formation. In the end of his book, however, Hale (covering the period 1450–1620) denied that war had any decisive effect on taxation, centralisation of states or bureaucratisation. Standing armies had not much effect on the political power of the rulers, nor was artillery an instrument for centralising power. Anderson (covering 1618–1789) described the increasing state control over armies and navies but had little to say about its causes or its effect on the growth of the state.[15]

Frank Tallett, author of *War and Society in Early Modern Europe, 1495–1715*, mentioned the idea of a military revolution briefly, but he was sceptical about interpretations which emphasise radical changes in tactics or technology in his period. Instead, Tallett preferred to stress continuities. In a chapter on 'the state and war' he expressed similar scepticism towards interpretations which give the rise of military forces controlled by the state a decisive role in state formation. He regarded them as traditional views, which – especially in the French and German cases – must be substantially modified as a result of recent scholarship on absolutism and the growth of the state. Military factors did not have a decisive role in establishing state dominance over nobility, warfare did not generally mean that estates were reduced in importance, and the role of the armed forces in the rise of (civilian) bureaucracy was limited, at least up to about 1650. In all these questions, Tallett emphasised that war might produce widely different results, thus making generalisations impossible.[16]

Somewhat paradoxically, surveys of war and armed forces published in the 1980s and 1990s did their best to reduce the role of their subjects in general history. The general impression is that political and (especially in Hale's study) social factors influenced the development of warfare, not that a military revolution (autonomous military factors) changed society and state. None of the authors attempted to formulate a new synthesis however, one that might for example argue that unique European social and political factors formed the military organisations that gradually brought large parts of the world under European control. Primarily, they argue against traditional (and often erroneous) Anglo-Saxon concepts of absolutism, bureaucracy and standing armies on the European continent. The three studies were explicitly limited to the European scene and only Anderson devoted some attention to navies. Whatever importance navies and warfare at sea may have had in early modern European history it is not reflected in surveys of the 'war and society' theme.

Long before the beginning of the Military Revolution debate, Frederic C. Lane, an American economic historian with Venice and Mediterranean maritime history as his specialities, began to formulate an economic theory which should explain the interconnection between war and the development of states. It is centred on protection cost and the possibility of reaping profit from efficient use of violence. It is probably no coincidence that Lane's studies of medieval and early modern maritime history made him conscious of the need to integrate violence, violence-control and protection cost in the analysis of economy. Low protection cost increases profits while high protection cost – which may be the result of attacks from competitors – decreases it. For a maritime historian, the idea that the use of coercion and protection in order to increase profit is an economically motivated activity is easy to connect with the realities of maritime trade and warfare before industrialisation. Lane suggested that economic actors may develop their ability to provide efficient coercion and protection at low cost as an integrated part of their entrepreneurial skill. The economically motivated demand for coercion and protection may also result in an increased role for the state which may (or may not) be the most cost-effective user of violence.[17]

However, his theory has wider repercussions. Lane asserted that states could be analysed as producers of a utility – protection – and as enterprises with interest in profits. In that, he formulated an economic theory of state formation which has remained largely unused by economists, sociologists and historians, including economic historians who seldom are interested in state formation problems. This is somewhat surprising as the quantitative growth in early modern state expenditure was closely connected with war. It is not at all a far-fetched idea to regard taxes paid to the early modern state as a price for protection (or an insurance premium) and the state as a seller of protection to the society. Many of these states were also involved in competition with other states, regional interests and private groups about the right to raise taxes for military and naval purposes, that is, a market for protection and coercion existed. Empire-building states also normally have to act as sellers of protection to several nations.

Of course, the 'customers' had normally not a free choice between various sellers of protection and as Charles Tilly has remarked, Lane may have been too much attached to neo-classical economic theory to fully work out the implications of his own theory.[18] But Lane's basic idea has been fruitful in Tilly's own thinking and they are close to his sociological concept of state formation as a result of bargaining about war financing between rulers and the elites. In that framework the customers may negotiate about *how much* protection they should pay for even if they have only one or a few sellers to turn to.[19] Elite groups may also choose between self-organised protection and protection sold by rulers, a fact which is very important in analyses of early modern state formation and maritime elite groups.

Violence and protection as utilities supplied by both states and private groups are probably most obvious in the maritime sphere up to the seventeenth century. Apart from Lane, Douglass C. North and economic historians working with his theories on institutions, protection of property rights and economic performance have studied the subject of maritime transportation and reduced cost of protection, but primarily in the post-1650 period when the institutional framework was different from the earlier period.[20] Another explanation of the connection between military and social change has been suggested by the American historian William H. McNeill. McNeill put special emphasis on the rise of bureaucratic (permanent, specialised and hierarchically controlled) armed forces as instruments of political control for rulers. Such forces could suppress opposition both from aristocrats and lower classes, which made it possible for the rulers to enforce a previously unknown level of domestic peace. This stimulated economic development and increased the tax base, thus creating a favourable circle of political stability, improved protection of commercial ventures, increased tax incomes and even greater political stability.[21] McNeill's interpretation may be described as a combination of Weberian sociology and Lane's ideas on governments and protection.

One of the leading European historians of the twentieth century, Fernand Braudel, who began his career with a monumental study of the sixteenth century Mediterranean, ended it with a *magnum opus* about European economic history from 1400 to 1800 with special emphasis on the development of capitalism. In his analysis Braudel has a marked tendency to minimise the roles of wars and states in early modern economic development. Braudel's approach, formulated in opposition to the political history which dominated up to the mid-twentieth century, is that early modern trade and economic interests normally circumvented blockades and other obstacles created by wars and politics. The impact of technology on war is underlined, but it is not related to demands from the state or the economic actors. States are mainly treated as unproductive extractors of economic resources from the society. However, in the final volume about capitalism (written in the 1970s) Braudel accepted Immanuel Wallerstein's idea that a country which acts as the centre of international capitalism must have a strong state. He also agreed with the German economist and sociologist Werner Sombart's idea that wars furthered capitalist development through the demands for weapons and large-scale credits. It is however impossible to argue that Braudel really integrated these ideas with his analytical framework.[22]

The American sociologist Immanuel Wallerstein, who in the 1970s began to analyse economic and political development since the sixteenth century from a 'world-system' perspective, put much emphasis on seaborne trade. As most large-scale trade was seaborne, this is only natural and Wallerstein is the most maritime of the sociological model builders. He asserted that the world-system needs a strong power in its core, a state with a strong government which could support the institutions that favoured the accumulation of economic surplus and investment opportunities to the core. Wallerstein identified Venice, the Spanish empire, the Dutch Republic and Great Britain as successive hegemonic powers. All were also leading seapowers which Wallerstein acknowledged, but he did not elaborate on this question. He did, however, emphasise that he regarded the Dutch Republic as a strong state with large and efficient armed forces on land and at sea. In this he went against a strong historiographical and sociological tradition which has made this republic into an antithesis to the absolutist, monarchical, bureaucratic and militaristic continental states, primarily France and Prussia. However, Wallerstein did not work out his argument in detail. In spite of his interest in Lane's protection cost theory, Wallerstein made no attempt to employ it for Spain and the Netherlands.[23]

A different interpretation has been presented by Jonathan Israel, himself a specialist in early modern Spanish and Dutch history. He regards early modern wars and political conflicts as important moulders of trade and economy. Israel especially emphasises the key role of trade entrepôts (regional or global centres for trade) – such as Venice, Lübeck, Antwerp and Amsterdam – in medieval and early modern trade. The entrepôt cities easily became power centres and empire builders in both economy and politics and this inevitably dragged them into struggles about international power. The entrepôt argument has similarities with Braudel's and Wallersteins's ideas, but Israel is critical of Braudel's interpretation of the role of the early modern state which Braudel regarded as inefficient and without ability to control the economy. To Israel, war, states and the use of politics and violence to promote mercantile interests matter in economics. Economic change cannot be studied only as a result of markets, productivity, finance and management. Israel's interpretation of the role of the state has similarities to those of Lane and McNeill although he has based them on his empirical research about Spain and the Netherlands in the sixteenth and seventeenth centuries. His ideas have been influential in reinterpretations of early modern Dutch history delivered in the 1990s.[24]

Lane, Braudel, Wallerstein and Israel have presented interpretations which are important to studies of maritime warfare, but only Lane himself was a maritime historian and only he has explicitly brought violence into a theoretical explanation. This explanation was apparently central to his understanding of the role of the Venetian state and its navy but he never attempted to write a broader interpretation of maritime history where the growth of the state navies might have been central. The present author's study of the long-term development of navies was in its theoretical assumptions inspired by Lane.[25] The present book covers a period when several navies were founded, but when it was far from self-evident that states should organise navies to protect seaborne trade and coastal territories. The question of *how* societies should organise protection at sea was important. Furthermore, the conflicting interpretations of the role of the state in the changing patterns of trade suggested by Braudel, Wallerstein and Israel must be taken into account. They have raised important questions about the role and efficiency of the early modern state, questions that merit much empirical research.

This book has its focus on actual warfare at sea: why wars were fought, how they were fought and where they were fought. It also attempts to describe and explain the transformation of maritime wars which took place between 1500 and 1650. However, this transformation was closely connected with other changes in the European societies which must be brought into the picture. The development of permanent navies, centralised state power and gun-armed warship technology were radical changes which occurred in the same period. They were also contemporary with similar changes in warfare on land, questions which have been extensively discussed in the Military Revolution debate. It is natural to assume causal interconnections between these changes, but the existence and direction of these connections are far from obvious – can we find any prime movers? Was it the rise of centralised states which created permanent armed forces and the systematic development of technology, or was it the opposite causal relationship that determined the development? In a similar way we may ask in what way the changes in maritime technology and the use of violence at sea were connected with the increase of maritime trade and the shift of the centre of that trade from southern to north-western Europe. Were the economic developments determined by technology and war or were those phenomena reflections of economic change? Empirical questions about when, where and how something happened may give us new answers to why something we already know of actually took place.

The fact that both commercial interests and political power were involved in warfare at sea has frequently made the ultimate aims of the wars a question of historical debate. Were they fought in the interests of political rulers, national security or the profits of merchants? Were domestic politics a more important cause of wars than international political and economic conflicts? Various interpretations along these lines have been given to the Anglo-Hispanic war 1585–1604, the Dutch-Hispanic conflict in the seventeenth century (especially the maritime war period 1621–48) and the three Anglo-Dutch wars 1652–74, for example. The Swedish expansion in the Baltic (1561–1660) has been explained either as a struggle for national security, for the ports and river estuaries where customs duties might be raised or for the surplus production of the Swedish peasants (easier to appropriate by the aristocrats and the king during a war).

The 'origin of war' debates often reflect the degree to which early modern wars at sea were increasingly fought by agents and national organisations and not by those who were immediately interested in the results of violence. It is important to focus attention on the fact that political and mercantile war aims usually were not in conflict and that this may have been important in integrating the interests underlying the establishment of permanent navies. Merchants, rulers and various interest groups found that this type of organisation was important for them and consequently they were willing to pay for it even in times of peace. Compared to earlier periods in European history this rise of integration behind a permanent state organisation for war at sea was an important change.

The importance of this integration process was so great that it was in itself a usual cause for war within states and between states. From 1500 to 1650 most European states underwent periods of civil wars and contests between groups with conflicting interests: the French civil wars (1562–98, the 1620s, the Frondes from 1648); the German wars, culminating in the Thirty Years War (1618–48); wars connected with the dissolution of the Nordic union (up to 1536); revolts against the Habsburg rule in the Netherlands (1568–1648); Portugal, Catalonia and Naples (from 1640 on); and the civil wars on the British Isles. The French and German wars had serious effects on these great nations' ability to develop sea power – Germany was finally dissolved into several practically sovereign states – while the other wars about sovereignty and integration had important effects on the development of navies and maritime warfare.

The book starts at a time when a series of rapid changes in technology, tactics, organisation and political framework began to demolish the stable medieval framework of warfare at sea. It ends, not with the general introduction of large bureaucratic battle fleets, but with the mid-seventeenth century. At that time, the technical and organisational framework for future development existed at least as 'blueprints', but it was far from clear to what extent they would be used and which the possible contenders were.[26]

2

TECHNOLOGY, TACTICS
AND STRATEGY

Technical development in organisations and networks

The role of technology in the transformation of Europe's armies and navies and the impact of this transformation on the rest of the world are often discussed by historians. Theories of technical change as a social and economic activity are usually not mentioned in these discussions which are centred on changes in tactics and strategy. Technology, tactics and strategy are closely related concepts in all discussions about warfare at sea but changes and structures in warfare can also be placed in their social, economic and political contexts where theories about technical change are relevant.[1]

The essential problem in *tactics* is how to behave when you are in physical contact with the enemy. A tactician is searching for the best combination of movement, protection and the ability to hit the enemy with something lethal. If the operational force is large the ability to control it in combat is also an important tactical problem. *Strategy* is primarily a question of distances, endurance, logistics and the choice of a favourable time and place for a battle. Both strategy and tactics might be predominantly offensive or defensive. Offensive strategy at sea often requires ships suitable for long-distance deployments and long periods at sea, while tactical offensive requires ships which are able to force an enemy to fight. *Technical change* is based on efforts to reduce constraints and increase options in human life. In warfare at sea technical change influences both tactics and strategy. As a warship must be built with a view to both strategic and tactical requirements, technical change often consists of better ways of *combining* various capabilities: firepower, staying power, speed, sailing qualities, endurance and habitability. Those who intend to use the ship or the navy must set the priorities and decide which combinations of capabilities they prefer. Is speed more important than protection, endurance more important than firepower, are restrictions on the draught of the ship essential to fulfil certain missions?

As all capabilities cannot be built into the same ship it is normally necessary to have more than one type and size of warship at the same time. In the early modern period (and in modern warfare until the Second World War) large ships were built in order to form concentrated striking forces (battle fleets) in strategically decisive areas. Smaller units were primarily built to exercise or contest control over long lines of communication (cruiser forces). Oared warships (galleys, later gunboats) had shorter endurance than sailing ships, but they could be built with a shallow draught and they were not dependent on the wind for mobility. Consequently, they were useful in coastal and amphibious warfare and in areas with calm weather. Oared warfare must be supported by an extensive network of bases or sheltered anchorages as oared warships, with their large crews in a very limited space, are inherently short-range vessels.

Several theories have emerged about how technology develops and how inventions and innovations (new combinations) are spread in society. Traditionally, much research has been based on theories which assumed that either demand (market pull) or supply (technology push) of technical ideas are decisive. Traditional history of technology as well as much military and naval history lean heavily on supply side explanations or even on pure technological determinism. Technology is regarded as something which is developed by specialists as a part of their profession and adopted by society. On the other hand, economists have stressed the importance of demand for technical development and they regard technical change as an economic phenomenon governed by market forces. In this perspective, technology is moulded by the possibility of transforming inventions into profitable business ventures.[2]

More recently, the *interaction* between technology and market forces, has been emphasised. Technology develops either within *organisations* (firms), which co-ordinate information about new technology and its potential application, or within *networks* of actors, who develop, use and produce technical products in close co-operation. Interaction explanations emphasise the value of a free and rapid exchange of information about ideas and experiences between users and producers of technically complex products. Close ties between users and producers make it easier to select between various technical alternatives. A firm organisational structure or a closely knit network may also make it easier to develop and retain essential know-how. In such a framework, visions and perceptions of new technology may overcome initially limited and inferior ability to handle the technology.[3] The last factor is essential to historians as a possible explanation of the fact that the centres of development often shift in connection with radical change of technology. New ideas may require new combinations of skill and these combinations may emerge and develop more rapidly in areas where the established technology is less firmly entrenched in the power structure.

Warships and guns were high technology in the sixteenth and seventeenth centuries and they were of great importance for political and economic development. It is therefore important to investigate if this technology was shaped by more or less autonomous technical skills in metallurgy and shipbuilding or by power politics, economic opportunities to use new technology, and social institutions constraining or promoting the use of innovations. The gradual development of navies as complex organisations is of special interest in this perspective. One of their roles was the *institutionalisation of interaction* between users and producers of naval hardware. The development of permanent organisations centred on warfare was a major innovation in this period and they might have appeared because they were a superior way of handling technology and co-ordinating it with the interests of the rulers. The new navies may have been structures where visions and perceptions of how new technology should be used might have overcome initial inferiority in established maritime skills.

The introduction of guns and gun-carrying ships made technology more complex. This required closer co-ordination and a more intense flow of information about experiences and new ideas. The hull, rig, equipment and armament of ships had large potential for improvements but it was best developed as a co-ordinated system and in close contact with those who used the new technology for war and trade. In the long run, the permanent navies proved to be the most efficient co-ordinator of the new technology for warfare at sea but this superiority belongs to a later age when the technology became mature. In our period, when a radical transformation took place, networks between entrepreneurs remained important for technical development, but it was new networks rather than those centred in the established maritime centres that provided the dynamics. In the maritime sphere this is observed in the fact that technical leadership shifted from the Mediterranean to north-western Europe.

In the early sixteenth century, the Italian maritime cities (Genoa and Venice) were still the leaders in maritime technology and the centres of extensive trading networks. England and France bought or hired Mediterranean armed merchantmen to fight wars. A century later the Dutch and the English maritime entrepreneurs (shipbuilders and shipowners) built the best merchantmen in Europe. Many of these were built to be armed with cheap but dependable cast-iron guns developed by private entrepreneurs. Such ships captured most of Europe's long-distance trade, they were hired by states (including Venice) as warships and the privately developed technology also influenced navies. Warship technology developed faster in Europe's new economic centre around the North Sea. New networks created around innovations and fresh combinations of interests were more efficient than established networks and accumulated experience and capital.

The development of technology for warfare at sea is often best analysed as an interaction process between the users (the operational forces), the producers and the political rulers of the state or the private investors in maritime armed force. These groups had to find compromises which provided the armed forces with the best possible weapon systems at the lowest possible cost. Unfortunately, early modern technology has left few written sources from which we may draw conclusions about how this dialogue developed. Technology was an art with much tacit knowledge and discussions about innovations in warship design and warship armament are seldom recorded in correspondence, minutes or memoranda. The best sources are often accounts but they require careful analysis before they yield any answers. Consequently, we can only seldom know for certain if a design feature was introduced by a technician, a private entrepreneur, an officer, an administrator or a ruler.

Furthermore, we lack much of the basic documentation about warship design before 1650. Only a few primitive drawings and a handful of (not very precise) models have been preserved. Dimensions are seldom on record before the late sixteenth century and only from that time were ships (primarily Dutch and English ships) reproduced in reliable pictures by skilled marine artists.[4] We are better off with early modern gunnery as several hundred guns from this period are preserved. Marine archaeology has also improved our knowledge of how warships were built in our period but the ships excavated up to now give only a fragmentary picture of a complicated process with many regional variations.[5]

The scarcity of sources on technology is itself a sign of the essentially pre-bureaucratic nature of the navies. Technology was an art and as such it was often preserved as family tradition among shipbuilders and gunfounders. The states and the navies relied on these semi-private artisans for their technical know-how. Only slowly did they begin to think in terms of technology as something which might be turned into a property of the state with detailed documentation of designs and training of technicians into bureaucrats. Consequently we are normally left with few traces of how an idea was born. Were users of technology asking for solutions to problems or was a new idea the brain-child of technicians that they were able to persuade users to finance? How intense and fruitful were the daily dialogues between those who produced naval hardware and those who used it? What role did social gulfs between rulers, aristocratic naval leaders and usually low-born technicians play in such dialogues? As for the private entrepreneurs in maritime violence, plunder and trade as well as the entrepreneurs in shipbuilding, naval stores and gun manufacturing, only scattered fragments of their activities remain. The large chartered companies for overseas trade and warfare are the major exceptions.

In spite of there having been much written about naval technology and tactics of this period, we are still seriously deficient in *comparative* studies which attempt to bring together the evidence from archives, pictures and archaeology from all those parts of Europe that took part in the development. Most existing studies have a tendency to place the centre of development in the region which the author knows best. The following brief text is mainly intended to cover the development of sailing gun-armed warships in England, France, Portugal, Denmark-Norway, Sweden, Spain and the Netherlands – the seven states which had major sailing-ship forces up to 1650. The Mediterranean galley fleets are mentioned only briefly. There was relatively little technical change in this area and the galley fleets had a fairly homogeneous technology based on long experience of oared warfare.

Guns at sea

From the latter half of the fifteenth century a number of inventions and innovations (new combinations) changed both tactics and strategy in warfare at sea.
The two main lines in this development were the introduction of heavy guns
at sea and innovations in sailing-ship technology. The latter improved the ability of the ship to stay at sea under adverse conditions and to use the wind as a
fairly safe source of energy. The combination of the heavy gun and the
improved sailing ship is usually regarded as a technological revolution of decisive importance for European expansion overseas as well as for naval strategy
within Europe.[6]

Guns had been used on ships throughout the fifteenth century, but at first
without much change in tactics and strategy. The early guns in use at sea were
small and primarily regarded as an infantry weapon which might inflict damage on the enemy crew or confuse them with their smoke. Heavy guns were
developed as weapons for siege warfare, and they had by the mid-fifteenth
century achieved considerable success against high but thin medieval fortification walls. Early guns were made of wrought iron staves formed into a tube (or
a 'barrel') fastened by iron hoops shrunk around it. The tube was open at both
ends and the gun was consequently breech-loaded. The loading mechanism
consisted of a separate chamber into which the shot and the powder charge
were placed. This mechanism as well as the thin wrought iron could not with-
stand high pressure from the explosive effects of gunpowder, and such guns
could only be fired with weak charges of powder. This type of gun was originally intended for stone shot, often of great calibre. Gradually, iron shot
became more common and during the sixteenth century stone shot was
largely phased out from military and naval service.

For a long time the alternative to the wrought-iron guns was a gun cast in
bronze: copper mixed with tin – they were often referred to as copper guns.
They became more common in the mid-fifteenth century. They could be
made lighter and yet were able to fire iron shot with greater effect than stone
shot of much larger calibre from wrought-iron guns. Copper was expensive
and the new technology was initially difficult to master. France and the
Burgundian centre of gun founding in the Southern Netherlands (from 1477
under Habsburg rule) were for a long period the most efficient producers of
heavy copper guns. The Ottomans employed excellent gun founders and by
the early sixteenth century Venice became a centre for high-quality production of such guns. The technology was gradually mastered by most European
states although there remained considerable differences in quality.

By the end of the fifteenth century heavy artillery was a well-established
part of warfare on land and recent successes in Spanish siege warfare in
Granada and during French operations in Italy showed that medieval methods
of fortification employing high thin walls had become obsolete. But heavy
guns were expensive and represented a large investment even for major states.

21

The number of such guns grew only slowly as a result of decades of new production and the accumulation of inventories in the arsenals. The artillery could
not be created quickly for a single campaign: it had to be organised by states as
a permanent force. Even in the great nations, heavy guns were counted in
scores and only gradually in hundreds, not in thousands. The number of skilled
gunners who could handle the new super-weapons with efficiency was also a
limiting factor. Consequently, the deployment of heavy guns in wartime was a
strategic question of great importance.

The heavy guns might also be used at sea. It is not entirely clear when this
idea dawned on European rulers, shipowners and shipbuilders. In itself it
might have been relatively trivial. The practical problems of arming a ship or a
galley with heavy guns were smaller than making such guns effectively mobile
on land. The ship was in itself a natural means of transportation for heavy guns
if a waterway was available. If the ship was to carry guns to a siege operation it
might be practical to try to use the ship itself as a gun platform. The early use
of heavy guns on ships was often connected with siege operations and bombardments of cities, rather than combats between ships at sea.[7] The early use of
heavy guns in ship-to-ship combat posed a major problem: until the late
fifteenth century sailing ships lacked much of the manoeuvrability required to
get a substantial number of hits against mobile targets. The very idea of fighting sailing ships in the open sea with a fresh wind blowing was only gradually
becoming realistic as a result of the development of sailing technology.

It would require much experience and several innovations to make the
sailing ship into a really efficient platform for many guns, but it was not
particularly difficult to arm a large ship with a limited number of heavy guns.
This required that openings be made in the hull to allow the guns to point
out, and an efficient method for closing them when the guns were not in use.
This hardly went beyond what a skilled ship carpenter could achieve without
claiming much originality. Small ships, such as the Portuguese caravels, might
be armed with a few rather heavy guns shooting over the rails. The galleys
were even easier to arm. With only minor modifications, one heavy gun could
be placed in its bow and this gun might be flanked with two or four medium
and light pieces. The armament pattern which became typical for galleys up
to the final demise of this type of warship around 1800 was there from the
beginning.

Heavy guns were, however, deployed at sea only gradually and in small
numbers. For a long time older wrought-iron guns were probably dominant
and ships might have had to surrender their guns if they were needed for siege
operations. The artillery of most states remained a specialised technical branch
of the armed forces, rather than being integrated parts of their armies and
navies. There is, however, little evidence for the belief that chivalric con-
tempt for gunpowder weapons or the inertia of established organisations
had much importance in delaying the deployment of guns at sea. Outside
the Mediterranean there was little established naval organisation or chivalric

tradition in warfare at sea, and in the Mediterranean the galley fleets *were* early users of heavy guns. Portuguese knights commanding fleets in the Indian Ocean from 1498 on, avoided boarding and used their superior gunpower to defeat enemies at sea and to bombard cities. Dutch sea officers were very seldom of noble origin, but they frequently used boarding tactics even in the mid-seventeenth century. In actual combats there were instances when men exposed to superior gunfire scornfully invited the enemy to board and fight as men but it is very doubtful if this should be taken as a confrontation between different attitudes to war. Both on land and at sea, aristocratic commanders used guns if that was to their advantage.

The third technical breakthrough in gun manufacturing was the introduction of the cast-iron gun. Owing to the higher temperature and more advanced metallurgy required, reliable cast-iron guns were more difficult to produce than guns made of copper. The great advantage was that iron was cheaper, although this effect was nullified if the production process was unreliable and a large number of guns failed on tests with high powder charges. Some types of iron ore were more suitable than others for use in gunfounding and this may have been one reason why English cast-iron guns were the earliest which were produced with success. The breakthrough was achieved in the 1540s and up to the late sixteenth century England had a monopoly on reliable cast-iron guns. They were important as armaments on Elizabethan and Dutch armed merchantmen trading in areas where the risk of being attacked was high. In combination with advantages in speed and sailing qualities, the cast-iron guns gave the northern sailing merchantmen an advantage in protection which could be turned into profits through trade. The first area where this was noticeable was in the Mediterranean where these northerners established themselves as important cargo carriers and occasional pirates in the late sixteenth century. From around 1600 the cheap cast-iron guns also became important for well-armed northern merchantmen trading and fighting in the East and West Indies.

By 1600 the Dutch had acquired the ability to produce cast-iron guns. This ability was transferred to Sweden where Dutch capital and entrepreneurship could join abundant resources of iron ore, forests and water power. A large-scale production of cast-iron guns developed in Sweden, to a large extent for export. In the early 1620s Spain started production of cast-iron guns. However, before 1650 cast-iron guns were not much used by state navies: they preferred copper guns. The English and Swedish navies which might have relied on domestic cast-iron guns nevertheless preferred copper guns, and the Swedes could also rely on large domestic resources of copper. Cast-iron guns were liable to burst and kill their crews if overheated in action, a problem that took a long time to solve. Copper guns were therefore preferred by navies which had to fight prolonged battles with sustained gunfire. Armed merchantmen had not enough men to reload and fire their guns rapidly and the risk of overheating was small. They were primarily armed with guns in order to fire a few broadsides against lightly armed attackers and for that purpose the cheap cast-iron guns of small and medium calibres (3- to 12-pounders) proved useful as a substitute for large crews. Merchantmen armed with cast-iron guns did however also fight fleet actions in the East and West Indies and up to the 1670s they were often hired by states for fleet service. After 1650 cast-iron guns rapidly became dominant as naval guns, probably because the increased demand for cheap guns stimulated technical progress.

Guns were made in various sizes and types. The two most common types of copper gun were short and large calibre guns (*cannons* or *kartaun/kartog*) and long, medium and small calibre guns (*culverins* or *schlangen*). Contemporary gunners believed that long guns had greater range but modern research has shown that little extra range was achieved with blackpowder gunnery if the guns were made longer than a certain medium-size length. Long-range gunnery at sea was in any case of limited use as the smooth-bore guns seldom hit a ship beyond a distance of a few hundred metres. Long guns had their advantages however. Guns were usually cast with their muzzles up and the density and strength at the bottom of a casting increased with the mass above. This made long guns stronger at the breech where the greatest strains would occur at firing and such guns could be fired with more powerful powder charges.[8] The variations in quality and experience among various gunfounders were considerable and explain some of the differences in fighting potential between different navies. The quality of gunpowder and gun-shot (which may be brittle if cast in an inefficient way), the design of gun carriages, and the routines for loading and handling guns may also have developed at an uneven pace.[9]

Standardisation of calibres was highly desirable and was gradually achieved in new production of guns during the sixteenth century. The total standardis-ation of guns to a limited number of types remained a dream in most navies, however. Guns had much longer lives than ships, old guns remained in service and captured guns or guns bought from various manufacturers were prevalent in the ordnance inventories. During wars, when everything that could be used had to be sent to sea, ships had to be armed with what was available, rather than an optimum armament specially designed for the ship. This must have lowered the efficiency of gunnery in combat, a fact which has to be taken into account when battles from this period are compared to those of later periods. The distribution of guns on ships may have been different than in later peri-ods when broadside tactics were predominant. In the sixteenth and early seventeenth century heavy guns, and, especially, long guns were probably often mounted in the extreme ends of the ships as bow- and stern-chasers. These guns may have been regarded as the main offensive armament in early gun-armed ships.[10]

Gun-carrying warships

The design and construction of gun-carrying sailing warships was one of the most demanding tasks undertaken in pre-industrial Europe. Such ships had to be able to fight with their guns, carry heavy loads high in their hulls, survive heavy weather and extended periods at sea, move in the desired direction at the best possible speed with the help of the wind and provide shelter for their crew. All this had to be achieved within the limits set by economy and technology. In warship design the strategic and tactical doctrines were expressed in hardware. The squeeze was tight and many designs turned out to be unsatisfactory because too much had been attempted in a ship with too small a displacement. But the period 1500 to 1650 saw decisive improvements in ship design which made battles with guns carried in sailing ships the dominant form of warfare at sea.[11]

Up to the late fifteenth century fighting at sea with galleys or sailing ships meant combats with infantry weapons − longbows, crossbows, light guns, pikes, javelins and swords, and soldiers and armed seamen were the fighting element of the crew. The galleys had a spur in their bow which might damage oars and penetrate into the light planking of the upper part of a galley in order to facilitate boarding − they had, however, no ram as in classical times. Battles at sea meant close combat, either with missile weapons or boarding, although the latter was often difficult in fresh winds. Both types of combat aimed at defeating the enemy crew and capturing the ship. Fighting power was approximately the same as men skilled in the use of infantry weapons, although seamanship was important in bringing a ship within boarding range, or close to an opponent.

An infantry warship had high fighting platforms fore and aft for men firing missile weapons. Their height was intended to give the ship an advantage in close combat. Such platforms could quickly be added to any sailing merchantman and a state or a city with a fleet of large merchantmen could easily organise a temporary navy. The most important offensive and defensive quality of a sailing ship was probably size. Even without soldiers, great size and high sides made a ship difficult to board. In offensive warfare the ability of a ship to carry soldiers and provide them with towering platforms from which they could fire missiles was proportional to its size. During the fourteenth and fifteenth centuries the ability to build very large ships improved. In the Mediterranean Genoa and Venice, the two leading maritime powers, had much of their carrying capacity concentrated in huge cargo carriers (often called carracks) whose size made them easy to defend against pirates. In the fifteenth-century Atlantic hemisphere, the development of large ships was combined with the development of the full-rigged ship with three or four masts.

When certain states began to build specialised warships in the late fifteenth century the technology to build large cargo carriers was useful as a starting point. Several of the earliest warships did at least superficially look like large cargo carriers transformed into floating fortresses, with high castles fore and aft and some heavy guns low in the hull. It is probable that this development process also included stronger hulls and better sailing qualities, but little is known about these. In the first half of the sixteenth century specialised warships were few, but much of the limited resources were invested in a few very large ships, some of more than 2,000 tonnes displacement. Such ships were built by Venice, the Ottomans, Portugal, Scotland, England, Denmark-Norway, France, the Order of St John and Sweden, and probably by mercantile interests in Genoa and Lübeck too.

A few of these giants are well-known in the literature but most of what has been written about them tends to assume that they were unique or very unusual. Actually they represented a common European trend in the first stage of the deployment of heavy guns at sea. Some were failures but several proved useful in action. The giants were built as combined artillery and infantry warships, with high superstructures and a limited number of heavy guns. Such guns could be mounted on much smaller vessels too. In the late fifteenth century the Portuguese were able to mount guns with 'ship-killing' capability even on larger types of caravel of only a few hundred tonnes displacement. As the efficiency of the gun was much dependent on the ability of the ship to point it in the appropriate direction, agile ships, easy to handle, might be at an advantage in combats with guns.

From the late fifteenth century on there were also smaller types of warship which attempted to combine some of the characteristics of the galley with those of the sailing ship. Several of these were called galleons or galeasses, two type designations which originally were regarded as more or less interchangeable. Some of these vessels were oar-powered hybrids between galleys and full-rigged ships (this type gradually became known as galeasses), while others were low-hulled sailing ships (later often known as galleons).[12] One common feature of these types seems to have been that they carried as many heavy guns as possible to fire forward and aft, probably in order to combine offensive tactical movements with effective gunfire. But also, the less agile great ships based on the large cargo carrier type seem to have concentrated as many guns as possible in forward and aft firing positions too.

When guns became more numerous and important, the size of the largest warships in most navies declined. Ships were no longer built to carry a large number of soldiers and with multi-tiered castles as platforms for infantry. In the latter half of the sixteenth and first half of the seventeenth century there were few warships above 1,500 tonnes displacement. Ships of a more moderate size, often about 800–1,200 tonnes, could carry several of the heavier types of guns and their size made them more agile, more weatherly and more flexible in various types of naval operation. Very large ships had a value as prestige ships and as fleet flagships, but only a few were required (and could be afforded) for such purposes.

Up to 1650 it looked as if guns had imposed an optimum on the size of warships and there was no sign of the race in battleship size which went on from the 1650s to the 1940s. During the latter half of the seventeenth century that race was fed by the increased availability of cheap cast-iron guns and rapidly growing fleets. Many actions were between concentrated battle fleets formed in close-hauled battle lines where increased size of ship meant better staying power as well as more concentrated firepower from heavy guns with great penetrating power. Before 1650 the ability to deploy a limited amount of gunpower at the right spot at the right time (for trade warfare and convoy protection, support of army forces and duels between individual ships during battles) was more important. That favoured medium-sized warships which were easy to manoeuvre, cheaper to build in greater number and could be risked in areas and seasons with much heavy weather.[13]

The development of the gun-carrying sailing warship was a long and complicated process and even by 1650 there was great potential for future innovation. The Mediterranean galleys represented a more mature technology which inherently was easy to adapt to guns. Older naval history, influenced by the Atlantic tradition, used to argue that guns mounted on the broadsides of sailing warships brought the end of galley supremacy.[14] In fact, up to the mid-sixteenth century it was the galley which benefited most from the new gun technology. Before the sixteenth century there had been few permanent galley forces in the Mediterranean, and outside that area oared warships had practically gone out of use. From around 1500 the number of galleys in the Mediterranean increased dramatically; France and England began to use galleys and galeasses in the Channel, while Sweden (1540) and Denmark-Norway (1565) introduced galleys in the Baltic. From the 1520s until about 1580 the galleys were, in terms of total displacement, the most important type of specialised warship in Europe.[15]

In the Mediterranean heavy guns rendered most existing fortifications obsolete. Gun-carrying galleys were efficient in attacking thin-walled fortresses close to the sea, but they could also act as mobile gun-carrying defence forces in the absence of modern fortifications.[16] Guns also made it easier for galleys both to attack and protect commercial shipping. With these tasks to fulfil, galleys were regarded as the most efficient weapon carrier in the Mediterranean during the sixteenth century. The sea powers in this area were well acquainted with modern sailing-ship technology and around 1500 they used gun-armed sailing warships. But after that they concentrated on galleys and from around 1540 large sailing warships practically disappeared from the Mediterranean, while their role in the Channel and the Baltic was supplemented by oared warships. As galley technology had not changed and sailing-ship technology was rapidly improving, the explanation for the increased role of the galley in this period must be the heavy gun.

The gun gave the low galley a weapon with which it could inflict serious damage on the high-sided hull of the large sailing ship, which up to then had had every advantage when attacked by galleys with infantry weapons. The galley was of course also vulnerable to gunfire, but with its low hull it was more difficult to hit than a high-charged sailing ship. As long as heavy guns were scarce, the fact that only one such gun could be mounted in each galley was not an important disadvantage. On a hull that could be manoeuvred by oars it could be fired with a certain precision. Unlike sixteenth-century sailing fleets, galleys could also manoeuvre in large formations where fleet and squadron commanders might exercise control and command. At Lepanto, the greatest naval battle of the age, more than 200 galleys fought on each side. Both as gun-carriers and as units of large fleets they were eminently suitable to current disciplined warfare with formalised tactics.

The disappearance of the sailing warship from the Mediterranean during a period of intense warfare and rapidly expanding navies indicates that early sixteenth-century sailing ships had serious shortcomings as gun-carriers. But their total abandonment of sailing warships also meant that the Mediterranean powers missed the opportunity of improving and developing this instrument of warfare. That development took place along the Atlantic seaboard and in the Baltic, areas where the galley was of limited use. The sailing ship of around 1500 may have been deficient, but it was a technical system in rapid development. There were continuous improvements in speed, seaworthiness, weather-liness (the ability to make progress against contrary winds) and endurance. The ability to carry guns and to resist gunfire were but two of several requirements that blended into the dynamic transformation of shipbuilding which produced the early modern gun-armed warship, the early modern cargo carriers and ships which attempted to combine fighting power with carrying capacity.

The fifteenth century had seen the development of the *full-rigged ship*, three-masters which combined the Atlantic and northern square sail with the triangular lateen sail of the Mediterranean. This combination meant increased speed, increased ability to sail close to the wind and increased manoeuvrabil-ity. With three masts the ship could be easily balanced on its course on any point of sailing and by unbalancing the rig the ship could quickly be made to turn on to another course. These qualities were essential in a warship in order to enable it to sail close to lee coasts in bad weather, to gain the wind from the enemy (i.e. to get to windward, for greater freedom of manoeuvre), and to manoeuvre rapidly during engagement, for example by tacking. In the early fifteenth century the typical rig in the Atlantic/Baltic hemisphere was one mast with a large square sail, while Mediterranean ships had one to three masts with one lateen sail on each. During the fifteenth century a three-mast rig with one square sail on the main- and foremasts and a lateen sail on the after (mizzen) mast became common in both areas. Towards the end of the century, small topsails became common on the main- and foremasts and large ships often had two small masts with one lateen sail each aft. The further development of the full-rigger consisted of additional sail area, its division into several sails, and improved methods of controlling the sails and the sail area. By the early seventeenth century major European ships had a practically standardised rig of three masts and ten sails: three square sails each on the mainmast and the foremast, a lateen sail and a square topsail on the mizzen mast and two small square sails on the bowsprit. This rig remained unchanged until around 1700.

The fully-fledged gun-armed warship required a *strong hull*, but the gradual development of that technology is only superficially known. The Mediterranean carvel building technique with planks placed edge to edge was spreading to the Atlantic and Baltic areas. From the 1460s to the mid-sixteenth century it replaced the traditional northern clinker building technique with overlapping planks in the construction of major ships. It is probable that there was also a diffusion of framework technique from southern to northern Europe, as the clinker building technique had been closely connected with the idea that the hull should be formed with planking and a framework added later. The spread of framework technique is little known, however, and we must avoid assuming that carvel hulls automatically meant that a fully-fledged framework building technique was also adopted.[17]

With carvel building and thick planking, a strong framework, well-supported decks and strong internal fastenings made of wood and high-quality iron, ships could both carry a large number of guns and survive intense enemy gunfire (staying power). Gun-armed warships carried the heaviest load on their decks and not in their holds, a fact which made warship construction demanding and increasingly separated it from the less complicated cargo carriers. A gun carrier required deck supports (beams and knees), transversal frames and longitudinal strengthenings dimensioned for heavy loads at places which were suboptimal for hull design and stability. In the Baltic, the word *kravell* (carvel-built ship) became (from the late fifteenth to at least the third quarter of the sixteenth century) synonymous with a specialised warship, an etymology which shows the importance of hull construction. The improved methods of hull construction might be analysed by measuring the ratio between the weight of the guns and the displacement of the ship, a subject which is little studied for this period.[18]

Much was done in *ship design* in order to increase speed, improve weatherliness and manoeuvrability and make the ship a steady and sufficiently stiff platform for gunfire. The height of the main gundeck above the waterline became important in gun-carrying warships and stability had to be estimated (by experience, as mathematical methods were only developed later) with great care in order to mount as much gunpower as possible on the decks. The height between decks had to be sufficient for the gun crews to work unhindered, a fact which increasingly separated warships from pure cargo carriers. The ratios between various dimensions (length, beam, depth, the rakes of stem and stern, the width of the 'floor', etc.) and the proportions of the rig had to be adjusted to the conflicting demands of speed, seaworthiness, weatherliness, manoeuvrability and stiffness. Optimum rather than maximum was desirable in many cases: stiffness was necessary if the guns on the leeward side were to be usable when the hull heeled over under the pressure of the wind, but too much stiffness made a ship roll violently, thus making it an unsteady gun platform.

The underwater lines of the hull were important for speed but also for the distribution of floating power to support the increasingly heavy armament. The lines of the hull at the stern determined the efficiency of the rudder. One common problem was that shipbuilders tried to achieve high speed with narrow hulls, rather than with sharp hull lines. Narrow hulls reduced stiffness and made warships into mediocre gun platforms. Only gradually did shipbuilders learn to give warships a generous beam and sharp underwater lines in order to ensure both speed and stiffness. The difficult process of finding the best compromise is reflected in many changes in dimension rules and design practices during the sixteenth and seventeenth centuries.

The decreasing importance of infantry weapons at sea made it possible to reduce the upperworks, but the extent to which this should be done remained a vexed question until the latter half of the seventeenth century. The general line of development went from higher freeboard to lower freeboard ships but it was far from straight and uniform. Radically lowered superstructures, such as those adopted by the English navy in the 1570s (the ships which were frequently called galleons), was soon rejected, but the concept returned in the 1630s and 1640s in small and medium-sized ships: the frigates built for the Spanish Armada of Flanders, the Dutch navy and the English navy. High and thick bulwarks were desirable to protect the crew from small-arms fire and guns were usually mounted under the protection of decks. In a gun-armed ship most of the crew would be below decks handling guns during battle. If an enemy was able to board with a determined force he might overpower the small deck crew, trap most of the crew below decks and take control of the ship. Most navies therefore preferred to have ships with both a forecastle and a substantial superstructure aft in order to have protected places where the crew could gather for an organised counter-attack into the waist if the ship was boarded.

These changes in rig, hull construction and ship design gradually transformed regional types of late medieval cargo carriers into a relatively homogeneous type of seventeenth century sailing gun-armed warship. There remained regional differences and various compromises between cargo-carrying and fighting capabilities, but they were variations on a common theme. The main armament was carried on a deck where the gunports were about 1.0 to 1.5 metres above the waterline when the ship was fully loaded. On medium-sized ships (with displacements of around 400/500 to 800/900 tonnes) this deck was usually covered with another deck, but there the guns were usually mounted only under the quarter-deck and in the forecastle. Larger ships usually had two complete battery decks with additional guns in the superstructures. A few very large ships (of around 2,000 tonnes or more) had three complete battery decks. When guns became cheaper, gunports were placed closer to each other. In the mid-seventeenth century unprotected upper deck areas, which earlier had not been used for guns, became armed and many ships built in the 1620s and 1630s gradually aquired an increased number of guns.

The development of the gun-armed ship also gave new opportunities for *combinations* of cargo-carrying and fighting power. Earlier, an armed merchantman had been a normal cargo carrier with weapons and armed men added for protection. A more specialised type was the famous Italian mercantile great galley which since the fourteenth century had served on regular routes within the Mediterranean and between Italy, Flanders and England. They required a large crew in proportion to their cargo and they disappeared from their traditional routes during the first half of the sixteenth century. In Venice and later in the Ottoman empire the type reappeared as an hybrid warship, the galeass, with auxiliary oars and heavy armament fore and aft.

In sailing defensible merchantmen, guns made it possible to substitute manpower with capital, a proposition which became especially attractive if the guns were cheap cast-iron ordnance. In the last decades of the sixteenth century a new type of economical armed merchantman suitable for trade in dangerous waters was developed in England and the Netherlands. It was a medium-sized ship with a substantial battery and with a crew numerous enough to fire at least a few broadsides against attackers which tried to board the vessel or fire continuously with chase guns in the bow and stern. Little is known about the early ships of this type but later they were shaped like warships with superstructures fore and aft, high bulwarks and with sufficient height between the decks to allow the gun crews to work unhindered. Their hulls were however not as strong as warships of the same size, they might be less steady and stiff as gun platforms and their dimensions might be compromises between warships and cargo carriers.[19]

The new type of gun-armed merchantman first appeared in substantial numbers in the trade between the Mediterranean and north-western Europe. In the late sixteenth century they were used by the Dutch and English when they entered the trade to the East and West Indies in armed struggle with the Iberian powers. Spain and Portugal began to use armed merchantmen in their America trade in order to protect it from the English and Dutch predators. The large Spanish merchantmen were built according to royal ordinances regulating their dimensions in order to make them suitable as warships.[20] In Europe armed merchantmen were used as auxiliary warships in the service of the states although as such they were often given additional guns and men. From the 1610s to the 1660s, the Dutch and to some extent the English developed a new type of business when fleets of armed merchantmen with guns and crews were hired out to Venice, France, Portugal, Denmark-Norway and Sweden. In Denmark-Norway and Sweden the states began to give customs preferences to ships built as armed merchantmen in order to create reserve fleets which might augment the regular navy in time of war. Much fighting from the late sixteenth century to the third quarter of the seventeenth century was done by armed merchantmen. Almost as much as the fully specialised warship they were the embodiment of sea power in a period when business interest was behind much of both the violence and protection which was the routine of warfare at sea.

Guns, strategy and tactics

The gradual development of guns and more advanced sailing ships gave new options for warfare at sea. Guns meant that manpower was substituted by capital and technical development in metallurgy and chemistry. It meant that fighting power (firepower from guns) could be stored during long periods and transported for long distances. Guns and effective propulsive power from the wind also gave ships the opportunity to fight at long range, far enough to eliminate or reduce the effect of infantry weapons. Advances in sailing-ship technology improved the ability of ships to sail long distances and to remain at sea even under unfavourable circumstances – heavy weather, dangerous coasts and so on. The ship and its crew became masters of the sea to a greater extent than before.

Guns and improved sailing-ship technology increased the strategic range of maritime warfare. Men required a constant supply of food and water, they required space to live in and they often fell ill or died on extended expeditions. Warships filled to capacity with fighting men could not travel long distances or stay at sea for long periods if they were to have the necessary strength to fight successfully. In contrast, guns and properly stored gunpowder could remain at sea for long periods and even travel across oceans without any reduction in their fighting potential. They did not require food, water or firewood, nor did they fall ill. The combination of wind power, effectively harnessed by the new full-rigged ship, and firepower from its guns enabled the ship to stay at sea for several months without any dramatic reduction in fighting efficiency. Gun-armed ships still required large crews, however, and the problems with health remained. Sometimes the latter became crippling and a fleet had to give up the attempt to deploy power in an area at a great distance from its base. But such events had become normal misfortunes in sea warfare. They were no longer signs that long-distance deployments were inherently impossible.

The consequences of this technically based change were far-reaching. Warfare at sea became interregional and even global. European states and commercial interests might send fleets to areas far from their bases, undertake prolonged blockades and launch attacks on trade and cities in distant waters. They could also defend long-distance trade in convoys protected by warships or by merchantmen armed with guns. This meant that power based on local resources was relatively reduced while the ability of a sea power to defend its interests and project power at long distances correspondingly increased. Naturally, it remained an advantage to have bases close to operational areas but the importance of that advantage had been reduced and was markedly less important than in warfare on land. As guns came increasingly into use in siege warfare on land the ability of a sea power to maintain a network of local bases (or allied cities) in hostile territories diminished. On the other hand, local power created by such fortified enclaves might be replaced by the power exercised by a squadron of gun-armed warships cruising off the coast. Outside Europe, where local power-holders had no effective siege artillery, networks of fortified trading posts supported by sailing fleets became important in the expansion of European maritime empires.

A second important consequence of the fact that guns could be a substitute for armed men at sea was that an invading army could no longer transform its manpower into efficient armed force at sea. Earlier, the fighting power of a navy carrying an invading army was the army itself. A defender might organise his own naval force and send it to sea with his army in order to stop the invasion by a decisive battle at sea but this was only one alternative. It was often not the best option for a weaker defender who would normally prefer to use the terrain and the attacker's logistical difficulties during an extended operation to beat off an invasion. The defender often found it a better alternative to concentrate his army in defensive positions on land rather than exposing it in a forward position at sea. With gun-armed warships a defender with a weaker army might prefer to meet the enemy at sea and try to defeat the invader while his stronger army could not act. In the fifteenth and sixteenth centuries the infantry became the dominating force in the armies and its reduced importance at sea meant that armies and navies became sharply distinctive organisations. Even inferior navies were often effective as anti-invasion deterrents because army commanders were normally reluctant to expose their forces to attack at sea until the enemy fleet was decisively beaten or effectively neutralised by blockade. With gun-armed ships the sea had become an excellent theatre for stopping or delaying an invading army.

A third consequence of the introduction of guns at sea was that warships acquired the ability to attack targets onshore. Ships might bombard fortifications and support army forces along the coast. Guns could of course also be used from land against ships but at least in our period when heavy guns were scarce and immobile and many old fortifications highly vulnerable to gunfire, the mobile firepower carried by ships was often important in seaborne attacks against cities and fortresses close to the sea. As cities and coastal areas became more vulnerable to seaborne guns, gun-armed navies also became more important in the defence of such areas. The states which could maintain such naval forces gained in power.

Technology, politics and economy interacted in the transformation of warfare at sea. The introduction of guns at sea and the development of efficient sailing ships created new tactical opportunities which in their turn created new strategic conditions which had important political and economic consequences. But economic and political factors in Europe were also favourable for

33

the evolution of new technology. It was not a simple relationship of new technology creating a new world (technological determinism) but rather a case of a rapidly changing world in which new technology was easily adapted, developed and integrated with the society. The fact that efficient guns and gun-armed warships for centuries remained practically a European speciality, which only to a limited extent was used by Asian seafarers, is a strong indication that technology in itself was not enough. The society must also have the necessary flexibility and dynamism to absorb technology and change the institutional framework in order to make the best possible use of them. There were also differences in adaptability within Europe. All European states were able to adapt to guns but there was no uniform efficiency in producing and using the new weapon system.

Much of the technical change must have been driven by ambitions to achieve tactical advantages and more ambitious strategies. The origin of the innovations, however, has been rather obscure. British authors have often taken it for granted that they had their origin, or at least achieved its practical breakthrough, in England. Henry VIII is regarded as a pioneer while John Hawkins, Francis Drake and other privateers and naval administrators who combined guns with swift and versatile ships developed the weapon system that defeated the Spanish Armada in 1588. Some (not all) students of the Portuguese activities in the Indian Ocean have found it obvious that gunnery was already the key instrument of long-distance oceanic warfare from around 1500. In that perspective, King Joao II (r. 1481–95) has been regarded as a great innovator. He sent gun-armed ships to sea in order to deter interlopers who interfered with the Portuguese trade to West Africa, but the same combination worked in the Indian Ocean.[21] Those (very few) who have seriously studied the naval wars in the Baltic of 1509–12, 1534–36 and 1563–70 have found that major battles were repeatedly fought with guns and that certain Nordic kings and admirals had a fairly clear grasp of the potential of the new technology. On the other hand, the experienced Dutch sea commanders whose gunnery defeated another Spanish Armada in the Channel in 1639 tried to use boarding during the war with England in 1652–54. The decades around 1650 were also the heydays of fireship tactics in battles at sea. The extensive use of fireships from the 1630s to the 1690s is a sign that contemporary tacticians were aware of limitations in gunnery tactics and were searching for alternatives.[22]

In several respects, guns were revolutionary weapons, but there were considerable difficulties in making full use of their potential power at sea. At present there is uncertainty about how guns were mounted and loaded in sixteenth- and early seventeenth-century sailing warships. There are a number of problems which remain to be investigated before we have a clear picture of how guns were handled in different navies and how this affected tactics. Up to the early seventeenth century there is scattered evidence that guns had to be loaded with one man working outside the ship, that is, in a very exposed position. Guns may have been lashed to the side rather than allowed to recoil for reloading. There might be more than one reason for this. Some guns (especially the long culverins) might have been so long that they could not recoil fully in a small ship. Second, armed merchantmen might have had so much cargo on their decks that there were no space for the guns to recoil. Third, some ships (especially armed merchantmen) had such small crews that they could not haul out the heavy guns if they were allowed to recoil. Fourth, the current tactical doctrine might, under these circumstances or other limitations, have presumed that guns should not be reloaded under enemy fire.

One interpretation of the Spanish manner of fighting in 1588 is that many of their guns were mounted in gun-carriages which were unsuitable for rapid reloading and that the Spanish crews were not trained to reload under fire and were consequently unable to achieve even a moderate rate of continuous fire.[23] On the other hand, early sixteenth-century naval gunnery was dominated by breech-loaders which could be reloaded fairly quickly from inside the ship. Is it conceivable that all navies would have adopted muzzle-loaders if this meant a dramatic decline of the rate of fire when all guns had to be loaded from outside the ship? Studies of ammunition expenditure in naval battles, to improve our knowledge of the realities of warfare in this period, would be welcome.

Tactics and fleet formations

The tactical consequences of guns in galley warfare are well known. The main difference from earlier galley warfare was that galleys now had a weapon for stand-off fights and for attacks on coastal fortifications. In battles between two galley fleets which were determined to fight, heavy guns became a useful additional weapon in the first stage of a battle before close combat with infantry weapons was joined. No change in the basic oared tactics, with galleys formed in line abreast formation, was necessary. Oared fleets could act with a certain sophistication in formation as they were not dependent on the wind. Galley fleet commanders might, for example, form the line of battle in a crescent in order to turn the enemy flanks or place one or more reserve formations behind the main line in order to concentrate the forces at a critical point as the battle progressed. Guns also allowed two galley fleets which were reluctant to fight a decisive battle to fight at a distance. In a chase battle, the chasing galley had an advantage as it could fire its guns from the bow while the fleeing galley had no guns aft. This may have made galley commanders with an inferior force more cautious to expose it to situations where battles might be difficult to avoid.[24]

The tactical formations used in sailing-ship battles are less well known. We have already seen that there are unresolved questions about how guns were actually handled. There are few surviving contemporary instructions and manuals about how to fight with sailing ships and those which exist have seldom been compared. The accounts of what actually happened during battles are

35

often brief and fragmentary. Many battle reports have not been compared with each other and with accounts of ammunition expenditure. It is, however, obvious that commanders of sailing fleets in this period faced three major problems. Sailing ships were inherently better in defensive than in offensive actions, major fleets were often heterogeneous and improvised, and it was difficult to keep the fleet in a coherent formation throughout a battle.[25]

Guns could only be used effectively if the gun-carrying ship was able to bring them to bear on the enemy. Against enemy ships built to resist gunfire only repeated hits would have any serious effect. This posed a problem in combining effective and decisive firepower with offensive tactical movement, a problem never fully solved with sailing warships. During the sixteenth century sailing tactics emphasised the importance of forward fire, so as many guns as possible were mounted in a forward firing position. The foremost broadside guns might also be canted in order to fire as close as possible to the axial direction of the ship. This combined fire power with offensive movement. Similarly, guns in the stern were important during retreats, but in both cases the amount of fire power was limited.

Broadside guns – which were probably few in number originally – may primarily have been regarded as an anti-boarding device. For a fleet which acted defensively broadside gunfire provided a new first zone of defence which had been largely absent in the age of infantry warships. To use the same guns for tactically offensive purposes – continuous fire in order to defeat an enemy – was more difficult. Our knowledge about how contemporary naval commanders thought about this question, before the general introduction of the battle-line after 1650 is deficient. The general impression is that for a long time they were thinking more in terms of the moral and material effect of hits from a limited number of well-aimed guns than of the effect of rapid broadside fire from well-drilled gun crews. This philosophy was realistic in duels between lightly built galleys and against merchantmen with hulls easily shattered by heavy guns. However, against purpose-built warships only a massive amount of gunfire would have decisive effect.

The heterogeneous and improvised character of major fleets was a problem typical of this period. It was largely eliminated in the decades after 1650 when major investments in battle fleets, the formation of permanent officer corps and the introduction of detailed fighting instructions provided naval tactics with a new framework. In the earlier period naval commanders had to do what was possible with combinations of specialised warships of greatly differing sizes, and temporarily employed armed merchantmen with different fighting qualities. The ships were commanded by an equally heterogeneous collection of more or less professional officers (often with an army rather than navy background), aristocrats with or without military or naval training, and civilian shipmasters with or without fighting experience. During the sixteenth century armed merchantmen were often armed only with light guns and were added to fleets primarily as carriers of infantry for boarding. As such they might assist purpose-built warships with additional soldiers when the fleet became engaged with the enemy. During the seventeenth century merchantmen serving in navies were built to carry a substantial gun armament, but they were inferior in fighting qualities to purpose-built warships of the same size. With ships and commanders of very different backgrounds and with little experience of co-operation, advanced tactical performance was not to be expected. Established doctrines of tactical behaviour were at best rudimentary.

With heterogeneous fleets and without a fighting doctrine which emphasised the decisive effect of continuous broadside fire, fighting instructions of this period seldom attempt to impose formations which the fleet could maintain once battle was joined. The signals systems in use were too primitive to enable commanders of large fleets to exercise any effective command when the fleets were actively engaged. Offensively minded commanders who attempted to fight decisive battles with sailing warships saw no alternative to close combat and *melée* tactics, where individual ships or small groups of ships would attack individual enemy ships and do their best to defeat them with guns, musketry, boarding or fireships.

Fighting instructions are often emphatic in their demand for support of ships heavily engaged with the enemy and they are often careful to divide the fleet into squadrons and groups of ships and to appoint senior officers in command of each sub-division of the fleet. Unlike later periods when this practice was intended as a command structure for the battle-line, the subdivision of fleets in this period seems to have been made mainly for reasons of morale. The senior officer of a group normally had a large ship, while other captains in the group had ships of inferior strength. The large ships were supposed to provide a kind of vanguard and break into the enemy formation, and the smaller ships in their group would support them to the best of their ability. Cohesion within groups of ships and loyalty to a group commander might compensate for the lack of professional training and the difficulties of controlling a major fleet from a flagship.

The choice between gunnery tactics or boarding might be made at a fleet level, as well as by individual commanders of ships. It was natural that a fleet which had a comparative advantage in infantry should try to board or fight at musket range while a fleet with a similar advantage in guns tried to fight a stand-off battle. Fleets with approximately the same fighting capability might leave it to the individual ship and squadron commanders, and the tactical circumstances, to determine how best to defeat the opposing enemy ships. The heterogeneous composition of the fleets made it impossible to give permanent and centralised instructions about which tactic every ship should use. However, there was not a free choice between the two systems of fighting. Gradually it became clear that a gun-armed warship was difficult to close and board by a ship of equal size and sailing qualities, especially from a leeward position. Attempts to board might normally be fought off with guns, as long as the ship remained manoeuvrable. Boarding might be attempted against damaged ships or against a numerically inferior enemy, although it was normally not to be expected that a much inferior enemy would join battle if it could be avoided. Especially from the 1630s, specially prepared fireships manned by well-trained crews provided another method of attacking gun-armed ships with small vessels.[26]

Naval commanders, however, were frequently careful in preparing formations which their fleet should keep when battle was joined. Like other questions connected with the naval tactics of this period these formations are imperfectly known. Still, a few main types of fleet formation may be discerned:

1 Line abreast formation inspired by army tactics and galley warfare. These formations were intended for boarding tactics after initial gunfire. The only formations of this type which are known with certainty are those of the English fleet in 1545 and the Spanish Armada of 1588.[27]

2 Groups of three ships (one large and two smaller) which might be formed into a wedge-formed column or a line of three-ship groups when the fleet attacked from windward or into one or two lines ahead when the fleet sailed close-hauled and awaited an enemy attack. The Danish and the Swedish navies developed such formations during the Nordic War of 1563–70.[28]

3 A group tactic where ships sailed in a line ahead formation and fired in succession at the enemy with bow guns and the broadside. After having fired, each ship tacked and reloaded her guns at a distance from the enemy, while the other ships in the group fired their guns, one ship at a time. This was the usual English formation against Spanish fleets and it assumed a passive and defensive enemy from which it was easy to gain the wind. Against ships of equal sailing quality it would hardly work.[29]

4 Line ahead formation. Essentially a defensive formation in this period, used for example by the Dutch against the Spanish fleet in the battle in the Channel in 1639.[30] Its use by the Portuguese in the Indian Ocean in the early sixteenth century is disputed.[31]

The fact that none of these formations had achieved a predominant position by 1650 suggests that they were far from ideal, especially for offensive action against serious resistance. Indeed, the first half of the seventeenth century seems to be especially barren in tactical innovations. Warship technology had by now developed to about the constant level it would retain until the end of the seventeenth century: warships were fairly manoeuvrable; they had an increasing number of broadside guns; and enough staying power to fight prolonged gunnery actions against ships of equal size. Up to 1650, naval commanders seem to have been little interested in the problems and opportunities which this increasingly sophisticated weapon system posed during major fleet engagements. Instead, they may have been increasingly interested in finding determined and loyal captains who could train efficient crews of good sailors and gunners. This was the most important requirement for normal naval duties in this period of long wars over the sea lines of communication: patrolling, escorting, blockading and attacks against enemy shipping. Major fleet contests were rare and if individual ships were manned by good teams of officers and men they would probably have the advantage in a *melée* type of battle. Naval commanders were responsible for decisions about when and where battles should be fought, and their tactical skill might be tested in preliminary manoeuvres to gain the wind from the enemy, but when the battle was joined the individual skills of the captains and their crews would be decisive.

It would require a period of intense and repeated fleet engagements, and a dose of tactical inspiration from the new type of warfare on land, to achieve a new tactical paradigm in the European navies. This occurred during the period 1650–80, with the three Anglo-Dutch wars as especially important trend-setters for naval reorganisation. Somewhat belatedly, guns were acknowledged as the main and decisive weapon at sea, and tactics were determined by the overriding importance of achieving massive and decisive effect on the enemy through continuous broadsides fired by well-drilled gun crews from battleships formed in line ahead.[32]

3

SEAMEN, SOLDIERS AND CHANGING MARITIME SOCIETIES

The sea – a violent place of work

For the individual, warfare and violence at sea were connected with opportunities and risks. The opportunities were the possibility of upward social mobility through success in warfare, profits from trade protected and promoted by violence, and the spoils of legal and illegal plunder. The risks were those usually connected with early modern warfare: death or illness due to hardship and contagious diseases and, less commonly, by wounds inflicted during combat. In addition, seamen had to face the risks of the sea: shipwreck and accidents at work. Many seamen became victims of violence. They were killed, robbed of their possessions, held as prisoners or enslaved.[1]

Although many sailors must have preferred to earn their wages through peaceful seafaring, the European mercantile and seafaring communities were not uniformly peaceful and innocent victims of violence and wars. Violence, used in acts of aggression as well as for protection, was part of the tradition and the professional skill of seamen. Coercion of competitors and various restrictions on trade, which had to be upheld by armed force, were common in medieval and early modern Europe. The long-distance sea lines of communication within Europe were controlled by the groups which were most efficient in protection and coercion. Private violence made the seas insecure and transportation more expensive for the European economy, but it was often profitable for those who used it with skill. This behaviour was also part of the profit-orientated use of violence which characterised European overseas ventures in trade, colonisation, piracy and the slave trade. From around 1500 the scope for such ventures increased dramatically and European seamen became involved in violent activities on a global scale. It is not an unjustified simplification to say that the chief European export product in this period was violence, and the technology and organisation associated with violence. To most non-Europeans of the sixteenth and seventeenth centuries, Europeans were men who came in ships in order to conquer, plunder, trade and enforce protection.

European sailors were bred in this environment where they were expected

to use violence. They had to defend valuable goods and the ship against predators and they had to sail into areas where they, as foreigners, might be met with
hostility and coercion. Neutral shipping was often captured during wars unless
it was well protected. The seas were largely beyond the control of the states,
and the coastal regions and maritime cities were often on the fringe of
centralised control from territorial states. The states were either too weak to
control maritime violence or allowed it in some tacit understanding with the
pirates, smugglers and interlopers in monopoly trade who lived in the coastal
regions. As long as these seafarers did not use violence against the rulers' subjects, states might close at least one eye to how they were earning their money
abroad. The eye which was kept open often looked more for how the state and
the ruling elite might share from the profits of violence rather than for how
the state should suppress it. Civil wars, rebellions and religious conflicts which
for long periods reduced the power of centralised states also had their consequences at sea. Seafarers were deeply involved in these wars and combined the
search for profit with religiously and politically motivated actions against
domestic and foreign enemies. To a large extent the sea had the character of a
violent and lawless frontier zone.

Private violence at sea might also be perfectly legal, at least within the area
where the seafarers had their domicile. The state might empower a shipowner
or a merchant to seek compensation for ships or goods lost to foreigners by
capturing ships from the country which was responsible for the losses. Such
'letters of reprisal' could be issued in times of peace and they naturally often
caused counter-reprisals. If formal war was declared the state might empower
privateers to carry out trade war and other acts of violence against enemies of
the state. States might also give commercial monopoly rights to chartered
companies together with legal rights to uphold the monopoly by violence.
This violence might be directed against other Europeans or against non-
Europeans who might be forced to trade under threat, subjected to European
'protection', or simply robbed. In practice, the legal and illegal uses of violence
at sea were mixed and intertwined in a complicated way during the sixteenth
and seventeenth centuries. Privateering and piracy were not fully separated
and the legal questions surrounding European behaviour beyond Europe were
not settled in this period. The concept of 'no peace beyond the line' was
invented to limit the political consequences in Europe of violence between
Europeans in America, Africa and Asia (that is, in areas considered to be
'beyond the line'). Even in the Mediterranean, an area which had been a centre of trade for many centuries, private and unofficial violence, small-scale wars
and piracy were common, and a serious threat both to peaceful trade and the
coastal population.

In this world, seamen in well-armed ships who were able to fend for themselves had better possibilities of surviving and get a share of the profit from
violence, protection and high-risk activities. European merchants and investors
often looked for profit from 'discoveries', colonisation, slave trading, long-

distance trade in dangerous waters, interloping trade in trade monopoly areas as well as piratical or privateering activities against European ships and colonies, but they had to find seamen who were willing to sail on these high-risk ventures. There are few signs that the number of such seamen was a serious limitation on their activities. Violence usually gave the individual seaman some chance of sharing the spoils, and wages on high-risk ventures were probably better than in other occupations. However, there must also have been a special culture and mentality in many European seafaring communities in which the use of violence against foreigners and people with different culture, language and religion was tolerated or even encouraged. Behaviour which would have been socially upsetting and morally revolting at home (pillaging of more or less defenceless ships or villages, for example) was acceptable if the victims were foreigners with a different language, religion or race.

Seamen, societies and states

The often intimate connections between private profit and efficient use of violence were important as a framework for the developing European navies. Much of the practical experience of warfare at sea, especially at long distance, accumulated within the private sphere of the societies. Merchants and investors in various ventures at sea gained considerable competence in how ships should be built, equipped and manned in order to be successful in defensive and offensive undertakings. The European tradition of convoys organised by merchants and cities was strong and continued in the early modern time both as a private form of protection and as an activity organised by states. State-controlled navies were developed as instruments for power projection, as anti-invasion and coast-defence forces, and as escort forces for trade. But the latter function of the navy was something the mercantile groups were likely to have to pay for and they might prefer to protect themselves rather than pay a state for a service which they could not control. The rulers of the states might on the other hand use this mercantile competence by hiring private ships for their navies and let the private interests organise provisioning and manning. They might also use it by integrating the private interests into the machinery of the state and give them the authority to organise navies with the competence they had gained in the private sector.[2]

One or more of these forms, as well as intermediate forms of integration between the states and the private groups, were tried by nearly all European states in this period. The growing navies of the state could thus profit from the wide range of experience which European seafarers had gained in their attempts to profit from their skills in using violence. Nations with a dynamic private maritime trade seldom had great difficulties in creating and expanding navies at surprisingly short notice. The human element in naval warfare, the experienced seamen and the maritime entrepreneurs were available. States which lacked such domestic resources might hire them from other parts of

Europe. The most successful maritime economy of our period, the Dutch Republic, created a state navy around the traditional private competence of convoy escorting but retained a highly viable sector for private violence at sea. Offensive warfare was to a large extent left to chartered private monopoly companies, the East and West India Companies.

Private entrepreneurs in warfare at sea had a market because the states often lacked the necessary administrative competence to run a navy. One of these competencies was the skill to create efficient teams of seamen to man the ships. Private shipowners normally had close contacts with the seafaring communities. They were in a good position to find skilled and experienced masters, pilots, boatswains and quartermasters who in their turn might find seamen with the combination of maritime and martial skills which made the crew efficient. Shipowners and masters, who were often members of the local elites, might have a good or bad reputation among seamen and this must have influenced their ability to recruit efficient crews. When the state searched for entrepreneurs who might supply a ship or a squadron for the navy they may often have been looking for persons who had a good reputation in a seafaring community. Such men could attract the often scarce resource of skilled seamen willing to serve, and they were also able to create efficient teams of these seamen. Even when navies searched for captains and crews of their own warships they might prefer men who had well developed networks in the maritime communities.

Some early modern states had ambitions to centralise and organise this competence for warfare at sea. Most gun-armed sailing navies began with investments in ships and guns. Gradually rulers found that these instruments of modern naval power could be markedly better used with efficient administration and a systematic organisation of the skills required to fight with sailing gun-carriers. Many of these skills already existed on the private market. If the state were to use its strategic position in the society for developing sea power it had to develop new social frameworks for the recruitment of seamen and the training of efficient leaders of warfare at sea. Arguably, this was the decisive element in a really efficient navy. The new framework had to provide incentives to make the seamen and the leaders disposed to act efficiently in the service of the state. It must also create bonds of loyalty to the state. However, unlike permanent armies and their soldiers (which required basic training in the use of weapons and continuous drill to become an efficient battlefield unit), seamen were a social group which already existed. They had a profession which made them useful on the civilian market and states which were based on viable maritime communities felt no urgency in hiring seamen permanently. What they required were mechanisms for the transfer of existing skilled seamen from civilian society to a state-controlled organisation for warfare at sea when this was required. The mechanism should also send them back to the civilian market when they were no longer required by the state.

The recruitment of leaders was another question. Men who led large numbers of subordinates in combat and warfare had normally been part of the elite group, the nobility or (at sea) a mercantile oligarchy. A position among the social, political and military elite made them effective as leaders, partly because their families had the means to provide them with military training, and partly because members of the elite could protect and help the men who fought under them. This combination of skill and patronage gave authority, an authority which of course was strengthened if the leader was brave, successful and inspiring. The loyalty of this elite to the state was often more dubious – they might instead use their power over men in their own interest. The transformation of military leaders from noblemen (and mercenaries who often were noblemen) into the modern officer corps is an interesting question but we are here only concerned with how it affected warfare at sea.[3]

The technical changes in warfare at sea created problems but also opportunities for the states. Except in Mediterranean galley warfare – and that is an important exception – members of the traditional elite were seldom professional seamen. A young nobleman might begin an army career as a common soldier to learn the profession, but he was much less likely to enter a navy as a common seaman. Some medieval noblemen were experienced sea commanders who understood naval strategy and tactics, but it is unlikely that many of them could have handled a ship without a master who had learnt his profession since his early youth. The increasing sophistication of ships and their new armament, the gun, made technical skills and the ability to organise teams of seamen more important in naval warfare. At the same time, the role of infantry in naval warfare declined and with that the importance of military skill at sea. The problem for the state was that traditional forms of mobilising social resources for warfare did not work well if the link between social status and the ability to command in actual warfare was weakened. Commanders of ships had to enjoy both the loyalty and confidence of the crew if the crew were to work as an efficient team. If the commander was not a natural leader it might be difficult for him to uphold discipline without high status in society, either through family connections or through the power given him by the state to punish or reward.[4]

But the possibilities for success in war created by the new instruments of naval warfare also meant that a new path to the elite was opened for those who *were* skilled in shiphandling and modern combat at sea. It also gave the state an important role in promoting men with new competencies to the elite or to give members of the elite an opportunity to gain new skills by learning shiphandling, naval gunnery and command of fleets. Service to the state might give social status and even nobility to skilled seamen, thus making them members of the elite. Service to the state might also give increased status to the seaman's profession, thus making it attractive for young members of the elite for the first time. The long-term practical solution was the creation of a new hierarchical elite group closely connected to the state, the permanent sea officer corps. For traditional and new members of the elite, the officer corps provided a framework giving them social status, salary and a share of the patronage controlled by states. For the states the creation of a hierarchical and bureaucratic officer corps proved to be an efficient way of increasing the loyalty of the elite group to the states. The officers controlled violence on behalf of the state, but they were also dependent on the authority of the state which legitimised both the taxes raised to maintain the armed forces and the authority they had over their subordinates.

The men who actually worked, fought and commanded at sea from 1500 to 1650 comprise a surprisingly neglected group in historical scholarship. There are also great gaps in our knowledge of social institutions connected with war and violence at sea: incentives and compulsion in recruitment of sailors; the social status of sea officers and seamen; and the professionalisation of sea officers. For later periods we have penetrating studies about social conditions in the navies, recruitment of seamen, the relations between officers and men, galley slaves, professionalisation and the naval career as a ladder for social advancement.[5] For this period, however, major studies about seafaring men are almost exclusively limited to biographies of famous fleet commanders. Some of them are important case studies of the problems in naval command and administration of this period.[6] But there are other interesting topics to study in a period which saw the initial phase of European seaborne expansion, the foundation of permanent navies and the shift of the maritime and economic centre of Europe from the Mediterranean to the Atlantic. As usual in maritime and naval history, comparative studies would be especially valuable.[7]

Such studies, however, are more complex than for later periods when state navies provided organisational frameworks as employers of officers and men engaged in maritime warfare. Men engaged in early modern warfare at sea were often not employed by navies. They belonged to seafaring communities, often living on the fringe of state control and having a dynamic of their own in projecting seaborne violence around the coasts of Europe and to other parts of the world. Economic incentives or the need to protect themselves, their community and perhaps their country made seamen into fighters on state warships, on armed merchantmen, on ships armed for piracy or privateering, or on ships hired by a state. The men who fought at sea were by no means always seamen. Medieval and early modern sailing warships often had crews where the majority were soldiers, not sailors. Most of the crews of the Mediterranean galley fleets were oarsmen – some of them free, others convicts, prisoners of wars or slaves. The fighting members of the galley crews were soldiers and gunners, while the skilled seamen were a small minority. The remainder of this chapter is intended only as a brief overview of two of these complexities: officers and the institutions for recruitment of crews.

Command of ships and fleets

Around 1500, fleets organised for war were platforms and means of transportation for soldiers. Galleys were traditionally fighting platforms for soldiers
with only a small number of skilled seamen. In sailing fleets mobilised for full-
scale wars the number of soldiers was usually larger than the number of seamen. Merchants, who wished to provide better protection for their ships than
the self-defence which armed seamen might offer, hired professional soldiers
who sailed on the merchantmen as a guarding force. Infantry soldiers provided
this fighting force at sea as on land, and soldiers at sea were commanded by
officers who often were noblemen. Large forces of soldiers at sea were usually
commanded by members of the ruling aristocracy who had the status to
enforce their will on other noble officers. Naturally, these aristocrats were also
the most likely commanders of the fleets.

Sailing ships – merchantmen as well as the few state-owned warships that
existed – were commanded by masters and a small hierarchy of men with specialised maritime skills: pilots, master's mates, quartermasters, boatswains. The
masters were seamen who knew the profession and who could supervise and
command the crew by virtue of long experience at sea. The shipmasters and
their subordinate officers were specialists who could handle the ship's complicated rig – one of the great inventions of this age – and convert the often
dangerous and capricious wind into a safe and efficient motive power. This
also enabled them to manoeuvre a ship and direct its guns during a battle. As
they were responsible for a valuable ship, its cargo and its maintenance, masters
were respected members of the seafaring and trading communities. But in
societies dominated by landowners, and with chivalric ideals and military skills
as the paradigm for social virtue, experienced masters of ships definitely
belonged to a lower stratum of the social hierarchy.

The practical consequence of this was that warships and merchantmen fitted
out for war had a command structure which often seems rather confusing.[8] The
officers of the embarked soldiers, and the shipmaster and his subordinates, represented two separate command structures. The latter was responsible for the
handling of the ship and its navigation, while infantry officers commanded the
soldiers during battle. The details of these command arrangements have been
little studied. Permanent armies were often as much in their infancy as the
navies and many of the officers who commanded troops were actually aristocrats and gentlemen, with limited military experience but with a social position
which made them suitable for command. If every ship were to have a captain in
command of both seamen and soldiers – we cannot be sure that this was the rule
everywhere as joint command was possible – a gentleman with or without a
background as soldier might often be preferred to a master. But masters might
have a prestige and social standing derived from family connections with rich
merchants or from their experience as fighting seamen. They might also be
regarded as suitable for command of a warship in the service of a state.

The circumstances under which a particular fleet was organised might have determined much of the real (possibly informal and probably often muddled) command structure. If a hastily assembled fleet of armed merchantmen embarked an organisationally coherent army with a firm command structure, it would be natural if that command structure took precedence over the individual masters of the ships. If a more or less established navy with ships commanded by masters or gentlemen officers with some experience of the sea embarked temporarily assembled units of soldiers, it seems rather natural that the soldiers were subordinated to the existing command structure of the ships. If the fleet were to be divided into small squadrons, or individual ships were to be sent out for cruising or escort duties, this command structure seems to be almost necessary. When army officers were in command we should not take it for granted that every ship in a fleet had a military 'captain' who commanded in each ship. The soldiers had to be divided according to the size of the ship and their officers may have preferred to stay on the larger ships which would be the most important units during battle.

Officer corps in their modern sense had their origin in our period.[9] The creation of a new corps of professional men who combined the skills of 'seamen' and 'warriors' with a hierarchical structure suitable for various levels of command and with a loyalty linked to the state seems so 'rational' and 'modern' that we may wonder why it took many generations to develop. We may explain this by arguing that states were for a long time too weak to create permanent structures of men with generous salaries, that the inertia and resistance created by the existing systems of social status were strong and that contemporary decision makers had greater difficulties than we have in perceiving the advantages of the modern officer corps. We must, however, also remember that men with skills as warriors at sea existed on the private market and that states might be satisfied with more informal bonds of allegiance, and contractual relationships with these groups. In the Mediterranean world, contractual relationships between galley officers of fairly high social status and various states were well established before 1500. The system survived up to the end of our period in a strong contractual structure within the Spanish sailing and galley fleets.

In western and northern Europe, maritime cities preferred to employ their native masters as commanders at sea, usually in combination with professional mercenary officers who commanded soldiers. The kings who began to create permanent sailing navies around 1500 were the rulers who were most likely to make experiments with new solutions. We may guess that they were the power-holders who had most to gain by creating a more permanent organisational structure which might compensate for a relative lack of maritime skills within their states. But in several of these navies the fully-fledged corps of sea officers did not appear until several decades or even more than a century after the state began to create permanent navies. There might have been a genuine lack of suitable commanders or it might have taken time to develop the idea that the state might create such men by giving them the opportunity to make a life-long career in the navy.

Nevertheless, from 1500 to 1650 the command structure and status system connected with warfare at sea underwent radical changes. In 1500 the professional commissioned sea officer hardly existed.[10] By 1650 sailing warships were commanded by men who formally and often also in reality were sea officers, that is, professional sailors and professional leaders of men in combat. The modern career path of the sea officers was barely established and only some navies had begun to give officers a permanent commission and rank. However, most navies had a pool of men who served as officers more or less permanently and these probably acted as a powerful interest group to which the states ultimately had to give permanent commissions in order to ensure their loyalty. Even large warships often had only a few officers – a captain and one or a few lieutenants. Some mid-seventeenth-century sea officers were noblemen who had chosen the navy as a career path, sometimes after they had tried the army. Other sea officers were of the same social background as masters and they might have secured a commission as officers as a reward for good service in the navy or because the expanding navies lacked sufficient experienced men to command their ships. Masters of merchantmen were often given a temporary commission as sea officers in times of war and the most successful of them might be rewarded with permanent commissions.

Masters, pilots and the old hierarchy of command based on experience of the sea still existed on warships in 1650 and, as the number of commissioned officers was small, they must often have had responsibilities which in later periods belonged to officers. However, the old hierarchy with its origin in merchantmen were now regarded as warrant officers and were subordinated to a new hierarchy of officers specialised for warfare at sea. We may now refer to this group as sea officers. A new group of specialists with their own small internal hierarchy had been added during the sixteenth century, the gunners. Warships still had soldiers in their crews, but they were now normally a minority. In most navies they were commanded by junior army officers who were subordinated to the sea officer commanding the ship. After 1650, some navies (England, the Netherlands, France) began to create regiments of marines which organisationally belonged to the navies.

Sea officers in most mid-seventeenth-century navies were apparently still primarily regarded as leaders during battle and as upholders of discipline. A good knowledge of the skills of the master, the pilot and the gunner was useful but officers were primarily leaders of men. They were also the representative of the state and as such they were responsible for the ship executing orders given by admirals or the government. Furthermore, they were responsible for the crew obeying laws and naval regulations, and the handling of money and victuals issued to the ships.

These tasks were not a formality in a period of relatively weak state power and many opportunities for private enrichment through plunder and peculation. An armed ship was a source of power which might be appropriated for various private uses if it was not properly controlled by the state. On sea as on land, warfare meant opportunities for enrichment by plunder. States had no illusions about their officers and crews, and their right to a share in the spoils of war was generally acknowledged. However, in a well-disciplined navy captured merchantmen were supposed to be taken to port where their legal status would be determined by a court. If it was declared a lawful prize the crew might divide the prize money according to the law.

Warships were also supposed to operate according to strategic demands and not in order to enrich officers and men. They should, for example, escort friendly merchantmen or blockade enemy ports, even if cruising for rich enemy prizes might be more profitable for the captain and the crew. If they captured a ship in a fleet combat they should continue to fight the enemy and not bring the prize to a port without the admiral's order. These were rules and norms of behaviour which it took a long time to establish and enforce and the rise of a professional officer corps was part of this story. Finally, a warship represented the power and dignity of the state and in contact with other states it was useful to have a commanding officer with a certain knowledge of diplomacy and international politics. Gentlemen were normally supposed to have such qualities in a higher degree than men with a background as plain seamen.

Much of the typical sea officer skills of a later period – shiphandling, gunnery, navigation – still primarily belonged to the specialists. This explains why men with no experience of the sea might yet often be given command of ships. If their social status or previous conduct in other appointments made it probable that they could command men in combat, enforce discipline and obey orders from superior officers, they might be suitable as sea officers. But the idea that the ships should be commanded by sea officers and not by officers who commanded soldiers was generally established by 1650. Increasingly, such officers also began their seagoing careers as young men and received at least basic training in shiphandling, gunnery and navigation before they obtained a commission as a sea officer. Towards the end of the seventeenth century this career path had become practically compulsory for future sea officers in the European navies, even for men from families with a high social position. The new professional sea officer must have the same competence as a master of a merchantmen in handling his ship.

The professional and bureaucratic corps of sea officers was a phenomenon which developed in the permanent navies. These navies had to 'invent' the sea officer in order to create a group of leaders who could combine a socially respectable position (which also gave authority over the crew) with the technical and maritime skills traditionally connected with men of a lower social position. Professionalisation meant that these sea officers became a well defined group – very similar in character in all navies – with special skills and a special code of conduct. Bureaucratisation meant that they were servants of a state who used the armed force of the state according to rules and orders given by the state. It also meant that orders were passed down a formal, hier-archical chain of command. This was in itself something of an innovation as it meant that the social hierarchy was subordinated to that of an organisation. A junior officer from an aristocratic family had to obey orders given by a senior officer who might not even be a nobleman. The rise of the sea officer was also closely connected with the rise of gunnery tactics and the decline of infantry as the decisive fighting force at sea. In many countries the army offi-cer corps developed in much the same way in this period, but this develop-ment was less complicated as infantry and cavalry officers could relatively smoothly inherit and merge with the traditional military role of the nobility. Sea officers were more comparable to the technical branches of the army, gunners and engineers, and just like them they were often of a less aristocratic origin.

In Denmark-Norway a group of royal sea officers developed gradually dur-ing the sixteenth century. Some were noblemen who chose the sea to fulfil their obligation to serve the king, others were commoners who were paid more or less permanently by the king to command ships.[11] A similar develop-ment took place in Sweden. During the wars in the 1520s and 1530s the Swedish navy was commanded according to old principles with 'army' officers and shipmasters. The next time the navy was fully mobilised for war, in the 1560s, ships were commanded by men who were called sea officers. It was not until the early seventeenth century that this corps of officers became a for-mally permanent service, but by then the modern career path of officers had been established in both the army and the navy.[12]

The English navy followed a more complicated line of development. In the early sixteenth century warships were commanded by captains (that title was already in use), who might be shipmasters or gentlemen with or without experience of the sea or command of soldiers. Fleets and warships were often fitted out on a more or less contractual basis. During the sixteenth century naval shipmasters, merchants with experience of armed trade, gentlemen and socially rising seamen with experience in private warfare, were used by the navy as captains. In the early seventeenth century gentlemen became predom-inant as sea officers, but during the Civil Wars in the 1640s (when the navy was controlled by the Parliament) these were almost entirely replaced by mas-ters, often men with experience from armed merchantmen. The formalisation of a permanent corps of English sea officers had to wait until the second half of the seventeenth century.[13]

In these three kingdoms, some members of the aristocracy and the gentry (the lower nobility in Scandinavia) were interested in becoming sea officers and, as such, they had to mix with men of more humble social origin. Members of the English gentry and a few aristocrats did, at least in the latter half of the sixteenth century, show a genuine interest in the seaman's profes-sion and the social prejudices against manual work connected with the sea – at least warfare at sea – seem to have declined. In the Dutch Republic the navy of the state developed in a distinctly maritime and non-noble environment and here almost exclusively masters with a mercantile background were hired to command the warships of the state. Many of these masters had considerable experience of fighting from service in armed merchantmen or privateers. From 1626 a corps of captains were given life-time employment, but the Dutch admiralties (or rather their captains) continued to hire junior officers on the open market, an arrangement that was still possible in the world's leading maritime power.[14]

In the Mediterranean world the profession of sea officer, in a sense, had already had a long history before 1500. The galleys were often commanded by men who had chosen this occupation as their career. They usually belonged to the nobility or its equivalent among the patriciate in city states. Service as galley officers was prestigious and attractive for younger sons of noble families. In the Mediterranean many Italian, French and Spanish noblemen served as entrepreneurs in galley warfare. As such they were owners and commanders of one or several galleys. Venetian (state-owned) galleys were commanded by members of the aristocratic families who ruled the republic and they sent out their young sons to serve as cadets on the galleys in order to qualify as galley commanders. The Order of St John on Malta developed into something of a cadet school for young noblemen from various European countries, primarily France and the Habsburg kingdoms in Spain and Italy, who wished to gain experience of the sea in a socially acceptable environment. Galley officers were primarily commanders of soldiers and their skills in shiphandling was probably limited, but service in galleys undoubtedly gave experience of the sea and of naval gunnery.[15]

The traditions of galley warfare have often been used as an explanation for the difficulties Spain experienced with the development of a professional corps of sea officers. This conclusion is a bit doubtful, however. It is obvious that far into the seventeenth century Spain had problems with the status and authority of men specialised as sea commanders. The galley tradition might have been an advantage if the highly regarded galley officers had primarily been identified as *sea* officers with an alternative role as commanders of sailing warships. Instead, Spanish warships were for a long time predominantly commanded by infantry officers. The early appointments to commands in sailing ships in sixteenth-century convoys to the West Indies were often given to men with military experience. In the permanent sailing navy which was established in the late sixteenth century two paths of career developed, one as seaman officer and another as infantry officer. Habsburg naval forces often had ships with a dual command of two officers, one from each hierarchy. Gradually, a command structure with single command – one officer in overall command on every ship – became predominant. Up to the mid-seventeenth century, however, it was much easier for an infantry officer – often but not always with seagoing experience – to be appointed to *capitan de mar y guerra*, that is commanding officer of both the seamen and the soldiers on a ship.

51

Men who had begun their careers as seamen had great difficulty in becoming accepted by the Castilian social elite, in spite of receiving support from the Habsburg kings who had realised the importance of an efficient corps of sea officers. The social elite of Castile had an ethos fostered in the *reconquista* ideals where military service on land was the norm. Seamen officers were primarily recruited from the mercantile and maritime groups on Spain's Biscay coast. Here it was entirely possible for a man who was regarded as a member of the gentry or lower nobility to serve as a sailor and learn the seaman's craft before he became a master and sea officer, but in the Castilian nobility this meant that he had been occupied with socially degrading manual work. Whether such men were to be preferred to men with army experience when commanders of ships and squadrons were to be appointed was often debated with some heat in the Spanish central administration. The low status of Spanish sea officers without an army background has often been used as an explanation for the relatively poor performance of Spanish warships in battle with English and Dutch ships.[16]

Spain had, by the early sixteenth century, already established a permanent army with a highly qualified, disciplined and politically reliable corps of infantry officers. This may have made the development of another corps of officers with different professional ideals more problematic than in countries without strong army traditions. Spanish infantry officers had, at least until the early seventeenth century, a well-deserved reputation as the best officer corps in Europe and this reputation appears to have been a strong argument in favour of giving these officers a wider field of authority.

The situation in Portugal seems to have been similar to that in Spain, although much less is known about it. Most of what has been written about the command structure on Portuguese warships is actually about the ships that sailed to the Indian Ocean. As these ships belonged to the Portuguese royal navy we may presume that they reflect the general conditions in this navy, but we cannot be certain. After Portugal's break with Spain in 1640 the new monarchy made attempts to reform the sea officer corps and promote experienced seamen to leading positions, but this ran into serious difficulties due to social prejudices.[17]

In Atlantic France, the seafaring population traditionally had low social status, although late medieval French kings tried to raise it. The social history of the officers of the sixteenth-century French navy during the Valois dynasty is little known.[18] When the ships of the navy disappeared in the turmoil of religious civil wars the officer corps continued to exist, as sea officers' commissions were among those offices which the French crown sold to provide revenues. When a real navy with ships was recreated by Richelieu in the 1620s these officers were little used. Instead, men with maritime and seagoing experience in trade and private warfare were preferred, many of them Huguenots from the coastal provinces. It seems to have been a matter of expediency – the state required a working navy quickly – rather than a conscious effort to prefer commoners. In the large French navy created by Louis XIV and Colbert (himself born as a commoner), noble officers dominated. In the Mediterranean galley fleet, noblemen had already been dominating as officers early in the seventeenth century. French noblemen with experience from the Order of St John at Malta played a large role in the seventeenth-century French navy, first in the galley fleet, but increasingly also in the sailing fleet.[19]

Venice and the Ottoman empire show the great structural difficulties in transformation of competencies from oared warfare to warfare under sail. In the sixteenth century both powers had had excellent galley forces commanded by highly skilled galley officers but their origins were markedly different. Where Venice recruited her galley commanders from the ruling oligarchy the Ottomans appointed their commanders either from professional sailors who had served in lower ranks on the state galleys or from men with privateering experience.[20] In the seventeenth century the two Levantine navies were compelled to use sailing warships, but they both lacked the technical ability to build such ships and men suitable to command them. Venice had to hire Dutch and English armed merchantmen with crews and officers and the Ottomans became much dependent on their North African vassals, who adopted the sailing ship technology in the early seventeenth century, partly with the help of renegades from western Europe.

The high command of the navies was a somewhat different problem from command of ships. Even by 1650 it was far from natural that admirals should be recruited from the sea captains. The commander-in-chiefs of major fleets and the positions as permanent heads of navies (Lord High Admiral in England, *Amiral de France* and other high admiral charges in France, *Riksamiral/Rigsadmiral* in the Nordic countries, *Admiraal-Generaal* and his deputies in the Netherlands), especially, were appointments where social and political considerations were important. Aristocrats were preferred and men with an army background were often preferred to sea officers. A few aristocratic families, such as the Howards in England and the Flemings in Sweden, produced several admirals. Some of these aristocratic admirals gained considerable experience as flag officers and showed notable success as strategists and tacticians. Denmark-Norway during the reign of Christian IV (r. 1588/96–1648) was a unique case in this period as the king (who was proud of being regarded as a professional seaman) often personally took command of the fleet and closely supervised its administration.

The Dutch Republic was the first European state where seamen officers of humble social origin reached the rank of commander-in-chief of a major navy. Piet Hein was appointed to that rank in 1629 and Maarten H. Tromp in 1637, but even in that bourgeois republic noblemen were appointed commanders-in-chief without much seagoing experience. In England, some of the Elizabethan privateering heroes, primarily John Hawkins and Francis Drake (who were both knighted), had come close to similar positions, but in the early Stuart navy social rank mattered more. In the latter half of the seventeenth century it became common in most European navies to select admirals from the experienced sea captains. By the early eighteenth century most admirals were men with a long career as professional sea officers, a career usually begun with a period when they had to learn the basic skills of a seaman. The modern career path of the permanent corps of sea officers was a fact.

Spain represents something of a paradox, as this navy surprisingly often appointed admirals with considerable seagoing experience. The best known Spanish admiral of this period is the Duke of Medina Sidonia who commanded the Armada of 1588. He, however, was a typical European naval commander-in-chief of the period, a leading aristocrat with a reputation as an energetic and reliable administrator, but without any experience of high command at sea. But Medina Sidonia was appointed as a last minute replacement for the deceased marquis of Santa Cruz, a man with a long seagoing experience who rose to the aristocracy in naval service. This Armada had several experienced seamen officers among its squadron commanders.[21] Seventeenth-century Spanish and Portuguese admirals are little studied but it seems that some of them had spent a considerable time at sea before they obtained senior commands. Most of them seem to have been galley officers or army officers who had had an appointment as sea captain before they were promoted to admirals but several came from the coast of Biscay and may have been experienced seamen.

The officers of the Ottoman navy represent a different tradition as hereditary nobility in the European sense did not exist in the Ottoman power structure. The Ottomans were pioneers in creating permanent corps of officials who served the sultan as officers on land and at sea and in positions as provincial governors and administrators. Their admirals were recruited from these high-ranking servants of the sultan or among successful privateers. Important expeditions might also be led by viziers, the most senior ministers. At least three of the sixteenth-century commanders-in-chief of the Ottoman navy, including the famous Hayreddin Barbarossa, had a background as corsairs in Algiers. More than any European navy of the age, the Ottoman navy was a social escalator for men of humble birth to leading positions.[22]

Impressment, volunteers and chained oarsmen

The mass of the sailors, soldiers, gunners and oarsmen who went to sea in this period did not enter a career path that took them to a higher social position. Some made the sea their occupation and they might develop skills which placed them a little above the bottom of the social scale. Others went to sea in hope of easy profits from plunder and violence, but many probably chose the sea just because this was a usual way to make a living in their community, at least for young men. Many were not especially skilled as seamen, but useful for heavy labour in a crew where other men could supervise them.

Unskilled men were especially useful for warships which needed large fighting crews. Most navies conscripted men for service at sea in national emergencies and this might have brought considerable groups of men with little or no seagoing experience to the sea. Navies were, however, primarily interested in skilled seamen and they used various political and social mechanisms to transfer them to warships at the lowest possible cost. It is interesting that while the militia tradition declined in importance on land in this period and was more or less replaced by mercenary and professional armies, its maritime form, the duty of seamen to serve the state at sea, increased in importance. In most states, the explanation is probably that seamen were professionals with an expanding civilian market. States, or mercenary army entrepreneurs, had to recruit and train men in order to get professional soldiers, but professional sailors already existed as a skilled labour force on the open market.

Throughout this period soldiers were an important part of the fighting force at sea, but their relative importance declined with the increased importance of guns. Even in battles where no boarding took place musketeers were useful in close-range actions and a force of trained infantry was essential if a fleet were to attempt an opposed landing, for a raid or for an attack against a fortified place. Special forces of marines did not exist before 1650, although soldiers serving in the Mediterranean galley fleets must be considered as specialised amphibious forces with considerable experience of fighting at sea. Soldiers embarked in sailing navies might also become used to war at sea if they served on ships for longer periods. They might do unskilled seaman work and they could be used as gun crews.

The most typical professional seaman in sailing ships was the young, agile and skilled topman who went aloft in the rigging to handle sails and carry out repairs. The importance of the topmen must have increased dramatically with the fifteenth- and sixteenth-century development of the full-rigged ship with its tall and complicated sail plan with two or three sails on every mast. Medieval ships with one large square sail or one or a few lateen sails did not need many men who could work aloft, as the sails could mainly be handled from the deck. The skilled topman could probably often hope for an appointment as petty officer and perhaps a career as master's mate and master when he grew older and less suited for work aloft. The step to the position as master did require other qualities as well, however, probably including the ability to read and write and a talent for business. Skilled topmen were usually a scarce resource in wartime, when the navies competed with merchantmen in securing their services.

Gunners were necessary in combats with the new gunpowder weapon. Originally, everyone who could handle and fire guns was regarded as a qualified specialist. Gradually, gunners declined to the status of ordinary seamen with some special training, and only the warrant and petty officers with gunnery training retained the status of a specialist. A gunner was usually supposed to lead a team of men who handled a gun. He was responsible for how it was loaded, aimed and fired, while the other members of the gun crew mainly supplied muscle-power to haul out the gun and train it on the enemy. The development of gunnery tactics in this period is still obscure and it is possible that it was not until the seventeenth century that such gun crews became the basic fighting teams of the warships. Carpenters and sailmakers were other specialists necessary for the maintenance of the ship and its propulsion apparatus. Their skills were especially necessary for repairs of damage caused by battle and gales.

We know little about how men were trained to become skilled specialists and to what extent the states took responsibility for the training of young men in naval service. When states became large shipowners they gained an interest in the maintenance and transmission of various skills connected with the sea and warfare at sea. In a fully-fledged naval organisation we would expect the navy to create these skills through training programmes and the early hiring of young men and boys as apprentices. We know that such systems existed later in the sailing navies, but to what extent they developed in our period has been little studied. J. F. Guilmartin in his seminal study of sixteenth-century Mediterranean galley warfare has suggested that we should look upon the specialised galley crews as parts of a social system in which men were trained through life-time experience rather than by military drills organised by the state. He emphasises that these skills were difficult to reproduce and that severe losses of skilled manpower in major battles might have serious long-term consequences in crippling the galley navy's operational capability. This, rather than the loss of galleys, might be the critical factor which made a galley battle decisive in a longer perspective. Galleys might quickly and relatively cheaply be built to replace losses, but if the cadre of skilled men were thin the vessels were of limited value.[23]

Guilmartin has not investigated how these skills were actually learnt, though he leaves us with the impression that they, like other traditional skills, were reproduced in social systems, perhaps within families where fathers and uncles brought up young men at sea. His suggestions do, however, reveal how little we actually know about essential parts of both sailing and oared warfare and their relations to the states of this period. We cannot say if the early modern state had gained control of the basic skills in modern warfare at sea or if they belonged to a maritime society outside the organisational framework of the state.

Practically all seaman skills connected with early modern warfare at sea did exist in the private maritime spheres of the European societies. When states mobilised their maritime resources for war these resources might be used, but the usefulness of a mobilised navy depended on how far the administration could concentrate these seamen with various skills and transform them into well-balanced teams, one for each ship. Gunnery might originally have been closely connected with states, but early modern gunners worked in an international labour market. This made it impossible for states to monopolise their skills and by the late sixteenth century both privateers and armed merchantmen were armed with high-quality guns and had qualified gunners. A state might invest in maritime skills by hiring more men and apprentices than immediately necessary for seagoing service. In later periods navies normally did that as part of the contingency planning for a possible mobilisation. There are few systematic studies of this subject and practically none available for this period.

Much work on a ship did not need specialised skills. Pulling and hauling on falls and tackles could be done from the deck by organised teams of unskilled men supervised by petty officers, the weighing of anchors required a lot of muscle power, boats required oarsmen and guns required a team of men to haul them out and point them. In a warship or a defensively armed merchant-man unskilled but able-bodied men were useful as a fighting force. Navies, privately armed warships and armed merchantmen were therefore often dependent on the labour market for unskilled men and they had to attract them with wages and the prospect of more or less legal plunder. The growing navies of the states seem to have been unable to rely only on these market forces to meet demand. Instead, most European states attempted to use their legal right to compel their subjects to contribute to the defence in order to recruit men to the navy.

Denmark-Norway and Sweden conscripted men from towns and other maritime communities, but it is possible that some of these men were more or less voluntarily recruited and that the state primarily required the local communities to pay them and provide them with lodgings during winter. Desertion does not seem to have been a great problem although little research has been done on the subject of naval conscription in Scandinavia. Conscripted men often stayed in the navies for several years, although they might stay at home when they were not required for service at sea. The Danish navy, at least, also relied on a force of permanently employed volunteers. When the navies were mobilised for full-scale wars they also tried to recruit foreign seamen in the Baltic area and in adjacent countries.[24]

In England, the navy also filled most of its demand for seamen through impressment although normally only for shorter periods. At least in the sixteenth century it does not seem to have been very difficult to persuade men to serve, and just as in Scandinavia pressed men were supposed to turn up for service without being put under some kind of guard. In the first half of the seventeenth century, however, the English navy faced a more difficult situation where seamen became notorious for protests, riots and mutinous behaviour. This was apparently the result of increased mismanagement which left seamen unpaid for long periods, but it may also have been caused by changed attitudes to impressment, better wages in the mercantile marine or fewer opportunities for plunder than in the Elizabethan age.[25]

Spain and Portugal in the sixteenth century were great maritime nations with considerable seafaring populations, but, as already mentioned, the status of seamen was low in the Iberian peninsula. The great maritime enterprises, stagnating population growth and the attractions of the colonies strained the maritime populations beyond their ability to produce and reproduce skilled seamen in sufficient numbers. Up to the late sixteenth century, the Spanish state relied to a large extent on hired and requisitioned merchantmen to form fleets in the Atlantic. Apparently this method also solved the administrative problem of recruiting sailors. When the state began to create a sailing navy the scarcity of skilled seamen became an increasing problem. In the early seventeenth century, the Spanish state made an interesting attempt to recruit young boys to schools where they were to be trained into seamen, but this turned out to be a failure. With increasing difficulties in recruiting volunteers, various forms of conscription became more common, especially from the 1620s, when an ambitious attempt at systematic registration of the seafaring population in *matriculas* was also started. The Spanish monarchy was composed of several constituent parts with different laws and customs and the possibilities of conscripting men for seagoing service differed considerably in various parts, even within Castile itself.[26]

The only navy which seems to have been able to rely on the market for mass recruitment of sailors was that of the Dutch Republic from the late sixteenth century on. During the sixteenth century the Netherlands developed into the largest concentrated labour market for seamen in the world and the Dutch mercantile marine, the East and West India companies and the navy attracted large number of foreigners, especially Germans and Scandinavians. The navy did not need to create a substantial permanent cadre of warrant officers, petty officers and skilled seamen as these were available at short notice. The key to their availability was, of course, high wages and the republic's good reputation as a reliable paymaster. The demands of naval warfare sometimes strained the manpower resources and the state frequently had to use a mild form of compulsion by prohibiting merchantmen from leaving the Dutch ports until the navy had found a sufficient number of seamen. But compared to other European navies, the Dutch system was a remarkable achievement for a state based on a limited population, especially if it is remembered that the same state also maintained one of Europe's largest armies through voluntary recruitment.[27]

Little attention has been paid to how the French navy manned its ships before the system of *classes maritimes* was developed in the age of Colbert. It is probable that the maritime regions and their traditional forms of manning were important for the navy but it has not been studied, in spite of the great interest for regional studies in French historiography.

While most sailing navies had to rely on systems for conscription which were ultimately based on principles of militia service or levies against national enemies, the oared galley fleets in the Mediterranean increasingly came to rely on chained oarsmen as their propulsive power. The use of convicts, prisoners of war and slaves as oarsmen had its breakthrough in the sixteenth century. Late medieval galleys – the period when Italian galley fleets dominated the

Mediterranean – had volunteers or militiamen at the oars. Such oarsmen were also part of the fighting crew. Venice continued into the seventeenth century to find as many oarsmen as possible through agreements with guilds (oarsmen in wartime in exchange for privileges to the guilds), or through voluntary or militia type recruitment in Dalmatia and on the Greek islands under Venetian control. But the steep rise in the number of oarsmen required by the growth of large permanent galley fleets under Spanish, Ottoman and French control outran the possibilities of recruiting free men to the oars. One consequence of this was a general change of the system of rowing the galleys. The traditional system, with one oar for each oarsman was replaced, from the mid-sixteenth century on, by a system where the three (or more) men on each bench served one oar. This was less efficient but required less skilled oarsmen which made it suitable for forced labour.[28]

No existing study gives a satisfactory answer to the question of the inter-connections between sixteenth-century Mediterranean warfare and the development of large forces of chained oarsmen. The change began in the western Mediterranean where rapidly increased wages in the first half of the sixteenth century forced the Spanish fleet to use chained oarsmen. In the east, where wages were lower, the Ottomans continued to use a combination of chained men, salaried Christians and conscripted or volunteer Muslims as late as the 1570s.[29] The economic problems of finding manpower for a dramatically increased number of galleys are obvious. But was it really good economy to have a huge number of chained men on the galleys who could only be used for propulsion and not as fighters? Why was it not better to have fewer galleys, with trained infantry serving at the oars?[30] How was the type of oarsman affected by the introduction of guns as a partial substitute for infantry? Were the chained oarsmen of this period primarily prisoners of war belonging to another religion or were they criminals and vagabonds sentenced to the galleys as punishment? To which extent were they slaves, that is, men captured from civilian populations in order to supply forced labour? The development of large Mediterranean galley fleets powered by forced labour was one of the major changes in early modern warfare, a development from market-orientated and militia-based systems of recruitment to a brutal and degrading use of human beings. What does it say about changes in mentality and economy in the Mediterranean world?

4

STATES, ORGANISATIONS AND MARITIME WARS

State formation and early modern navies

This chapter is an attempt to characterise the political and economic landscape of early modern Europe as seen from a maritime point of view. It is to a considerable extent based on economic history and historical sociology. This is necessary as warfare at sea from 1500 to 1650 was not a straightforward contest between well-integrated political units (states) fighting for national interests defined by their rulers. In this period, centralised and well-integrated territorial states were exceptions to the rule, loosely connected empires and city-states were still important, and the classical European system of great powers had not yet developed. Especially at sea, conflicts up to 1650 are often better understood as contests in protection and coercion between interest groups and coalitions of such groups. Many rulers had no ambition to exercise an efficient monopoly on violence at sea and to deny their subjects the right to fight for their private interests at sea. Most European states only gradually and unevenly developed the administrative competence required for large-scale warfare at sea. For those who used the sea lines of communication in order to explore economic opportunities, efficient use of violence was one of several entrepreneurial skills which were necessary for profit.[1]

Integration of political and economic interest groups and the different geographical areas loosely forming a state might be called state building or state formation. In early modern Europe the two main types of interest groups were the landowners and the merchants. The latter were often located in maritime cities or coastal regions where shipping and trade were important sources of income. State formation has important legal, religious, ideological and cultural aspects, but the core of the process in early modern Europe (c. 1500–1800) was the growth of centralised resource extraction for war, and the rise of complex and permanent organisations connected with warfare: armies and navies. The growth and transformation of early modern states were usually connected with an interaction process (conflicts, coalitions, compromises) between rulers and subjects about how the resources of the society should be used to organise defence and preparation for war. The interaction process often took the form of bargaining between rulers and the elite groups, in early modern times usually feudal power-holders and cities. The rulers and the elite group had to find compromises about how to co-ordinate their interests behind the state, and the organisational structures developed by the state.[2]

For the successful early modern states the result of this bargaining and interest aggregation process was twofold. The central state obtained increased administrative ability to penetrate the society and extract resources from it. The state usually had to make compromises with local elites in this process, but one way or another it extracted more resources from society. It also required increased ability to use these resources in organisational patterns created by the state. This was important as the state no longer had to rely on local elites to organise the resources for war. State formation or state building expressed itself in *organisational structures* of which armies and navies were the most important consumers of extracted resources: men and money. But in the early phase of state formation, coercion, violence-control and protection might also partly be organised through various networks or coalitions between the elite groups in society. In the maritime sphere, private investments in enterprises based on violence and armed protection were common. Rulers or representative institutions might mobilise, hire or co-operate with armed forces organised by private groups: militia, mercenaries and armed merchantmen. This had been typical for medieval society where the states had often been frameworks for political decision making and sources of legitimacy, rather than administrative centres of power.

Historical sociology has made several attempts to find connections between economic and social structures and long-term political development. The explanations have often been centred on state formation, the importance of war and the armed forces and the ambitions of states to obtain an effective monopoly on violence. The attempts at generalisations presented by most historical sociologists from Max Weber on are solidly based on continental experience: agriculture, feudalism, princes, armies and fiscal-military bureaucracies. In this study we are mainly interested in possible relationships between the maritime economy and maritime interest groups, territorial states with coasts, the use of violence at sea and European expansion overseas. From a maritime perspective, state formation is mainly a question about how states waged war at sea and in what way warfare at sea affected the growth of organisation and resource extraction connected with states. Were there any marked differences in state formation between typical continental states and typical maritime states and how do the European states which by geography are *both* continental and maritime fit into attempts to generalise? Europe consists of one large and several smaller peninsulas and the continent has a very long coast in proportion to its territory. This unusual geography must have increased the possibilities for continental and maritime influences to meet and cross-fertilise with each other. From a maritime perspective, the most interesting sociological question is perhaps to what extent this special geography drove Europe into its globally unique position as a centre for a world-wide network of maritime lines of communication.[3]

The most useful sociological framework for explaining early modern European state formation, from a maritime perspective, is that provided by Charles Tilly in his *Coercion, Capital, and European States, AD 990–1990* (1990). Revising his own and other sociologists' earlier attempts to provide a single path of state development, Tilly suggests that there were two types of social interaction which formed the basis of European state formation. One was the logic of coercion in which administration and violence control human activities in a territorial setting, especially extraction of resources from peasants. The other was the logic of capital, which controls human activities on the market, especially trade, finance and transport. In a comparative framework, state formation can be studied as the interplay between these two forces where states follow different patterns of development depending whether capital or coercion dominates the process. Tilly formulates two ideal-type trajectories of state formation: the coercion-intensive path – usually a monarchical territorial state – and the capital-intensive path, usually a city-state. Most European states were compromises between these ideal-types and, very interestingly from a maritime perspective, a third pattern emerged in Europe (and only there). Tilly calls this pattern capitalised coercion: territorial states which incorporate cities and capital in a productive way. A state based on capitalised coercion does not simply extract resources from capital but also use its power to promote the growth of capital and the market-orientated type of economy in which capital is accumulated.[4]

This framework of analysis integrates maritime Europe into historical sociology but it is not appropriate to use it without a critical discussion. The main problem from a maritime point of view is that Tilly tends to make coercion (the use of violence and war) into a predominantly territorial (feudal, monarchical) phenomenon, while capital (cities, merchants) in his framework tends to become inherently peaceful, or at least low-profile followers in the development of armed forces. Simplifications of this type are normally necessary in models used in social sciences, but sometimes they require a momentum of their own. In Tilly's own practical application of his theoretical framework this is illustrated by the manner in which he classifies mercantile and maritime republics like Venice and the Dutch Republic. They are discussed as states following the capital-intensive path with substantial concentrations of capital but with weak, intermittent armed force. Immanuel Wallerstein is taken to task for not having explained how Dutch seventeenth-century hegemony in trade could have been based on 'a wispy national state' like the Dutch Netherlands, a state which according to Tilly lagged behind its coercion-intensive neighbours in the creation of a standing army and a large bureaucracy.[5]

Questions of standing armies are not the concern of this study although in passing it must be emphasised that the Dutch Republic throughout the seventeenth century maintained one of Europe's largest armies, that this was one of the earliest permanent armies on the continent and that it in proportion to the Dutch population was far larger than those of the major European states.[6] Here, permanent navies and the role of the maritime states in the protection and promotion of trade are more important. It must then be questioned whether Tilly's capital-intensive trajectory is the proper place for maritime states if the historical record shows that they repeatedly used violence to promote and protect their commercial interests. His 'capitalised–coercion' trajectory seems to be a better alternative. This is not to deny that the maritime states might have used violence according to a capitalist logic, that is, with profit as the ultimate guide. But the assumption that these states were unable or unwilling to create strong permanent organisations for the efficient use of force is difficult to reconcile with historical facts.[7]

The role of navies in the state formation process has often been neglected compared to that of the armies.[8] The role of the continental states and the development of permanent armies is much better understood. One reason is that navies accounted for a smaller part of the European resources for war. Another and probably more important reason is that the nations which became the leading naval powers have an historiography in which state formation took place somewhere else, on the 'continent' or in the 'absolutist' states. Dutch and Anglo-Saxon historians have usually supposed that their states were 'limited' and 'weak'. This interpretation is highly questionable.[9] In one perspective, the role of the maritime powers in the European state formation process was in fact crucial. Efficient state formation is to a large extent a concentration and systematisation of strategically important resources and competencies in order to convert them into something which gives muscle to political power. In a long-term perspective technology has been one of the most important factors in the development of the modern world. Among the strategic competencies which mattered in early modern Europe were the abilities to design, build and maintain warships, to produce dependable and cheap guns, to create efficient crews out of men with various skills and to lead fleets in combat and during long-distance expeditions to little known parts of the world. Naval technology, naval administration and naval leadership were scarce resources which could be developed only by strong and sustained demand for these resources. Technical competence is usually little appreciated in state formation studies, but if navies and their dynamic role in early modern Europe and European relations with the rest of the world are brought into the picture this marginalisation of technology is difficult to sustain.

When competence is to be assessed the question of efficiency must be asked. It is not difficult to find a wide range of efficiency in the use of resources for war during the period 1500–1650. Gradually, it became the great age of the middle-sized states which in some cases, particularly the Dutch Republic and Sweden, achieved a power status far out of proportion to their bases in population and economic resources. It was the way these resources were organised by the state which mattered, not the amount of resources in society. The efficiency of a state depended on both its ability to mobilise its resources and its ability to organise them for war. In this perspective, representative institutions, elite participation in administration and decision making, and the organisational forms used in armies and navies are often interconnected. In our period, it is necessary to look for efficient connections between resource mobilisation and the use of resources, rather than to study fundraising and naval and military organisations as two separate phenomena. State formation succeeds only if resources can be raised and deployed in a quantitatively and qualitatively efficient way. Representative institutions with some direct power over the use of the resources, elite participation in central administration, and more decentralised or contractual forms of armed forces might be sensible solutions to the problem of securing support for such forces. A 'modern', centralised, bureaucratic and technically advanced navy might be useless if the society which it was supposed to serve suddenly fails to support it.

The degree to which established elite groups took part in the administration of the new organisations of the states has attracted surprisingly little scholarly debate. It does not seem to be regarded as an important problem to study whether there were marked differences in efficiency which might be explained by the attitudes and degree of participation of old elites in new structures.[10] A casual look at elites and early modern state formation makes it tempting to argue that efficient interest aggregation around centralisation of resources for the armed forces was best achieved in states where the representative institutions and the groups they represented were brought into the decision-making process and compelled to share responsibility for its security policy. Their degree of *active participation* in the state formation process might be of crucial importance. If the social elite was given a stake in the success of the central state they were likely to use their social influence, their capital and their patronage to further the interests of the state.

Venice is an early example with strong maritime connections. In our period, the Netherlands and Sweden are illustrative examples and in the following century the same process took place in Great Britain. The elite groups took part in the administration of the states and shared the prestige of its success; they used the bureaucracy and the armed forces to exercise their patronage and they invested their savings in the state debt. Early modern Spain and France, where the social and economic elites were less involved in the central administration of the states, periodically had larger armed forces than the smaller states, but seen in proportion to their populations these great powers were markedly less able to centralise their resources for war or mobilise loans from domestic sources. However, not all representative institutions acted as state builders. Poland and Catalonia are examples of nations with strong representative institutions which failed to integrate the elite with the state, while post-1650 Denmark-Norway and Brandenburg-Prussia are examples of states with strong armed forces without any representative institutions. The latter were, however, good examples of states where the elite groups participated in state administration.[11]

Territorial states and maritime centres

From a maritime point of view, the European political and economic landscape was formed by the naval power of the states and the economic power of the centres for shipping and maritime trade. Both navies and maritime centres were able to exercise control of the sea lines of communication through violence. Their incentives to do so were not the same however. Territorial states were interested in the sea as a highway for power projection and as a forward area for anti-invasion defence. They were usually interested in protecting trade to their own ports and in the plunder and destruction of enemy trade. Territorial states might also develop navies in order to protect trade as a source of income. This protection was not always desired by those who had to pay for it, for example the Sound Toll to Denmark or the protection money paid by seafarers in the Indian Ocean to the Portuguese. For rulers of territorial states, warfare at sea was usually a part of the state formation process, one of several ways of strengthening the state in competition with domestic and foreign competitors in a dynastic and imperialistic power struggle. Centres of maritime trade used violence at sea primarily in order to protect and promote trade, sometimes in trade war against competitors. For rulers of these centres, violence was a means to make capital invested in trade and shipping profitable. Convoys, in which the shipping interest pooled their protective resources for mutual support, were a common form of city-state naval activity.

Fifteenth- and early sixteenth-century Europe had several centres for large-scale interregional shipping. They were often, but not always, closely connected with the centres for merchant capitalism. These shipowning centres provided the bulk of the long-distance shipping around Europe and the Mediterranean and they had the resources to organise convoys and other forms of protection of trade when necessary. Most large ships were also built in these areas. In the Mediterranean, Venice and Genoa were the most important of these centres and they were also leading centres of mercantile and financial capitalism. The eastern part of the Spanish Biscay coast, especially the Basque provinces, was another important area which also played a leading role in the development of the full-rigged ship. Brittany and Normandy were important ship-owning centres as were several cities in the northern Netherlands, especially in Holland. In Northern Europe cities like Lübeck, Hamburg and Danzig were important shipping and trading centres and, together with smaller Baltic cities, they formed the Hanse, an organisation which acted as a cartel and an alliance in control of maritime trade. Small-scale shipping was common along the European coast, but it was the major centres which owned most of the great ships (in Italy the big merchant galleys also), which in wartime might be converted into powerful warships.[12]

The importance of these ship-owning centres for late Medieval and Renaissance seapower is visible from the fact that the French and English kings in the fifteenth and early sixteenth centuries often hired or bought great carracks from Genoa and great hulks and carvels from the German Hanse cities when they went to war.[13] Sweden bought an entire fleet from Lübeck in 1522 and Denmark-Norway acquired several North European merchantmen when war with Sweden started in 1563. Castilian kings traditionally relied on their northern seafaring communities to provide them with temporary warships, and this tradition was the mainstay of Spanish Atlantic sea power until the 1580s. In other forms (construction and leasing of warships) the Biscay area remained a centre for private entrepreneurship connected with Spanish sea power far longer. But Spain also relied on the Mediterranean maritime centres to procure warships. Some of the largest (although not the most powerfully armed) ships of the Armada of 1588 were Venetian merchantmen. In the Adriatic, Ragusa (Dubrovnik) developed as a ship-owning centre and from the late sixteenth century it was an important supplier of warships on long-term lease to the Spanish crown.[14]

In the Mediterranean, the galleys had traditionally been used by both maritime cities and territorial rulers. In the sixteenth century, when large permanent galley fleets were established, the three great galley powers were the Ottoman empire, the Spanish empire and Venice. France dropped out of the race for Mediterranean naval power in the 1560s, while Genoa was primarily an important centre for entrepreneurs in galley warfare who supplied Spain and other powers with galley squadrons on a contractual basis. But the contacts between the galley fleets and the established maritime centres on one hand and the innovations which created the new gun-carrying sailing navies on the other, were limited. Venice, which in 1500 was the only European state with a large permanent navy, proved to be very slow in efficiently adapting to the great naval innovation of the age, the gun-carrying sailing ship. A permanent Ventian sailing navy was not created until the 1670s. Innovations which threatened to transform an existing social power structure met more resistance than in regions without any established naval structure at all.

The most important and dynamic development of early gun-carrying warships did not take place in the traditional centre of European maritime activity, the Mediterranean. Instead, it was a number of western and northern European monarchies which took the lead from the late fifteenth century on. Portugal, France, England, Denmark-Norway and Sweden were the states which first built specialised sailing warships with heavy guns and created permanent organisations to maintain and develop this weapon system.[15] This process was a part of the growth of centralised state power, rather than a transformation and modernisation of existing maritime power. The French sailing navy, which was organised by the provincial admiralties in Brittany and

Normandy, was the only one with connections to major ship-owning centres. The other four navies were created by the four European monarchies where the capital city was also the leading mercantile port of the nation and the main centre for the royal naval and military power. Lisbon, London (the Thames estuary area), Copenhagen and Stockholm did not count as major ship-owning centres in the early sixteenth century but they appear to have provided fruitful combinations of maritime and military competence, concentrated royal authority and market-orientated activities. The navies and their administrations in these cities were close to the rulers, close to information about new maritime and military technology and close to the markets for naval stores.

The rulers in these states also had strong incentives to use new technology in order to increase their authority at home and abroad. The fact that geography and royal initiative in these countries had combined the naval centre with the centre of the state probably strengthened the permanency of the navy. It was more likely to survive periods of reduced royal authority. The fact that the French navy, located on the periphery of the monarchy, disappeared during a long period of royal weakness (c. 1570–1625) points in that direction.[16] But, as the Venetian and Ottoman example show, concentration of maritime and naval activities in the capital may not be an unmixed blessing. It may ensure continuity and survival for the navy but it might also tie it to a stagnating state power.

The activities of the rulers of the houses of Aviz, Valois, Tudor, Oldenburg and Vasa are especially interesting if they are compared with those of the rulers of Spain (the kingdoms of Castile and Aragon) and the Burgundian Netherlands, which from 1516 were united under the Habsburg dynasty. In Spain, Ferdinand and Isabella in the decades around 1500 had made rapid progress in state building and even founded a transatlantic empire in America, but they had not created a sailing navy administered by the state. The Valois dukes of Burgundy had maintained a small navy but their Habsburg successors (from 1477) left naval matters entirely to the provincial admiralties and the regional maritime interests.[17] In Spain, up to the 1580s, the Habsburgs continued to rely on the maritime interests to provide sailing naval forces when they were required. For most of the sixteenth century the emperor-king Charles and his son Philip II were the mightiest rulers in Christendom, they controlled several of Europe's major shipping centres and they were the rulers of a growing transoceanic empire with its European entrepôt in Seville. But until late in the century they had no permanent sailing navy of their own and they relied on contractors when they needed sea power. The first real Habsburg permanent sailing navy was that of Portugal over which Philip II took control in 1580.[18]

The implication of all this is that permanent gun-armed sailing navies were a phenomenon of the European periphery, mainly created by rulers without strong ties to the leading maritime interests. To them, heavy shipborne guns and specialised warships were interesting, perhaps fascinating, innovations on which they spent scarce resources in order to increase their political and military leverage at home and abroad. In order to build, maintain and efficiently use these innovations they had to create shipyards, naval bases, ordnance depots and a staff of personnel with specialised skills: shipbuilders, gunners, shipmasters and pilots. In domestic politics a royal navy meant that the ruler had created a new type of organisation for protection against invasion and blockade, an organisation which might provide a motive for raised taxes and increased royal power. Abroad, a navy meant better possibilities of projecting power and extracting protection money from shipping (relevant in such different areas as the Indian Ocean and the Baltic). The difference between the permanent sailing navies and the naval power temporarily organised by maritime city-states and rulers of maritime centres (like the Habsburgs) gradually emerged during the sixteenth century. It was the permanent navies which accumulated technical and organisational know-how in modern warfare at sea. As investments in power they proved to be very rewarding: in the long run the permanent navies proved to be the only viable form of sea power.

This does not mean that private interests were already marginalised as efficient users of violence at sea in the sixteenth century. It was the *established* maritime centres (primarily those in Italy, Spain and Germany) which lost their pre-eminence in maritime warfare. Other private interest groups adapted to the new technical conditions and made efficient use of them. They could act through market-orientated networks of contacts between entrepreneurs in armed trade and plunder, shipbuilding, and weapon manufacturing which developed in areas which by the late sixteenth century rapidly took the lead in Europe's mercantile and technical development. Northern Netherlands and England were at the centre of this development, while Atlantic France and northern Germany appear to have been at its periphery and Sweden entered as an exporter of cheap cast-iron guns, especially useful for armed merchantmen. But it was the province of Holland, seconded by Zeeland, Friesland and part of the English maritime community, which took the lead. They challenged both the established centres of shipping and trade in Europe and the Iberian state monopolies on trade with America and Asia – challenges which had to be supported with a combination of commercial superiority and efficient forms of violence and protection. It was to a considerable degree these northern mercantile interests which used and developed the most advanced maritime technology.[19]

The Dutch federal state which emerged in the 1570s and 1580s out of a revolt against the Habsburg ruler was extremely dependent on its maritime resources from its inception, for both warfare against the Spanish forces sent by their Habsburg prince and for the economic survival of the republic. More than any other European state the Dutch Republic was connected with the new entrepreneurial activities and their networks of contacts. This state, which a long historiographical tradition has described as 'weak', soon proved to be the most formidable sea power Europe had seen up to that time. Its success against Iberian sea power was both economic and naval and Dutch sea power was always closely co-ordinated with commercial interests. But, although the republic's mercantile marine was the largest in Europe, the Dutch state primarily relied on warships of its own for service in Europe. For war and trade outside Europe it relied on chartered monopolistic companies. The capitalist and bourgeois Dutch state built, maintained and manned its own warships, while its Habsburg adversary to a large extent came to rely on chartered warships. The Habsburgs mainly followed dynastic and imperial goals, but they used market forces to administer their navy. The Dutch Republic was sensitive to demands from profit-orientated maritime groups and it purchased naval stores and recruited seamen on the open market. But the administrative infrastructure of both the navy and the companies for overseas activities were organisations, ultimately dependent on political control. The most market-orientated state in Europe was perhaps run by businessmen too good to leave the administrative function to the market.

Organisations, markets and networks

One of the radical changes in warfare that separates the Middle Ages from modern times is the growth of *organisations* specialised in warfare. Medieval warfare was based on social institutions, rather than permanent organisations managed by the state. The feudal levy, the local militia on land and at sea, the armed merchantmen, the city wall and the private castle were all part of the local and regional power structure and they might be used against the state as well as against internal and external enemies. The ruler had the right of co-ordinating the armed forces of the society, but he was not in charge of a central administration of the armed forces. He might have ships, weapons and armed retainers of his own but so had many local power-holders.

Armed social institutions (militia, feudal levy, etc.) had for long periods been insufficient or incompatible with the demands of ambitious rulers and threatened societies. But the alternative was not solely permanent organisations run by the state. There was also armed force leased on the market. The central role of military entrepreneurs and mercenary soldiers in warfare on land, from the late Middle Ages until the seventeenth century, is well known. At sea, where ships owned by market-orientated mercantile groups were instruments of warfare, the market might seem the natural solution for the organisation of war and protection. On a practical level, armed social institutions, mercenary forces and permanent armed forces might be complementary. But in a theoretical and long-term perspective on European history they are competing systems and we may ask if there are any theory available to explain why centralised armies and navies administered by the state finally became the dominant form.

Such explanations may be found in organisation theories, primarily in ideas derived from Max Weber. Central to Weberian organisation theory is the idea that an organisation is an instrument for central power-holders to exercise power over a large area or a large number of individuals, in order to achieve centrally determined aims. The organisation must have a system of command and control which gives the centre of the hierarchy the power to enforce its orders down to the lowest level of the hierarchy. The organisation must be independent of outside and competing socio-economic interests. The officials of an organisation must obey the centre of the organisation, rather than local elite groups, and their careers must be determined by their usefulness to the organisation and not on socio-economic connections. The officials of the organisation must not appropriate the assets of the organisation for private economic or political purposes and they must separate their private affairs and property from those of the organisation. They should be salaried officials who identify their goals with the organisation. In order to ensure control and continuity much of the decision process must be documented in writing. Organisations normally produce archives – which make their activities attractive subjects for historians.[20]

Historical sociologists who have studied state formation and the rise of early modern bureaucratic states are usually aware of these basic criteria for an organisation. The development of the centralised early modern state and its armed forces is clearly an example of the separation of a hierarchical organisation from the rest of the society.[21] But few if any historical sociologists have been interested in later development of organisation theory and its implications for early modern state formation. It is one thing to say that organisations develop as instruments of power – it does not answer the question why they have proved *superior* to other forms of power. These questions have been asked by economists who have left the main stream of their subject and turned to sociology and history in order to explain phenomena which are central to economy. Interesting answers have been given by, among others, Ronald H. Coase, Herbert Simon, Alfred D. Chandler and Oliver E. Williamson.[22]

Common explanations for the growth of complex organisations (companies) emphasise that transactions and information gathering are costly processes and that rational decisions based on full information are impossible to achieve. The capacity of an individual to develop skills and gather information is of necessity limited and, although decision makers may be rational, their rationality is bounded by their experience and the information they have access to. Human beings create organisations in order to reduce these limitations. An organisation may employ various specialists who might co-operate and develop their skills. An organisation may also acquire and process a larger amount of information than an individual. If the organisation is permanent it may develop complex and advanced technical and administrative systems which makes it superior to a hastily assembled and temporary organisation.

The best known alternative to organisation are transactions on the open market. In economic theory, the market has the great advantage of providing competition. Buyers can make choices and sellers must improve their competence in order to be attractive. Economic theory which attempts to explain the

70

growth of organisations does not deny the great importance of the market, but claims that it cannot be superior under all circumstances. Organisations might provide a superior form of control if market conditions are characterised by great uncertainty, if there are few suppliers, if long-term contracts are necessary, if a high degree of 'asset specificity' is involved and if there is a high risk that instructions from the buyer are interpreted in an opportunistic way.[23] Complex and large-scale activities under uncertain conditions (such as warfare) are best co-ordinated by the visible hands of decision makers in an organisation than by the invisible hand of the market. In such a situation an organisation, working with officials whose careers are closely tied to the success of the organisation and its owner, might be superior to outside entrepreneurs whose interest is determined mainly by private profit. An organisation may provide higher quality, it may ensure that the necessary assets (tacit knowledge, specialised skills and complex hardware) are always available and it may ensure that operative decisions are implemented without the complications of various contractual limitations and conflicts of interpretation.

On the other hand, if products or services are standardised and their quality and quantity are easy to check, they may be bought on the open market where competition could reduce prices and give producers incentives to lower costs and improve quality. Organisations may also develop inertia and rigidity. An organisation built around a specialised technology or a firm doctrine might, in the long run, become path-dependent, governed by vested interests and increasingly unable to adapt to a changing environment.[24] An organisation might also become so complex that the central authority cannot control it efficiently and maintain its original purpose. In that case the various parts of the organisation, each in possession of highly developed skills, might begin to sub-optimise and develop in a way which suits their part of the organisation rather than its common goal.

Much of this may not look surprising to historians who may identify the early modern states, their armed forces and, not least, their navies as complex organisations of the type which the theories intend to explain. The development of the early organisations might be better understood if certain basic concepts from unorthodox economic theory are used. The navies gradually became technologically and administratively the most complex organisations in early modern Europe and they also developed in a way which was uniquely European. From a modern perspective the advantages of established organisations in waging wars seem so obvious that the alternatives may look inherently inferior. But in the early modern period the European states were involved in a search process to which there were no easily predictable answers. Would armed social institutions, the market or the organisation provide the best protection and the most efficient use of violence to society? The creation of organisational competence through bureaucracy and the permanent officer corps was in itself a new idea and it required permanent financing of a type that existing political interest aggregation often could not cope with. The

71

obstacles provided by armed social institutions whose existence was closely related to the power structure in society might be formidable. But there are also reasons to suspect that the open market was not exactly as unco-ordinated and opportunistic as some theories of organisation presume.

Private entrepreneurs who produce complex products and services may often be dependent on close relations with customers and with producers of complementary products. Customers and producers may develop *networks* in which they communicate and co-ordinate their activities. Such networks may rapidly provide the individual entrepreneur with well-focused information and critical know-how and these may be of decisive importance when producers and users of complicated products wish to improve the product. Networks may act as non-hierarchical and informal co-ordinators. Networks of this type are much less likely to leave well documented archives than formalised organisations. In the early modern maritime world we may suspect that shipbuilders, shipowners and manufacturers of guns developed ships and their armament through informal dialogue which has left few traces in the record. The role of organised navies in this process is far from clear. A possible but tentative answer is that technical development gained momentum in environments where there were *both* viable private networks and efficient organisations which might interact with each other.[25]

The economics of trade, violence and entrepôts

In this period Europe's main export product to Asia may have been violence and protection. Europeans used violence to get monopoly rights to trade, they sold protection to Asian and European merchants and ships and they sold their superior technology for war to Asians who were in conflict with other Europeans and other Asians. In exchange, Europeans received various valuable Asian products which they shipped to Europe or (which is often forgotten in Europe) sold in other parts of Asia. Europeans often made profit as intra-Asian traders because they were efficient in the use of violence both for their own protection and as a commodity which might be sold. Except silver (which Europeans mainly imported from America) there was little else that they had to offer Asians in the sixteenth and seventeenth centuries.

If violence was such an important commodity in Asia that a very small number of Europeans sailing in ships and living in fortified ports made a noticeable impact here, what can we say about the importance of violence on maritime trade within Europe? In Chapter 1, pp. 11–12, Frederic C. Lane's protection cost theory was briefly presented. Its central message is that protection from violence contributed to economic growth and that costs for protection inflicted upon competitors reduce their potential for economic growth. Protection and violence are economic factors just as capital, labour, natural resources and transaction cost (transport, information costs, insurance, etc.) are. They influence the prices of various goods just like the rate of interest and the price and quality of labour. Protection cost may be regarded as a transaction cost (partly inter-changeable with insurance costs), and innovative behaviour in protection and violence may contribute to profit just like innovations in production and trans-portation.[26]

In the early modern maritime world protection and violence depended on both private entrepreneurship and political willingness to mould foreign pol-icy and naval strategy to the interest of capital engaged in trade. If successful, such a policy would reap profit for society through economic growth. Private entrepreneurship in violence and trade might also contribute to economic growth. Seaborne protection and violence are embodied in ships and teams of men forming their crews. Successful entrepreneurship requires networks between shipowners, masters and ship-builders in order to channel experi-ences and requirements into optimal ships. It also requires masters and crews who combine efficiency as seamen with efficiency as fighters. If we wish to study how maritime innovations, entrepreneurship and the maritime and naval policy of the state work in practice, warfare at sea must be investigated.

As economic factors, violence and protection had economic consequences which ought to be taken into account in economic history. Violence was an important means of economic competition in Europe and between Europeans outside Europe. Efficient protection lowered the costs of transportation, thus widening markets by making distribution cheaper and giving consumers access to goods from areas which otherwise would have been difficult to reach. Violence might protect or break trading monopolies which themselves protected inefficient mercantile and industrial groups. In our period, the English, French and Dutch armed incursions into the Iberian trade monopo-lies in America and Asia were often economically supported by the fact that the West European could buy and sell at prices that made them highly com-petitive. But a comparative advantage in violence and protection might (alone or together with other advantages) create monopolies or oligopolies which for a period give high profits and rapid accumulation of capital. Such accumula-tion may shape new power structures in industry and trade. Protection and violence might also channel trade according to the interest of states or cities, thus supporting mercantilistic regulations and tax-raising.

In a maritime perspective on European history the role of warfare and pro-tection in the rise and decline of *entrepôts* for trade are especially important. In the industrial society the distribution of goods can normally be arranged through networks of transportation where the buyers and sellers can control the transactions from a distance. Rapid information makes it possible to follow prices and transactions on a global scale. Ports and stores for goods are in themselves not centres of power and the 'market' is an abstraction. Early mod-ern trade was different. It had to cope with the fact that the flow of goods from one region to another was irregular and unpredictable and that informa-tion about demand and supply could only be transferred slowly. It was often not possible for a producer to know where the demand for his products was most intense. Weather conditions made it impossible to plan transportation with sailing ships with any precision. In order to achieve some kind of steady distribution, a reasonable balance of demand and supply and a degree of price stability, concrete market-places, entrepôts, were formed where goods were stockpiled for further transportation.

The great entrepôts were the classical European trading cities with their ports and storehouses: Venice, Genoa, Seville, Lisbon, Antwerp, Amsterdam, London, Hamburg, Lübeck. Naturally, these entrepôts also became centres for trade, finance, shipping and insurance. Men engaged in large-scale trade had to live and work in the entrepôts in order to keep themselves in touch with the flow of information and to take decisions which might quickly be implemented by loading goods on to ships. The great importance of these entrepôts gave them or their territorial rulers economic and political power. The entrepôts could use this power to curb competition but they also became attractive objects for envious political and economic competitors who wished to reduce their power.[27]

Venice, Genoa, the German Hanse and the Dutch Republic are the classical European cases of maritime states and power structures created around great entrepôts. Of these, Genoa and the Hanse disappeared as important political powers during our period, Venice declined to a regional centre while the Dutch entrepôt (with Amsterdam as the leading city) rose to become the centre for trade on a global scale, the first of its kind. This period also saw the rise and decline of Lisbon, Seville and Antwerp as great entrepôts. As these three cities were under Habsburg rule for long periods and as Genoa was closely related to the Spanish power system from 1528, the rise of the Dutch entrepôt and the decline of the others is interesting. From 1568 to 1648 the Dutch were involved in war with Spain (including Portugal from 1580 to 1640), a war that gradually became more and more maritime and global. The war began as a struggle against Habsburg domestic policy in the Netherlands but it developed into a contest about empire and the control of world trade. In that contest, seaborne coercion, protection and efficiency in trade and shipping were joint instruments of competition.

Economically, politically and geographically, an Iberian- and Habsburg-dominated system of European entrepôts with Lisbon and Seville as termini for the Asian and American trades and with Antwerp and Genoa as great regional centres for trade and finance (for northern and southern Europe, respectively) would look very natural. The success would of course depend on whether the House of Habsburg with its agglomeration of states in Europe and colonial empires overseas was able to protect the sea lines of communication to these four cities. With great military and maritime resources, great incomes in silver from America, the experience of being pioneers in colonialisation overseas and widespread contacts with German and Italian financiers and merchants, the Spanish Habsburgs seemed to have the best cards.

As we know, they were not able to play them well. The Dutch rebels, with a population only one tenth of that over which the Spanish Habsburgs ruled in Europe, won the maritime power struggle in economy and warfare. By 1650, the entrepôt of the world was located in Holland and Zeeland. The Spanish system of entrepôts and lines of transoceanic trade were reduced in importance and increasingly infiltrated with foreign capital. During the same period, Venice had lost her position as an important entrepôt for trade between the Levant and Europe, to a large extent also to the Dutch (and the English and French). These transfers of entrepôts were the most obvious signs of the change of supremacy in trade and economy from southern to north-western Europe which took place in this period. War, trade and efficiency in protection were far from the whole explanation. We also have to take efficiency in production into account. The Dutch had advantages in industrial efficiency too. But this is a complementary rather than an alternative explanation, as Dutch supremacy at sea was also based on industrial and technological efficiency in shipbuilding and arms production (including the successful transfer to Sweden of Dutch know-how in iron gun founding).

Politically, it was a triumph of a state which followed the logic of capital as much as the logic of coercion. The Dutch Republic cannot be described as subservient to capital. It was also a nation which fought for its political independence and the integrity of a political decision making system which the ruling elite believed in. But profits from maritime trade and the financial means to win the war were two intertwined phenomena and it was natural for this state to mould its strategy to the interests of the maritime groups. This was probably the key behind the success of the Dutch entrepôt – its growth answered a national interest of the highest priority. In the power struggle with Spain, the destruction of the Iberian-controlled entrepôts had also been a Dutch national interest.[28]

The Dutch success was also a triumph of a fresh combination of interests with low barriers against innovative change. With limited means, focused by profit interest rather than reputation and widespread imperial ambition, the Dutch Republic had secured their political independence and mercantile supremacy. Much of their success may have depended on the fact that the republic had no strong traditions of political and economic supremacy to defend. Rapid development of maritime technology gave them the opportunity to create political and economical frameworks moulded by the entrepreneurial conditions which were best suited to exploit these opportunities. New ideas may require new combinations of skill and these combinations may emerge and develop more rapidly in areas where the established combinations of technology, political institutions and organisations for war and economy are less firmly entrenched in the power structure. In the decades after 1650, the Dutch repeatedly became the victims of envious competitors and in the next century they also had to cope with an increasing economic and political inertia in structures and institutions which had once been the foundation of their success.

5

THE PORTUGUESE IN MARITIME ASIA, 1498–1600

A small power in a great ocean

In the early decades of the fifteenth century the Indian Ocean was the scene of a remarkable case of maritime power projection. From 1405 to 1433 the Ming emperors of China sent seven large fleets into this area. Some of them carried almost 30,000 men and the major ships of the fleets were at least as big as the largest cargo carriers of Europe of that time, the Genoese and Venetian carracks. The aim of these huge expeditions was neither territorial conquest, nor mercantile hegemony. The fleets suppressed piracy, negotiated treaties with local rulers who were induced to pay tribute, they brought emissaries to the emperor and they promoted trade between China, South and Southeast Asia, Arabia and Africa. The presence of the mighty fleets must have given foreign rulers and seafarers a visible proof of the power of Imperial China. But the Chinese did not acquire any naval bases outside metropolitan China, nor did they permanently deploy any warships in the Indian Ocean. Armed force and the ability to send large fleets far from their bases were not transformed into commercial profit or a Chinese maritime empire.

The most populous and technically advanced empire on earth in the fifteenth century had for a brief period turned its attention to the ocean south of its territory but it had not found anything which induced its rulers to create a permanent power structure in this area. In fact, the naval expeditions were very expensive for the Imperial treasury and that in itself is an explanation for why they ceased. Chinese cargo carriers continued to sail to Southeast Asia as they had for centuries but they seldom appeared in the Indian Ocean and they were not protected by the Chinese state.[1]

The lack of political or commercial legacy left by the Chinese naval efforts in the Indian Ocean stands in marked contrast to the intrusion into this area of the Portuguese which began with the arrival of Vasco da Gama's little fleet of three ships and around 150 men in 1498. Portugal did not count as a great power in Europe. It was not even one of the most important shipping nations of Europe. Technically, Europe was backward in many respects compared to Asia, and for centuries Europeans were more interested in Asian products than

Asians were interested in importing from Europe. In shipping tonnage and number of men the sixteenth century Portuguese presence in the Indian Ocean area was smaller than that of the fifteenth century Chinese fleets. But, unlike the Chinese, the Portuguese had ideas of how naval power might be used with profit. The Portuguese introduced the European idea of using seaborne violence and protection as an export commodity. The Indian Ocean proved to be a surprisingly receptive market. The European innovation in maritime violence gave the foreigners a role as warriors and merchants in a multifarious and ever-changing political and economic environment. Various interest groups began to interact with the Europeans, fought them, sought their protection or shared their know-how about local conditions in exchange for their fighting abilities. Major rulers, such as the Mughals in India or the Safavids in Persia usually co-operated with the Europeans who were regarded for a long time as useful partners on the maritime fringes of their essentially land-orientated empires. The Ottomans sometimes challenged them but with relatively small forces.[2]

Portugal projected a new combination of seaborne armed force, political control and economic ambition that had its impact on Asia. The impact may have been local and limited and hardly noticed by most Asians but it was the first step in a process where Europeans first gained control of the maritime lines of communication by armed force and then continued to take control over Asian and African territories around the Indian Ocean. In the nineteenth century this ocean had, politically, become a European lake bordering European colonies and protectorates. This was only a transitional phase in the history of European–Asian relations but it must be regarded as important. Many of the formation processes behind the present states around the Indian Ocean have their origin in European sea power. It was the Portuguese who brought the European innovation of sea power as an instrument of state policy to this part of the world.

This chapter will mainly discuss the Portuguese use of armed force in Asian waters up to about 1600. Asian resistance to Portuguese power is mentioned only briefly as is warfare and violence at sea between Asians. This leaves much of the maritime interaction process between Asians out of the picture – Asia was for most of the pre-industrial period the main area for large-scale maritime trade. But available evidence shows that Asians were less accustomed than Europeans to using violence at sea. Major rulers in Asia were normally intransigent to maritime enterprise and traditions of organised naval defence or aggression were lacking. Piracy existed and seafarers were prepared to meet it but Asian merchants seldom used violence as a mean of competition. In the Indian Ocean, Islam had for centuries acted as an integrative force among merchants from different nations. Further east, maritime trade was dominated by Chinese merchants who preferred to co-operate rather than fight each other in foreign waters.[3]

The Portuguese intrusion into the Indian Ocean was based on several factors that made the Europeans unique in their behaviour at sea. Trade, protection and plunder were closely related phenomena in Europe and the control of maritime trade had been the cause of major wars between states such as the late medieval wars between Venice and Genoa. Portugal also represented a recent European political ambition where rulers of states attempted to enforce a monopoly of violence at sea and if possible raise taxes for armed protection of seafarers. Furthermore, Portugal could profit from recent European innovations in sailing-ship technology and gunnery. Portugal also had an unusual know-how in long-distance sailing in unknown waters gained during the fifteenth century explorations of the Atlantic islands (the Azores, Madeira, the Canaries) and the African west coast. The ruling Portuguese dynasty, the House of Aviz, was interested in mercantile enterprise and had developed a small trading empire in West Africa. Finally, the Portuguese elite had a tradition of crusades against Muslims. During the fifteenth and sixteenth centuries it was kept alive with expeditions against Morocco where a network of coastal forts was maintained. In fact, Morocco drew more military resources than the spectacular power projection into the Indian Ocean. This venture would also end in a national catastrophe when the main Portuguese army was annihilated and king Sebastiao killed by the Moroccans at the battle of Alcácer-Kebir in 1578.

The final and systematic Portuguese attempt to find a direct maritime route between Europe and India was made in the 1480s and 1490s by the Kings Joao II (r. 1481–95) and Manuel I (r. 1495–1521). The driving forces behind the expeditions were to find eastern Christian allies against the Muslims and to create a profitable Portuguese-controlled trade in Asian goods, primarily pepper. Up to 1500 that trade went through Egypt and Syria, territories controlled by the Mamluk sultans who raised a considerable part of their incomes from customs on the trade in exchange for protection. In Europe, Venice had, after long struggles with Genoa, gained preponderance as middleman between the Levant ports and the European consumers. This position was based on the city's geographical position and its skill in trade protected by armed force. A direct sea route from the production areas to Europe, eliminating middlemen and armed protectors of trade might both be profitable for the Portuguese and financially disastrous for the Muslim ruler who controlled Jerusalem. The last consideration was important for king Manuel who was driven by religious zeal and an intense desire to reduce Muslim power.

The Portuguese enmity against Muslim groups greatly determined their Indian Ocean policy. It was not obvious that Portugal should become a political and naval power in this area and this was probably not the original idea. If trade in pepper and other Asian goods had been the only consideration, economy might have induced the Portuguese to act as traders who only used force for defence. Maritime trade in the Indian Ocean was open to anybody who could pay for the goods and a combination of diplomacy, capital (partially from Genoese and Florentine investors) and restrained shows of force against

Muslim competitors might have given the Portuguese the opportunity to organise a fairly peaceful trade. As events were to show, Asian competitors were unable to defeat well-armed Portuguese ships.

But Portugal soon found that seaborne trade in the Indian Ocean was dominated by Muslims: Arab, Indian and Malay traders who usually belonged to the religion that stirred up Portuguese enmity and crusading zeal. During da Gamas's first explorative voyage of 1497–99 and the second and more ambitious expedition sent out under Pedro Alvares Cabral in 1500, serious conflicts had already arisen, mainly in contacts with the Hindu ruler of the great entrepôt city Calicut on the west coast of India. He was sympathetic towards the Europeans as merchants but he rejected Portuguese demands that all Muslim traders should be banished. When Muslim merchants began to attack the Portuguese in Calicut, its ruler was held responsible. The Portuguese quickly began to use their guns against Muslim and Indian ships and cities in order to enforce their will. In this they were successful and these successes set off an aggressive pattern of behaviour. The Portuguese had understood that no strong naval forces were available to resist them if they resorted to offensive actions. Furthermore, they had found that the lightly built Asian ships were highly vulnerable to gunfire.

The third Portuguese expedition, which sailed under Vasco da Gama in 1502, was instructed to leave a squadron in the Indian Ocean as the first permanent Portuguese fleet there. It was a fateful decision and a remarkable proof of the self-confidence and ambition, which now prevailed in Lisbon. Da Gama came with well-armed merchantmen and caravels and quickly began to assert his position with naval power. Blockades, patrols with cruising vessels, bombardments of cities and acts of pure terror were used to control the trade on the west coast of India. Asian ships had to buy licences (*cartazes*) from the Portuguese if they wished to trade in this area. The ruler of Calicut and the Muslim traders assembled a large fleet of both major ships with several hundred men and a large number of small craft which, in February 1503, attacked da Gama's fleet off Calicut. With a vast superiority in manpower the Indian-Muslim fleet naturally attempted to board the Portuguese ships but this was successfully repulsed with gunfire. It was a clear demonstration that the new European combination of easily manoeuvrable sailing ships and heavy guns really worked. From 1503 Portugal sent squadron after squadron of ships into the Indian Ocean and gradually built up a large naval power in the area. The show of force began to pay off when minor rulers along the Indian west coast, primarily that of Cochin, allied themselves with the Portuguese and provided them with bases, ports for trade and access to the pepper-producing areas along the coast.

In a few years, Portugal seriously disrupted the trade in pepper and other Asian products through Mamluk and Venetian controlled ports and re-routed it around the Cape. The Mamluk rulers naturally responded in an attempt to regain the trade which had been such an important source of tax incomes.

With technical help from the Ottoman empire, an Egyptian galley force armed with guns was created in Suez for use in the Indian Ocean.[4] It arrived in 1508 at Diu in northern India where it joined the naval forces of the Sultan of Gujarat. Gujarat was a major Indian state whose merchants had a large stake in trade throughout the Indian Ocean. Initially the fleet defeated a small Portuguese force which attacked, but it failed to launch the offensive along the west coast of India that would have been necessary to break Portugal's naval control in that area. In spring 1509 the main Portuguese fleet under the viceroy Francisco de Almeida attacked Diu and destroyed the Egyptian-Gujarat fleet. This ended the last seaborne attempt to oust Portugal from the Indian Ocean before the arrival of the Dutch East India Company a century later. A gun-armed European battle fleet had taken control over a large ocean at a vast distance from Europe.

Up to 1509 the Portuguese presence in Asia had been purely maritime and no territorial conquest had been attempted. Lonely islands and ports controlled by friendly rulers were used as naval bases. From 1509 to 1515 the governor-general, Afonso de Albuquerque, led a campaign to create a maritime empire where a combination of a permanent fleet and fortified entrepôts and naval bases at strategic choke points would give Portugal control of the major lines of trade in the Indian Ocean. In 1510 he captured Goa on the west coast of India. This city was developed into a centre of trade and it became the capital of Portugal's *Estado da India*. In 1511 the Portuguese fleet sailed east to the city of Malacca (Melaka) which was also taken after a siege. Malacca was the most important entrepôt for spice trade in Southeast Asia and its location in the narrow straits which controlled the most convenient route between the Indian Ocean and the China Seas made it into a strategically very important base. In 1513 a siege of the equally important city of Aden at the entrance of the Red Sea failed. Portugal was never able to gain full control over the Red Sea route and in the latter half of the century this would become a serious gap in their control of the pepper trade. However, in 1515 Albuquerque was able to stage a coup by which he took control over Hormuz (Ormuz) at the entrance of the Persian Gulf, another very important entrepôt and strategic city.

In fifteen years, Portugal had established a new power structure in the Indian Ocean. The Portuguese crown had gained control of the pepper trade in the Arabian Sea and much of the pepper production along the Malabar (western) coast of India and channelled it to the new route around the Cape of Good Hope. Pepper trade became a royal monopoly (periodically leased to private investors) and all trade around Africa had to be carried in armed merchantmen owned by the king. Gradually, these grew in size until, by the latter half of the sixteenth century, they had become the largest European merchantmen in use. The huge *naus* (often called carracks) were a return to fifteenth-century technology when size rather than guns served as defence of cargo carriers. Size was useful in Asia, where the threat often came from small ships using boarding tactics, but it made the ships unwieldy sailers and vulnerable to more manoeuvrable European ships armed with guns.

Apart from the pepper trade, Portugal had also established herself as the seller of protection to Asian seaborne trade and to several small principalities around the Indian Ocean. The Asian merchants in this area had not asked for Portuguese protection and originally the *cartazes* sold by the Portuguese provided little but protection from the Portuguese themselves (sometimes not even that). Portuguese naval control was normally fully effective only along the western coast of India and in the straits of Malacca, but even that was a remarkable achievement in the sixteenth century. Gradually they organised the trade along the Indian west coast in convoys, perhaps as much in order to control it as to protect it from pirates.[5] From the 1510s Portugal began to use specialised warships, galleons *(galeaos)*, to exercise naval control, together with the smaller caravels. The latter type was also developed into a larger form of cruising warship, the *caravela redonda*.[6] For local patrols, light oared and sailing craft were used, including vessels of local type. The number of Portuguese in the east was small, possibly never above 10,000 men (including Eurasians) available for naval and military service. Naval control was therefore essential to supply and reinforce forts and enclaves threatened by local rulers.[7]

The Portuguese were unique as the only sea power with a presence throughout maritime Asia. No Asian power attempted to establish a similar position but they were sometimes successful in resisting or challenging Portuguese power. In 1517 the Portuguese fleet failed when it attacked a Muslim galley squadron in the port of Jiddah in the Red Sea under unfavourable tactical circumstances.[8] An attack against Diu in 1531 also failed although three years later the Portuguese were able to gain the fort in this important port in exchange for help to the Gujarat ruler against the Mughal invaders. Portugal thus gained better control over the flourishing sea trade of Gujarat. By this time, however, another imperial power, the Ottomans, had begun to show interest in the Arabian Sea. In 1516–17 the Ottomans defeated the Mamluk rulers of Egypt and added Syria, Palestine, Egypt and Mecca to their empire. This was partly an unintended result of the loss of Mamluk customs revenues which King Manuel of Portugal had hoped for when he attacked the Muslim spice trade in the east. Neither in the East or West was there any Christian power with the necessary armed force to benefit from the decline of Mamluk power – it was the Ottomans who gained.

In contrast to the Mughal rulers in India, the Sultan in Constantinople had a large navy and could re-direct considerable maritime resources and skills to the Indian Ocean. Potentially, the Ottomans represented a combination of skills, resources and ambition which might have defeated the Portuguese, but the threat never materialised as the rulers in Constantinople had other priorities.[9] However, in the 1530s a substantial Ottoman Red Sea fleet was created and used for offensive purposes. The Sultan of Gujarat allied with the Ottomans who, in 1538, sent a large galley fleet from Suez with an army and strong siege artillery. It first took Aden from its local ruler and then sailed to lay siege to Portuguese-held Diu. This operation ended in a conflict between the two Muslim powers and an Ottoman retreat, however, but the latter had gained control over the Red Sea. This they were determined to retain, not the least because it was necessary for the protection of the holy cities of Mecca and Medina from Christian attacks. An ambitious Portuguese naval attack against their base in Suez in 1541 failed. The Red Sea was difficult to navigate with large sailing ships and they did not return to it. In the early 1550s the Ottomans were active with a fleet based at Basra in the Persian Gulf. They made successful attacks in 1551–52 but were defeated when they attempted to take Hormuz in 1554.[10] In 1585 and 1588 the Ottomans made raids along the east African coast which forced the Portuguese to establish firmer control there.[11]

Ottoman seapower in the Indian Ocean mainly consisted of Mediterranean-style galleys which were unable to challenge the Portuguese sailing fleet far from their bases. This may be attributed to limited maritime ambition as well as to technical conservatism, but the galleys were powerful in the areas where they could operate. Ottoman control of the Red Sea made it possible for Asian merchants to reopen the trade between Asia and the Levant. The most active oceanic challenge to the Portuguese from the 1560s on came from the Sultanate of Aceh on northern Sumatra. Aceh could buy spices from the Moluccas islands in the eastern Indonesian archipelago and the Sultan co-operated both with Gujarati merchants from whom he gathered advanced sailing-ship technology and the Ottomans from whom he received gun-founders and artillerists. For the Ottomans, the alliance with Gujarat and Aceh became a method of challenging the Portuguese using limited means. Well-armed Aceh ships (some possibly owned by Gujaratis) began to break the Portuguese attempts to enforce naval blockades on Aceh and the Red Sea. Aceh also established a network of trade in the Bay of Bengal which was beyond Portuguese control. The Sultan of Aceh even became a serious threat to the Portuguese base in Malacca which was attacked in 1568 and repeatedly in 1571–5. The Portuguese navy was able to counter these threats but various plans for blockades and sieges of Aceh were not fulfilled.[12]

Aceh represented the most serious maritime threat against the Portuguese in the sixteenth century precisely because this state imitated their own technology – strongly-built sailing ships armed with heavy guns. Interestingly, neither of the two Muslim powers from which Aceh received support, Gujarat and the Ottomans, themselves used this combination of modern technology with success, a fact which illustrates that new combinations of skills may develop more efficiently in areas where the established technology is less firmly entrenched in the power structure.

Apart from the *carreira* trade around Africa and the protection selling empire, Portugal also had a mercantile presence in maritime Asia. The crown organised a number of intra-Asian *carreiras* which were gradually replaced by trading voyages contracted out to Portuguese, usually to officers and administrators who recognised the possibility of gaining commercial profit as a reward for their service to the crown. When the Portuguese acquired knowledge about this part of the world and its opportunities for profit, many of them also began to act as traders and mercenaries to Asian rulers without permission from the state. This type of activity was common around the Bay of Bengal where the Portuguese state exercised less control. Portugal also began to establish a presence in Southeast Asia (Indonesia) and the Chinese hemisphere. In Southeast Asia pepper and other spices were the most important products. The Portuguese never claimed any monopoly in this area but with well-armed ships they were able to establish profitable trade and gain influence over local rulers of islands such as Ternate and Tidore. Attempts to use force against the Chinese in the early 1520s were repulsed but special circumstances soon made it possible for the Portuguese to develop a profitable trade in this area. The Chinese emperor had forbidden his subjects to trade with Japan, but the imperial bureaucrats in southern China began, in their own interest, to allow the Portuguese to act as middlemen. From c. 1557 they were also allowed to create a trading factory at Macao. The yearly voyage with one great *nau* on the route Goa-Macao–Nagasaki became the most valuable of all concessionary voyages. In this part of the world, the Portuguese acted as peaceful traders who used arms only in defence against pirates.[13]

Few efforts have been made to prove whether the armed protection of the Portuguese state really was necessary to give the Portuguese the opportunity to trade profitably in maritime Asia. It is possible that Portuguese merchants might have been able to use European technology (ships and guns) profitably as a mean of defence even if their state had abstained from monopolistic protection selling. Trade east of Cape Comorin (the southern tip of India) where the *Estado* had a limited role was attractive for private entrepreneurs. But it was the kings who made the early investments in discovery and the gathering of maritime skills. Portuguese control over great entrepôts like Hormuz, Diu, Goa and Malacca may also have given Portuguese merchants advantage in information and the possibility of making decisions with greater certainty. The control of entrepôts ultimately depended on the armed force of the state, primarily the navy which controlled the sea lines of communication between them.

The organisation of a new trade route around Africa, the enforcement of a practical monopoly of violence at sea based on fortresses and a permanent fleet, and the development of European trade in Asia were remarkable achievements for a medium-sized European nation. The three facets of the Portuguese network of trade and power were based on the geographical, political, technical, maritime and mercantile skills and the control of major Asian entrepôts which the Portuguese state had developed during its dynamic drive to the east. Could this combination be developed into something which raised Portugal's position in Europe? Venice had earlier become prosperous on well-protected trade, the Dutch and the British later created positive circles of development around their overseas enterprises, and the Danish kings used the Sound Toll as a financial base for state formation. It might have been possible to achieve something similar if the three components had been connected into a system that promoted Portuguese capitalism, enriched the Portuguese state and created know-how which had given the Portuguese a lasting role as naval and maritime innovators. This might have given Portugal political and economic leverage in Europe and a leading role in the union with Spain when the Habsburgs had to develop competence in naval shipbuilding, and professionalism in warfare at sea, for the European power struggle in the late sixteenth century.

Something went wrong. In early modern Europe a limited population was no serious obstacle against a European state becoming a great power. Venice, the Dutch Republic and Sweden are examples of that. In the early sixteenth century Portugal had the ambition, but after a promising start it left the game. The Portuguese navy did indeed play an important role in the Habsburg war effort in Europe, but it proved a blunt instrument for offensive warfare against the English and the Dutch who by the late sixteenth century had developed more advanced instruments of sea power.[14] There is no definite historical explanation of why the Portuguese navy stagnated and there is also a serious lack of studies of this navy as an organisation: its technology, logistics and personnel and its role as an instrument of state policy. Studies of the anatomy of Portuguese sea power might be rewarding as they might increase our understanding both of the great Asian societies which did not develop naval organisations and the European societies which did. Recent research on the *Estado da India* has concentrated on other questions but we can try to find partial explanation by looking at various interpretations offered by recent scholarship.

Historical interpretations

The Portuguese imperial and mercantile enterprise in maritime Asia, its rise and subsequent decline during the seventeenth century, has attracted interest among historians from several countries. A common traditional interpretation was to contrast the heroism and ruthless efficiency of the early conquerors with a supposed unenterprising and corrupt mentality among later generations of Portuguese administrators, soldiers, seamen and merchants. Various explanations based on race, religion and the negative effects of Portugal's union with Spain (1580–1640) have been offered from historians with different backgrounds. The large-scale destruction of archival sources during the earthquake at Lisbon in 1755 has made it difficult to reconstruct the anatomy of the Portuguese naval and mercantile efforts in Asia.

During the latter half of the twentieth century, the economic history of the Portuguese empire and its role in Euro-Asian trade have been investigated. Frederic C. Lane's interpretation was that Europe's main export product (excepting money) to the East in the sixteenth and seventeenth centuries was violence. Portugal attempted to create a profitable Cape route by violence which was intended to increase the protection cost of her competitors to a prohibitive level. The Portuguese did not choose the alternative of employing violence only to protect their own trade with the aim of reducing the transport costs to Europe and lowering the pepper price, thus increasing demand and eliminating competition. Instead, the price was kept high and attracted competitors, an attraction that in the end destroyed the Portuguese pepper monopoly.[15]

However, not all economic interpretations put an emphasis on violence and warfare. Vitorino Magalhaes Godinho's studies of the economy of the Portuguese empire were made within a Braudelian framework with a stress on geography, trade routes and variations in market conditions (*conjouncture*). Violence, protection cost and different combinations of protection and transport were not discussed. Godinho did, however, emphasise that the Portuguese state and the knights who ran the empire were driven by feudal ambitions and a non-mercantile ethos.[16]

In the early 1970s, Niels Steensgaard made Lane's protection cost theory into the centre-piece of his analysis of the transformation of European-Asian trade around 1600. In his interpretation, the Portuguese *Estado da India* was essentially a redistributive enterprise which sold protection at sea to small-scale Asian merchants who had to submit to the normally enforced protection. The Ottoman empire, Persia and (up to 1517) the Mamluks provided the same service along the caravan routes between East and West. Steensgaard agreed with Godinho and the Dutch sociologist J. C. van Leur in describing the Portuguese presence in Asia as based on traditional feudal and non-capitalist norms of behaviour. The Portuguese also eventually gave up the attempt to gain a monopoly on pepper trade between Asia and Europe and preferred to extract as much money as possible on customs duties on the trade that followed the traditional routes. In contrast to this, the Dutch and English East India companies which appeared around 1600 were capitalist enterprises primarily using violence to protect their own trade. Violence was a cost which had to be kept down to increase profit. The companies did not sell protection to others or use violence, unless it furthered their mercantile ambitions and the accumulation of capital.[17]

Michael Pearson has developed another theme in his studies of the attitudes of Indian territorial rulers to seafaring trade and of Portuguese behaviour in the Indian Ocean. Indian rulers were not interested in promoting maritime trade, they derived little income from customs duties and they were not interested in profits from protection. Seaborne trade was not protected, nor was it disturbed by local rulers. In contrast, Portugal introduced politics and armed force at sea. Pearson is influenced by Steensgaard and emphasises that the Portuguese did not markedly change the Asian patterns of trade – they were superior as warriors at sea, but not as businessmen. However, Pearson seems so impressed by Steensgaard's interpretation of a decisive structural break around

1600 that he reduces the importance of his own researches, which are essentially studies of state formation. If Portugal brought a radically new idea of the role of the state at sea to Asia around 1500, that might also be described as an innovation with far-reaching consequences.[18]

Research in the 1980s and 1990s has attempted to revise the picture of the Portuguese as unenterprising in their approach to trade and as stuck in a medieval framework of redistributive tribute-raising. Sanjay Subrahmanyam, a specialist on early modern Indian trade, has emphasised that the Portuguese society was not a monolith and that the Indian Ocean empire underwent evolution. There were discussions and conflicts about the aims of the empire, policy changed more than once and many Portuguese traders and entrepreneurs did quite well. They were dynamic, adaptive and enterprising as well as rapacious and corrupt. They also interacted with Indian rulers and merchants and learnt much from them. Summarising his own and others' (especially Luis Filipe Thomaz') research, Subrahmanyam has been critical of Steensgaard and Pearson. They are accused of using a schematical weberian framework of development from irrationality to rationality, with the Portuguese seen as representatives of medieval (and Catholic) irrationality. Subrahmanyam does not regard the Dutch East India Company as different from Portugal in its use of seaborne violence: both powers could be rational, dynamic and profit-orientated, but also violent and irrational. However, he has not attempted any systematic comparison between Portuguese and Dutch attitudes to trade and violence or the differences in social and economic structure between the two societies.[19]

James Boyajian has made a study of the Portuguese empire in the east during Habsburg rule (1580–1640). He regards the Portuguese discoveries as the start of a commercial revolution. Gradually an increasing number of Portuguese merchants became important and changed Portugal's overseas venture from plunder, tribute and privileged trade into large-scale commercial trade. Some of these merchants were capitalists of the same type as those in Italy and the Netherlands, and in the 1620s and 1630s they became, for a time, important as financiers of the Spanish crown. Several of them were New Christians, members of Iberian Jewish families who (at least officially) had converted under the pressure of religious persecution. But Boyajian also emphasises that the merchants had little political power in Portugal where they were regarded more as suitable objects for taxation and suppliers of forced loans than as members of an elite group with scarce competence essential for the development of the country. The Portuguese state was dominated by landowning and aristocratic interests with limited understanding of the potentials of trade and capitalism. The commercial expansion was regarded as a threat to the established social order rather than as an opportunity to stimulate investment in manufacturing and agriculture.

The Portuguese framework of state maritime policy was not smoothly adaptive to mercantile interests. The royal monopoly on trade between Asia and Europe was a problem which the merchants had to circumvent with purchases of small lots of freight space belonging to Portuguese officials. The result was that many of the huge *naus da India* were overloaded to a dangerous degree, apparently because their captains had too little authority to regulate their loading – the passengers brought in too much baggage, including goods. These royal cargo carriers were also increasingly inferior in sailing and defensive qualities compared to the rapidly improving armed merchantmen which the Dutch and English used. An increasing number of *naus* were lost due to shipwreck or enemy action, with catastrophic financial results. The Portuguese merchants were not allowed to organise their own protection – a monopoly from which the state and its administrators derived income – nor were they given any influence over how the state organised the protection of their trade: convoys, commanding officers, naval technology and the design of armed cargo carriers. Boyajian has not put his results in any comparative framework, but his Portuguese capitalist merchants obviously lived in a different environment from their Dutch competitors who to a large extent ran the Dutch state in their own interest and who were also able to organise an East India Company as a semi-sovereign capitalist state where trade and protection were integrated.[20]

The various interpretations have shown that there was a lack of communication between the ruling (landowning and violence-controlling) elite and the merchants in both the Indian Ocean area and in Portugal. In Asia the ruling elites were uninterested in maritime enterprise and warfare and left the ocean to foreign intruders without a determined fight for supremacy. The Portuguese elite groups were interested in maritime enterprise and profits from seaborne trade, protection and oppression, but, as far as we now know, they remained locked in a feudal framework of ideas where a social and political transformation based on economic change was alien. In Portugal, capitalism and maritime technology, determined by the logic of mercantile profit and capital accumulation, faced problems in developing. In Charles Tilly's terminology, the Portuguese followed a coercion-intensive logic. The protection money raised in Asia and the monopoly profits on trade (if they really existed) were not used to create a strong Portuguese state with a dynamic society. The empire in the east was overtaken by Europeans whose capitalist enterprise had access to political power.

Why, then, was Portugal *initially* so successful as a wielder of violence and protection in the Indian Ocean? Most authors have expressed the opinion that the Portuguese naval successes were based on superior technical competencies: ships and guns. This argument was central in Carlo Cipolla's study of naval technology in the European overseas expansion. It is also used by Geoffrey Parker in his *Military Revolution* study, although he attaches little weight to European achievements overseas before 1600.[21] To Cipolla, the Europeans' superiority depended primarily on their utilitarian attitude to technology which was seen as an instrument for material achievements and was quickly adapted to military and naval use. In Asia socio-cultural factors were an obstacle to successful assimilation of the same technology. A few authors have expressed doubts. In 1980 P. J. Marshall emphasised, in a cautiously argued article, that the European naval and military superiority over the Asians was thin until the Industrial Revolution. At the same time, Geoffrey Scammell attacked the received orthodoxy more boldly and claimed that Portuguese success did not depend on ships and guns but on their ability to exploit conflicts in indigenous societies. Portugal ruled by internal allies and to a large extent with the help of Asians in their service.[22]

Criticism of the central role of technology in European expansion seems to underrate two obvious facts. The Europeans in Asia were always extremely few in comparison to the Asians, and among these no power in the entire Indian Ocean attempted to create a navy which challenged the Europeans. The Portuguese frequently fought numerically much superior forces with success and it seems strange to argue that they repeatedly won by accident rather than through some kind of qualitative or structural advantage. Scammell's argument that the ability to rule by internal division among the Asians, with indigenous support, does not take into account that Portugal *first* had to show its ability to control the sea lines of communication before it could gain allies and hire Asians as soldiers, sailors and shipbuilders. Regional power struggles, and many Asians' willingness to serve a power which could pay, gave the Portuguese technology a leverage which multiplied their influence far beyond what the number of men, ships and guns alone might have achieved. But they never fought an Asian power who attacked their bases and sea lines of communication in a systematic way. They never met an Asian maritime strategy to defeat them throughout Asia. This had to wait until the seventeenth century when other Europeans arrived and challenged the Portuguese in that way. Until then, the Portuguese were always able to use the sea lines of communication to concentrate their very limited resources on the area for the time being under threat. Their main enemy at sea was often the monsoon wind system which determined naval operations and periodically made it difficult to supply threatened fortresses and enclaves from the sea.

But both adherents and critics of the role of technology have often had a rather narrow focus on hardware and minimised its context. Technology must be studied in its institutional and organisational framework: how is the hardware used and which social and economic incentives exist to promote development and efficiency? The Portuguese combined guns, gun-carrying ships, tactical ability and an organisational framework where specialised, gun-armed warships were the core of naval strategy. The Portuguese came to Asia in such ships and they must have been aware that their skill in handling this instrument of power was decisive for their survival. No Asian power was dependent on ships to the same extent in order to survive. This dependency on a special technology may have focused the attention of Portuguese warriors on its use and development in ways that explain much of their success.

The Portuguese ships and the guns were primarily owned by the state. This makes the Portuguese enterprise look strikingly modern, but little research has been given to the sixteenth century Portuguese navy as a coherent organisation. It is regarded as part of the Indian enterprise but it was also an Atlantic and European force. The navy of the House of Aviz was a pioneer in several respects and in the early sixteenth century it may have been the most advanced operational force of its kind. But it seems that the Asian adventure gave it a different direction than other European royal navies which gradually developed into professional and bureaucratic organisations for formalised European warfare. The Portuguese naval efforts in the east were not driven by the logic of interstate rivalry but by the European tradition of trade, plunder and violence. That made it possible for warriors to go to sea, not to become seamen (a relatively despised job even in Portugal) but in order to gain honour and wealth. With no strong naval opponent in the area, the Portuguese officials in Asia could use a royal fleet, financially based on incomes from protection of Asian ships, to enrich themselves by trade, plunder and oppression and to defend their own position as rulers over small coastal enclaves.

This combination of seaborne warriors, trade, new technology and a centrally controlled organisation which co-ordinated naval and military activities throughout maritime Asia was new to Asians. Even to Europeans it was an enormous undertaking in terms of distances but it had its late medieval forerunners in Venice, Genoa and the Hanse. The really innovative behaviour was that of the two Kings Joao II and Manuel who during the decades around 1500 behaved like merchants rather than traditional territorial princes. Their successors had other priorities and they were unable to continue the dynamic development of the Portuguese armed forces and the Portuguese society which these two rulers had initiated.

Naval warfare in the hemisphere of Confucian bureaucracy

There was nothing self-evident in European behaviour at sea. Technical ability to build large ships and manufacture guns did not inevitably lead to warfare at sea and power projection. Long-distance trade was not inevitably connected with violence. Strong and well-organised states were not always selling protection at sea. In Eastern Asia, Imperial China had a very different attitude to trade and foreigners. China was a technically and economically advanced nation with a well-developed bureaucratic state and a huge population. It had all the necessary preconditions to develop a maritime empire in Asia and even in America and Europe. But the Chinese government was dominated by a suspicious attitude to the border areas of its territory, where Chinese might interact with foreigners and threaten the established order. China's coastal provinces were also regarded as border areas where barbarian foreigners might appear. Chinese attitudes were also generally defensive and the Chinese state did not maintain any naval forces other than regional coastguard flotillas. At the same time, Chinese merchants were very active in international maritime trade. They were not protected by the Chinese state, however, and the government was prone to restrict trade at the slightest suspicion that it might cause overly close relations with foreigners.[23]

Sixteenth-century Japan was a nation involved in fierce internal power struggles and civil wars between various war lords. In this turmoil, the Portuguese were able to gain a foothold in Japan as merchants and missionaries from their first arrival in 1543. They introduced the musket to Japan and this weapon as well as (probably) wrought-iron guns were used during the internal wars. As Japan was an island kingdom, sea power had a role in these struggles, but there are no signs that heavy guns made of copper or cast-iron, or gun-carrying warships, were introduced. By 1590 Japan was unified under the rule of the military leader Toyotomo Hideyoshi. To an expansionistic ruler of a large island state, areas like the Philippines or Southeast Asia might have been tempting. The land forces available to the Spanish, Portuguese and Asian rulers of these territories were very small compared to the large and war-experienced Japanese army. But Hideyoshi had no navy for long-distance deployment and his ambitions were fixed in another direction. He wished to conquer China.

This may look fantastic. But Ming China had had many difficulties with the containment of the Mongols and half a century later it would succumb to the Manchus. Japan was inherently stronger than these northern barbarians and, provided the Japanese could control the sea lines of communication, an invasion might be successful. In April 1592 Japan launched an invasion of Korea with an army of 130,000 (or perhaps up to 200,000) men, the largest seaborne invasion ever in any part of the world in the early modern period. Korea was invaded because it was close to Japan and could serve as a bridge to China for a Japanese army which had to rely on fishing boats and other small vessels for its transport overseas. Hideyoshi hoped that Korea might offer no resistance or perhaps join his forces. In fact, the Koreans fought back but the army could not stop the musket-armed Japanese from overrunning much of the peninsula.[24]

More effective resistance came from the Korean navy. Korea had armed forces organised according to the Chinese pattern with a permanent army and navy and a hierarchic and bureaucratic officer corps. Korea also shared the same technology and culture as China. The navy was a coastguard force divided according to the Korean provinces. The southern coast of Korea is archipelagic with several islands, peninsulas, sounds and inlets. The navy in this area was divided in an eastern and western squadron of which the first offered little resistance. The western squadron, that of the province of Chollado, was based on a peninsula in the city of Yosu under command of admiral Yi Sun-Shin. Since early 1591 it had undergone an intense training and rearmament programme centred around the introduction of warships armed with broadside guns and powered with oars during combat. The heaviest guns in use were made of copper and may have had a weight of around 300 to 400 kilograms.[25] Such guns were not large by European standards but they were optimal against small and lightly built vessels where a larger number of light guns are better than a few heavy pieces. The new ships were exclusively built for gunbattles and had a protective upper deck above the guns and the oarsmen. It was covered with large iron spikes to discourage boarders. The shape of the upper deck gave them the name 'turtle-ships'.[26]

With a striking force of turtle-ships and smaller vessels, in May and June 1592 admiral Yi Sun-Shin launched a series of successful attacks against the Japanese transport vessels spread out in the Korean archipelago. The Japanese gathered a more organised combat fleet but it was largely annihilated in the battle of Hansan Bay on 8 July 1592. In August, Yi attacked the Japanese transport fleet at Pusan and destroyed many vessels although Japanese gunfire from land hindered Korean attempts to eliminate this force. The numbers of vessels on both sides were very large in these battles but most ships were small. The Japanese fleets were improvised, with few real warships. During these actions the Korean gun-armed warships had shown that a large number of light vessels with many men had no chance against the systematic use of gunfire. Contemporary accounts describe how the turtle-ships penetrated large formations of Japanese vessels and destroyed them. Japanese arms could not penetrate their sides, nor could they be boarded. The Japanese were also handicapped by a lack of unified command. There was no organised navy and ships were sent out under several commanders without any fixed command structure. On the Korean side, Yi Sun-shin began as a provincial fleet commander but he was given command of all operational Korean warships as the struggle developed.

After a few months the Koreans had gained command of the sea and to a large extent cut off the invading army from Japan. At the same time a Chinese army arrived to counter the Japanese. A cease-fire was signed in June 1593 and most of the Japanese army evacuated Korea. However, Hideyoshi had not given up his ambitions and in 1597 he launched a new invasion of Korea, again taking the shortest route from Japan to the Pusan area. The Japanese still had no organised navy but they had by now begun to use guns on ships. The Korean navy, of which admiral Yi had been removed from command, was mobilised for a counterattack but suffered a severe defeat during a night action in a narrow strait at Chilchonryang on 16 July 1597. This time the Japanese were able to board the Korean vessels and only twelve warships escaped, apparently all turtle-ships. Admiral Yi was quickly recalled to command. The small force that remained was able to destroy a large number of Japanese vessels attempting to open a logistic route from the south to the main Japanese army which operated in central Korea. This time Yi used his knowledge of the strong tidal waters in the Korean archipelago to his advantage. In 1598 Hideyoshi died and the Japanese began to evacuate their army from Korea. During these operations a combined Korean-Chinese fleet under Yi's command inflicted a crushing defeat on the Japanese fleet at Noryangjin on 19 November 1598. Admiral Yi was killed during the battle.

Gunpowder weapons played a decisive role during the Japanese-Korean wars, but their distribution was strange from a European perspective. The Japanese army was well equipped with muskets while the Koreans fought with bows. At sea, the Koreans had effective guns carried by innovative warships: broadside-armed oared ships, suitable for archipelago warfare. Europeans might have described them as a kind of galeass. Their existence and tactical usefulness obviously came as a surprise to Hideyoshi. He was not unaware of European gun-armed ships and he had in fact attempted to buy such ships from both the Spanish and the Portuguese when he planned his invasion.[27] In the end, he improvised his naval forces and had to find out the hard way that gunfire was supreme at sea. In a larger perspective, the war showed that Korea and Japan, and probably also China, might mobilise huge armed forces for modern warfare on land and at sea. The bureaucratic and Confucian states in Eastern Asia were organisationally and technologically at the same level as Europe at this time. But after 1598 they were usually at peace with each other and with the Europeans, and no further development of their naval technology took place until they were seriously challenged by the Europeans and North Americans during the nineteenth century.

6

THE MEDITERRANEAN
The failure of empires

Zonchio 1499: a decisive battle

By late 1498 it had become clear that the Ottoman sultan, Bayezid II, was preparing an amphibious offensive.[1] Venice feared that her Greek possessions were in danger and mobilised an impressive fleet of 12 great (merchant) galleys, 44 galleys (normal size) and 28 sailing ships, including four very large ships with a displacement of around 2,000 tonnes each and armed with heavy guns. The fleet was manned by 20,000 to 25,000 men and during the summer of 1499 it moved south to the east coast of Morea (the Peloponese) where it met a large Turkish fleet which had earlier assembled in Constantinople. According to Venetian estimates the main components of this fleet were three great galleys, 60 galleys, 30 small galleys and 20 large and medium-sized sailing ships. Among the latter was a ship which was larger than the Venetian giants, probably with a displacement of 2,500 to 3,000 tonnes.[2] This fleet was believed to have around 37,000 men and was under the command of Daud Pasha, a former Grand Vizier.

The Turks intended to land heavy guns at the strategic Venetian fortress of Lepanto, then under siege by an Ottoman army led by the Sultan himself. The Venetian fleet led by the Captain-General Antonio Grimani had the task of preventing this in order to save the fortress. For more than a century, Venice had been the leading sea power in the Mediterranean. As late as 1489 it had added Cyprus to its empire and in 1495–96 Venetian galleys had been important in the defeat of the French invasion of Naples. In the summer of 1499 the Venetians had mobilised the largest fleet they had ever sent to sea and now it had reached the area of operations in time to frustrate the offensive move of the Sultan. Venice expected a victory at sea, a new confirmation of its naval supremacy over the Asiatic Turkish warriors who had occupied Anatolia and the Balkans and created a continental empire.

After a few weeks of manoeuvring against each other, Grimani saw an opportune moment for attack on 12 August. Daud Pasha had adopted a defensive attitude and sought protection in the Bay of Zonchio (today the Bay of Navarino and well-known as the scene of another naval battle of 1827). The

Venetian attack failed miserably. Two of the largest Venetian ships grappled with the largest Turkish ship. They caught fire and all three went up in flames. Another Venetian ship and a galley were sunk by gunfire. However, most of the Venetian galleys and ships did not seriously attack the enemy. This unwillingness to drive home a decisive attack on the Turks demoralised the fleet. Although the Venetians were joined by a French squadron, it failed to gain any success in further attacks against the Turks who slowly moved northward along the coast. The Venetians used fireships and gunfire, but avoided close actions, possibly with the frightful scenes of burning ships at Zonchio fresh in their memory. The Ottoman fleet reached the Gulf of Lepanto and the Venetian fortress surrendered when the defenders realised that the enemy was between them and their own fleet. The Turks placed guns at the entrance to the gulf and made it their base for the next year's campaign. The Ottoman main fleet had established a forward base in the Ionian Sea, hitherto a Venetian preserve.

The failure of the Venetian fleet has been explained by its complicated command structure, lack of discipline among the officers who were also political decision makers in the Republic, financial problems and the difficulties of co-ordinating sailing and oared warships in offensive actions. To this may probably be added good gunfire and well-disciplined defence on the Turkish side. In 1500 a further fleet action at Zonchio on 24 July ended with another Venetian setback, not least due to Turkish gunfire. This time only the galleys could be brought into action as the wind was too light for the sailing warships. As the Venetians were unable to control the Ionian Sea, the Ottomans took their fortresses at Modon, Coron and Zonchio in the Morea. In the following years Venice received support from France, Spain, Portugal, the Pope and the Knights of St John (Rhodes) and with improved discipline in the fleet, some successes were achieved. But the Ottoman conquests could not be rolled back and in 1502 Venice had to accept a peace in which the Republic tacitly admitted Ottoman naval superiority in the Levant.

The Venetians retained a strong commercial position in the area but could no longer hope to control the sea lines of communications outside the Adriatic by naval force. They could no longer coerce economic competitors with naval power. Their dependence on friendship with the Sultan for their trade neutralised the largest Christian fleet in future wars involving the Ottomans, except when Venice was attacked (1537 and 1570). Two other factors also made Venice and the Ottomans into reluctant allies. As established empires with trade and territories which were closely intertwined with each other, they shared an interest in the maintenance of law and order in the Levant. They both struggled for the monopolisation of violence by central government and discouraged the use of violence by private interests. Furthermore, the Portuguese intrusion in the Indian Ocean made Venice dependent on Ottoman success in that ocean for her supplies of spices from Asia.

The battles around Zonchio and Lepanto of 1499–1500 and even the Turkish-Venetian war are often left out of general accounts of political and naval history. Instead, events like the battle of Lepanto in 1571 and the Armada campaign of 1588 are given wide coverage. In political, naval and technical significance, these events are fully comparable. The Ottoman rulers derived much of their prestige and power within the Muslim world from their abilities as military leaders. A defeat around 1500 would have lowered their prestige, and a continued Venetian naval superiority in the Aegean and the Levant might have made the dramatic Ottoman conquests in the following decades less probable. Instead, the Ottoman empire emerged as the leading sea power of the Mediterranean, a new situation which would be of great importance for the power struggle during the sixteenth century.

From a naval perspective, the actions of 1499–1500 are interesting as an illustration of the state of the art of warfare at sea at this time. The two most powerful navies in the world had met in combat, guns had been widely used, and their efficiency had limited resort to close combat. Sailing ships, even of very large size, had been used, but they had failed to convince the participants of their value in battles at sea. In future sixteenth-century wars in the Mediterranean they were little used and all efforts were concentrated on galley construction. The amphibious and short-distance character of Mediterranean warfare was highlighted. Most maritime operations were closely connected with attacks on, or the defence, of fortresses. In 1500, this was the dominant form of warfare at sea in Europe.

Declining and rising empires: Venice, the Ottomans and Spain

The decades around the year 1500 saw major changes in the political and maritime structure of the Mediterranean world. Old empires declined and new ones emerged. The old empires were Italian, maritime and centred on mercantile cities. The new empires were based on resource extraction from large territories east and west of Italy. Spain and France competed for hegemony in Italy while the Ottomans rapidly created a world power with large territories in Asia, Europe and Africa. As empire builders in an area connected by sea, the warriors of the rising empires had to adapt to maritime warfare. They did so by creating permanent naval forces, a part of the state formation process which made empire building a practical possibility. Gunpowder weapons were an important part of the change, although their relationship with progress in state formation remains a complex question. The navies were part of the organisational structure which enabled rulers to enforce control over violence and to raise taxes by selling protection to hitherto independent political units, thus creating empires.[3]

The new Mediterranean empires were not maritime societies with dynamic merchants and large-scale shipowners. In a Mediterranean perspective, this was something new. For centuries the Italian city states had been dominant in both maritime trade and maritime warfare: northern Italy was economically and technologically the most sophisticated area of Europe; Venice and Genoa were great maritime entrepôts and shipowning cities; and Florence was a flourishing economic centre. Naval control of the Levant, in combination with a long experience of trade, also made Venice a middleman between Asia and Europe. Both Venice and Genoa owned territories and trading posts in the Levant. Venice and Florence had networks of trade using well-armed merchant galleys, while Genoa specialised in trade with huge and defensible sailing ships. Sea power, mercantile dominance and economic prosperity seemed to be inextricably interconnected.[4] Would the new territorially-based empires be able to repeat this performance, provide security at sea in order to lower transport costs and stimulate investment in the maritime economy? Was the radical political unification of the Mediterranean a preparation for its rise into a leading centre of an emerging world economy, encompassing Europe, Africa, Asia and America?

Large-scale empire building began in the East. After the conquest of Constantinople in 1453, the Ottoman sultans began to develop Turkish naval power as a new means of imperial expansion in the Black Sea and eastern Mediterranean. They could make good use of the seafaring population in Anatolia and on the Greek islands which had once been the source of strength for the Byzantine navy. Naval bases were created and a permanent force of galleys and galley crews were established. When combined with heavy guns and efficient Janissary infantry, Ottoman galleys became a formidable weapon for imperial expansion, but the long war with Venice from 1463 to 1479 showed that the navy lacked experience. It was this inferiority which was rectified in the war with Venice between 1499 and 1502.[5]

The Sultan used his navy for protection and regulation of trade, control of islands and coastal areas and support for imperial expansion. The activities of both Christian and Muslim corsairs were curtailed and the Mamluks of Egypt were supplied with gunners and naval experts against the Portuguese threat in the Red Sea and the Indian Ocean. Under Selim I (r. 1512–20) a dramatic expansion took place. Persia was defeated in 1514 and during 1516/17 the Mamluk sultanate was conquered, giving the Ottomans control over Egypt, Syria, Palestine and the holy cities of Mecca and Medina. The Mamluks had no navy, and the Ottoman navy was mobilised as a logistic and flank-supporting force to their army in this campaign.[6] Ottoman sea power was also indirectly important for Selim's triumphs. It meant that no Christian power was able to interfere with this struggle for domination in the Muslim world. France and Spain, the two rapidly rising great powers in the west, had for decades played with the idea of expanding their power to the Levant. In Portugal, king Manuel had attempted to intervene from the back door, through the Indian Ocean. With the growth of centralising forces and state formation in the Christian west such expansion had been possible. The consolidation of Muslim territories under Ottoman rule and the rapid state formation within this empire put an end to such ideas for centuries.

In 1522 the Order of St John, the last vestige of the western crusades, was forced to leave Rhodes after a long siege. This eliminated an irritating base for privateering and a potential base for large-scale western actions against Ottoman hegemony in the Levant. In 1526 the Turks also conquered most of Hungary, the first of several campaigns in this area where naval control of the Danube was essential for the logistics of the army.[7] In a few decades, an empire with practically the same geographical configuration as the eastern half of the Roman empire had been created. Large parts of it were easily accessible from the sea and control of the sea was essential for trade and the transfer of resources between one part of the empire and another. The maritime axis Alexandria–Constantinople was especially important, as it provided the capital with Egyptian grain and made it possible to transfer resources between the two central parts of the empire. The ability to mobilise and concentrate resources was essential for early modern state and empire builders such as the Ottoman sultans. This, together with a strong desire to regulate trade and prices and ensure the supply of food and essential goods to their subjects, seems to have driven the great conquering sultans of the period 1451 to 1566 (Mehmed II, Bayezid II, Selim I and Suleyman I) to create a permanent navy. They were among the first territorial princes in Europe and Western Asia to make a serious attempt to create a working state monopoly of violence at sea through a permanent organisation.[8]

In the western Mediterranean another empire was forming in the same period. The union between the crowns of Aragon and Castile established during the 1470s by the marriage of Ferdinand and Isabella released dynamic forces in state formation which made it more than a dynastic alliance. The two rulers developed Spain into an early modern military state, but this state also had a maritime dimension. Aragon ruled over Sicily, Sardinia and the Balearics, and the *reconquista* continued after the conquest of Granada in 1492 with attacks on Muslim North Africa. The new empire also faced two other challenges where control of the sea lines of communication was essential. Columbus' discoveries in the West Indies became the starting point for a Castilian colonisation of America based on a successful claim of Spanish-Portuguese monopoly of the trans-oceanic discoveries. From 1494, France, hitherto mainly engaged in wars with England and Burgundy, began to project power into Italy and attempted to gain control over Naples, later also over Lombardy. A French-Italian conglomerate state might become the most powerful empire in Europe.[9]

The Italian wars (1494–1559) are a classic topic in military history, but attention has overwhelmingly been concentrated on the battles on land. The sea lines of communication were, nevertheless, also of great importance and in the maritime perspective the conflict was decisive for the future power structure in the western Mediterranean. The first French attack on Naples

(1494/95) had been a rapid progress down the peninsula. This is often explained by the massive French use of modern siege artillery. It was, however, also a result of close co-operation between the French army and the navy, a largely improvised force of sailing ships and galleys. A considerable part of the army was sent by sea and the fleet made demonstrations along the coast to open the way for the army. At Rapallo, 4,000 soldiers were landed and successfully attacked the enemy forces in their rear.[10]

The main French army soon had to be withdrawn northwards, however, leaving only garrisons in important fortresses. Spain and Venice (and other powers) allied against France, a Spanish fleet brought in an army from Spain, while Venice sent galleys to support the counter-attack and the blockades of cities occupied by the French. The French fleet was too weak to challenge this combination, and the isolated French garrisons capitulated. In the next phase of the Italian wars, from 1500 to 1504, both France and Spain maintained fleets of sailing ships and galleys to secure their lines of communication to southern Italy but they did not meet in any major battles at sea. The kingdom of Naples was gained for Spain by victories on land – these were the years when the Spanish infantry gained its reputation – but the operations were based on control of the sea lines of communication.

The Ottomans, the Habsburgs and France, 1510–59

In 1516, the new Spanish Mediterranean empire was inherited by the Habsburg prince Charles. Three years later he also inherited the Habsburg territories in Austria and the Netherlands and was elected German emperor as Charles V. The new western empire was mainly connected by sea lines of communication. In the very centre of the Habsburg territories lay the other European great power, France, rich in population and often regarded as an archetype for the 'modern' national state. For two centuries, the Habsburg 'encirclement' of France became the chief determinant of French foreign policy. Much of the circle around France was in fact open seas in the Atlantic and the Mediterranean. For the Habsburgs, the sea would be essential for the free transfer and concentration of resources for military actions and state formation, and their ability to develop a coherent maritime and naval policy would be crucial for the future of this conglomerate of European and American possessions. For France, efficient sea power might cut the Habsburg lines of communication.

Initially, the conflict at sea between France and the Habsburgs was concentrated on the Mediterranean, and early rise of Habsburg naval power was practically identical with the growth of the permanent galley fleets within the Spanish empire. This growth was also stimulated by Spanish ambitions in another direction. In order both to continue the *reconquista* of Muslim territories and to secure the lines of communication between Spain and Italy, a series of amphibious expeditions were launched against cities in North Africa. They were especially intense in 1509/10 when Oran, Bougie, Tripoli and the harbour fort in Algiers were taken. After that Spanish expansion in North Africa began to meet effective resistance. This came not from the local inhabitants but from a group of highly skilled corsairs, led by the brothers Oruc (killed in action 1518) and Khizr (or Hizir), both usually known as Barbarossa. They began operations from La Goletta (close to Tunis) but soon extended their control to other ports. In the late 1510s the corsairs paid allegiance to the Ottoman sultan who provided them with arms and men and appointed Khizr, (by now known as Hayreddin or Kheir-ed-Din: Defender of the Faith), governor of Algiers and commander of the western Ottoman fleet.[11]

Algiers had been taken by the corsairs from the local inhabitants in 1516 and Spanish attempts to take that city in seaborne assaults in 1516 and 1519 failed when gales destroyed their fleets. In 1529 the Spanish fort which controlled the harbour of Algiers fell to Hayreddin Barbarossa's forces. Initially these forces had to fight both Spain and the local Muslims. Many of the warriors were refugees from Granada, and together with seamen of east Mediterranean origin, they formed an efficient maritime state in North Africa. Hayreddin was born on the island of Lesbos in the Aegean and like most of the corsairs he was of humble social origin. Some were to make a fortune as corsairs – a few rose to high positions in the Ottoman service.[12]

From 1521 to 1529 Spain and France were involved in a large-scale war over Italy. It was to a considerable extent fought at sea, predominantly in the form of close co-operation between armies and navies along the Italian and French coasts. Galleys and sailing ships – oared vessels now began to dominate – provided gunfire, amphibious capability, blockade forces and flank support during sieges and military operations. Warfare and diplomacy were substantially questions of gaining support or submission from the Italian states, where Genoa was a chief object of interest on the maritime side. Up to 1528, the most important entrepreneur in galley warfare, the Genoese Andrea Doria, served the king of France. His galley squadron was the most efficient part of the French fleet, but he was not given command of that fleet and he became dissatisfied with French policy towards Genoa and his own business interests. In 1528 Doria suddenly entered the service of the king-emperor Charles when his contract with France ended. He changed sides shortly after his galleys had won a victory over Spain. As a maritime *condottiere*, Doria understood how to show his value.

In his new contract he was given the overall command of the Habsburgs' Mediterranean fleet: the galley squadrons of Spain, Sicily and Naples, Doria's own galleys and other galleys hired from Italian entrepreneurs. In the same year, Doria staged a coup in Genoa, which politically and economically became attached to the Habsburg camp. For the Spanish king, Doria and his family became guarantors of Spanish control over the sea lines of communication between Spain and northern Italy (and further north to Austria, Germany and the Netherlands, later called the Spanish Road) and free access to the strategically important harbour of Genoa. For Genoa, Spain provided military security and a profitable market, while Doria in his position as galley entrepreneur and commander of the fleet gained access to a large patronage system and a flow of money. This ensured his leading position in Genoa and enabled him to enforce political peace in an earlier much disunited republic.[13]

Doria's change of sides in 1528 gave Spain control of the sea, and the French blockade of Naples (hitherto supported by Doria) was lifted. France had to admit defeat in Italy and signed a peace in 1529. The peace gave the Habsburg King-Emperor Charles an opportunity to launch offensive actions against the Ottoman empire, both in order to relieve his Austrian lands from military pressure and to retake territories in North Africa lost to Hayreddin's forces. One part of this was the transfer of the Knights of St John – homeless since 1522 – to Malta and Tripoli in 1530. They made Malta into a heavily fortified naval base in a strategically important position. In most operations against the Muslims, the galleys of Malta as well as those of the Pope were to co-operate with Spain.[14]

Andrea Doria began to attack North Africa, but his forces were met by a competent defence. Another Spanish idea was to stir up a revolt against the Turks in Greece, thus making this Christian area a counterpart to North Africa. In 1532 Doria conquered Coron in the Morea (Peloponese) and defeated a hastily assembled Ottoman fleet which was sent out to meet the intruders. Sultan Suleyman realised that this navy required better leadership, and in 1533 Hayreddin was called to Constantinople and appointed Kapudan Pasha: commander-in-chief of the navy. The two most famous sixteenth century Mediterranean admirals, who recently had connected two maritime states to the growing empires, were now in command of the imperial galley fleets.

Hayreddin wasted little time. During 1534 Coron was retaken and his fleet ravaged the coasts of southern Italy and occupied Tunis. In 1535, the King-Emperor Charles was not preoccupied with other urgent tasks and he decided to concentrate his military and naval power in a large expedition to Tunis, led by Charles in person. Seventy-four galleys, 30 small galleys (*galeotas* and *fustas*) and around 300 sailing vessels with about 20,000 men carried an army of almost 30,000 men which took the city, installed a client ruler and placed a Christian garrison in the fortress La Goletta close to Tunis. Portugal, the Pope, Malta and Genoa sent contingents to the fleet. Hayreddin was unable to counter this invasion but his fleet attacked Minorca instead.

France and the Habsburg empire again went to war in 1536. The first major operation was an invasion of Provence and an unsuccessful siege of Marseilles led by the Emperor and supported by the fleet. In 1537 France and the Sultan decided to invade Italy.[15] It is an interesting example of the restrictions in radius of Mediterranean galley warfare that the Turks regarded it as necessary to conquer Venetian Corfu – the base nearest the Italian peninsula – as a first step in their Italian operation. The attack failed, but brought the Venetians into the war. In 1538, Venice, Spain and the Pope formed a formidable fleet, but it could not unite until late in the season, as Doria with the Spanish fleet did not arrive at Corfu until early September. The allied fleet had quantitative superiority over Hayreddin's fleet, possibly 130 galleys against 90. Both fleets were now almost exclusively oared – the attendant sailing vessels were regarded as transports.

The Ottoman fleet was in the Gulf of Prevesa on the Greek coast south of Corfu. It was a classical place for naval actions – the battle of Actium was fought here in the year 31 BC. The narrow entrance to the gulf was protected by a castle and shore batteries, which made it difficult to enter. The Christian side was joined by an army of 16,000 men in sailing ships on 22 September, but it was too late in the season to begin a formal siege. The allied forces under Doria's command attempted to make amphibious assaults on the castle to clear the way for the fleet before its supplies had run out. These failed and, with supplies running low, the Christians had to use a northerly wind in order to retire during 27 September. Some galleys and several sailing ships straggled and were attacked by the Ottoman fleet. Doria could not counter-attack to support them. The Christian losses were not great, but the Ottomans had showed that with an inferior force they could fight off a combined Spanish–Venetian attack. In the following decades they were supreme in the Levant and a serious threat to the western Mediterranean.[16]

That was the long-term effect. In the short run, Mediterranean galleys showed their fragility. During the weeks after Prevesa, the Ottoman fleet was decimated by a sudden storm off the Albanian coast, although the crews seem to have been saved. Doria used this opportunity to capture Castelnuovo near Cattaro in October 1538. It was retaken in the summer of 1539 by Barbarossa's fleet, which was larger this year and could dominate the Adriatic.[17] France had left the war in 1538 and Venice did the same in 1540. Spain and the Ottomans continued their struggle. In 1541 Charles V was in the unusual situation of enjoying peace in both Germany and Italy. He decided once again to lead a great amphibious expedition, this time to Algiers, the centre of North African corsairs. A fleet of 65 galleys and 450 other vessels of various size with about 12,000 seamen and oarsmen, was collected to carry 24,000 Spanish, Italian and German soldiers across the Mediterranean. In order to prevent the superior Ottoman fleet from interfering, the attack was launched in the autumn. It was a gamble with the weather that the emperor lost. In a gale, 15 galleys and about 150 ships with stores and artillery were wrecked against the open coast of Algiers. The defence of the city was efficient and, after four weeks, Charles decided to evacuate with the loss of 12,000 men.

France again began to fight Spain in Italy in 1542. The new power balance at sea was shown when an Ottoman fleet of 110 galleys was sent to the western Mediterranean and spent the winter of 1543–44 in Toulon.[18] It co-operated with the French in the siege and capture of Nice in 1543, but next year Hayreddin declined to take part in a projected siege of Genoa. He apparently hoped that the French would help him to retake Tunis, but, when they declined, he preferred to chase Spanish galley squadrons and ravage enemy coasts in Italy. This was the last expedition of Hayreddin who died in 1546. His rise from a humble sailor to state builder, commander of the largest fleet in the world and one of the Sultan's viziers, was probably the most remarkable early modern career of a seaman. France left the war in 1544 and sent its Mediterranean galleys to the Channel for a projected invasion of England. A truce was concluded between Constantinople and Spain, but the war continued at a lower scale with corsair raids and attempts to capture bases in North Africa.[19]

In 1551 this type of warfare escalated when the Ottomans took Tripoli from the Knights of St John. Next year, France was back in the war and about 100 Ottoman galleys went to the western Mediterranean.[20] They surprised Doria's fleet of 39 galleys on its way to Naples with soldiers, but he was able to escape with the loss of seven galleys. In 1553 the Ottoman fleet returned and invaded Corsica, but the island was retaken when the Muslim fleet returned to the east. Large Ottoman fleets appeared in the western Mediterranean in 1554–56, expeditions which culminated in 1558 when 130 galleys took part. These fleets dominated the sea in the centre of the Spanish empire, although their strategic importance for the war in Italy is little known. Spain won the war in Italy, in spite of the French-Ottoman control of the sea. The Ottomans and the French did not establish any effective co-operation in which their fleets could be used for systematic sieges of fortified places. The Ottomans achieved little visible success except devastation along the coasts, but they may have tied up considerable forces in coastal defence, created difficulties for Spanish communications and interrupted trade.

The Ottoman fleet did not use North Africa for logistics and winter ports, and this reduced its efficiency in the western Mediterranean. Apparently the Ottoman logistical system in North Africa was too weak for expeditions of this size which had to be based in Constantinople. The Ottoman failure to establish a really strong base system in the western Mediterranean made it difficult for them to dominate this area with a galley fleet. Galleys had short radii of action, and none of the two great empires had found any solution to this problem other than increasingly expensive sieges of fortified ports which might serve as bases. From such bases, local squadrons of oared vessels could launch raids, which in the long run might weaken the enemy. The idea of developing gun-armed sailing vessels as front-line warships with a longer range had more or less disappeared in the Mediterranean after the early sixteenth-century experiences which apparently were disappointments. The next decades witnessed the apogee of large-scale galley warfare in the Mediterranean, but were also a period when the limitations of galleys as instruments for control of sea lines of communication became obvious.

The apogee of galley warfare, 1559–80

In April 1559 the peace of Cateau-Cambrésis was concluded between France and Spain.[21] Philip II, the new king of Spain, could not know that this marked the end of the period known to posterity as 'the Italian wars' and that France would disappear as a naval power until the 1620s. But he – and even more the viceroy of Sicily and the Knights of Malta – hoped that Spanish resources could now be concentrated on counter-measures against Ottoman sea power. They hoped to use the galleys and soldiers freed from the war with France to make a surprise attack against Tripoli, another attempt to improve the strategic situation with the capture of a galley base. The expedition took much longer to organise than expected and did not start in earnest until early 1560. It arrived first at the island of Djerba, half-way between Tunis and Tripoli, which originally was intended as a temporary base. Sickness and bad winter weather changed the plans and it was decided to stay at Djerba and fortify the island.

The Ottoman navy under its commander, Piali Pasha, had quickly organised a force of around 85 galleys which made a rapid voyage from Constantinople to Djerba. It arrived on the morning of 11 May 1560 and surprised a disorganised Christian force. Many galleys were not manned and their commander, the 20–year old Gian Andrea Doria,[22] panicked and lost control. The Christian fleet was never formed for serious resistance and lost 27 to 30 of some 45 galleys and around half of its 29 sailing ships. The army was left on Djerba with no possibility of escaping or receiving supplies. It held out until the end of July 1560 when it capitulated. The total Christian losses of soldiers and seamen at Djerba are uncertain, one (high) estimate puts it at 18,000. The main cause of the catastrophe was an underestimation of the Ottoman ability to respond quickly and with superior force to a Christian attack in mid-Mediterranean. Spain and her smaller allies had also displayed inefficiency in mobilising their forces, and thus lost the advantage of surprise.[23]

For Philip II the Ottoman navy had now become the main threat to his empire. France was in serious political difficulties, and his own troubles in the Netherlands were yet to come. But the Ottoman galleys might still capture his North African possessions, devastate the coasts and stir up rebellion in Granada. He decided to expand the permanent galley force and its readiness for combat, and made the Pope agree to a taxation of Church property in exchange for a promise that Spain would maintain 100 galleys in service. During the following years many galleys were lost in minor actions or in gales, and some of these losses may be attributed to lack of experienced crews, partly a result of Djerba.[24] The expected Ottoman expedition to take Spanish-held Oran far in the west appeared in 1563 but it was relatively weak, 30 to 40 galleys, and was forced to retreat by the Spanish fleet.

In 1565 the Ottomans launched their long-expected major offensive. Its target was Malta, which was attacked by 140 galleys and an army of around 30,000 men. The defenders had about a tenth of that strength, led by the

Grand Master of the Order of St John, Jean de la Valette. The siege of Malta from May to early September 1565 belongs to the epics of Christian–Muslim confrontation in the Mediterranean. For Spain, the problem was how best to use her limited forces. Her fleet was too weak to intercept the invaders at sea or protect the transfer of a major army to Malta. The Spaniards chose to leave the Turks to spend as much of their men and ammunition in assaults on the walls of the Knight's strongholds at Malta as they would and to hope that the defenders would survive a few months. In late August, a Spanish relief force was sent from Sicily. It was twice forced back by bad weather, but when it arrived, it found the Turks in the process of evacuation. They had been so decimated that they were unable to fight the Spanish forces either on land or at sea.[25]

The following years saw no major actions at sea, although both sides mobilised large fleets and the Ottoman numerical superiority at sea was obvious. It is, however, also obvious that they had difficulties in translating their superiority into lasting conquest in the western Mediterranean. This may be the logical explanation for their decision to attack Venetian-ruled Cyprus in 1570.[26] They must have calculated that the addition of the Venetian fleet to the enemy forces meant less than the fact that Cyprus was situated so far from the main Christian bases that it would be difficult for their galleys to prevent the attack. The Turkish invasion force, supported by about 150 to 160 galleys, reached Cyprus in July and rapidly occupied the island, except the city of Famagusta. The Venetians had quickly mobilised their fleet, but they were inferior in numbers of galleys and infantry to interfere directly with the Ottoman invasion. In late August the Italian squadrons of Philip II's galley fleet (49 galleys) and the Pope's squadron (12 galleys) arrived in the Levant, bringing the Christian force up to about 180 to 190 galleys. The three fleets found it difficult to co-operate; they believed that their forces were too small for a relief of Cyprus and could not agree on a less ambitious plan, such as attacks on Ottoman territories in Greece or the Adriatic. They achieved little, but in January 1571 a small Venetian squadron was able to bring in supplies to Famagusta, which made it possible to continue the resistance. The Sultan dismissed Piali Pasha as commander of the Ottoman navy for his failure to keep up an efficient blockade during the winter.

In Spring 1571, Spain, Venice and the Pope formed a closer alliance, the Holy League. They agreed to maintain a force of 200 galleys, 100 sailing ships, 50,000 infantry and 4,500 cavalry during the years 1571–73 in order to wage war on the Ottomans. Philip II's half-brother, Don John of Austria, was appointed commander of this force. It took the whole summer of 1571 to gather the Spanish part of it and bring it to the Levant. Famagusta had capitulated in early August and the Turkish conquest of Cyprus was complete. During September the combined fleet was finally organised under Don John, who, in spite of his youth, proved to be an efficient leader of a force that was full of political and personal antagonism. Totalling around 206 galleys and six

Venetian galeasses (converted merchant galleys), it was organised as a coherent fleet with a unified command structure and a formal battle order where galleys from different states were mixed in the same squadron. The well-trained Spanish infantry was partly distributed on the 108 Venetian galleys which were weak in manpower. The Ottoman fleet, about 220–230 galleys and at least 50 to 60 small galleys, was in the Gulf of Lepanto under the command of the new Kapudan Pasha, Müezzinzade Ali Pasha.

The two fleets met on 7 October 1571 in one of the largest and best known battles ever fought at sea. It was unusual as both sides deliberately sought offensive action without having any important strategic purpose to seek battle for. It was too late in the season to make use of a victory and neither side threatened any vital interests of the other. Both sides are said to have underestimated the strength of their opponent and the Ottomans had an express order from the Sultan to fight. On the Christian side, Don John might have fought for glory but also with a conviction that the alliance would not survive one more year of hesitant inactivity by the united fleet. Lepanto was primarily fought because political logic required action.

Following this logic, the two fleets charged each other in two long lines abreast spread across the Gulf of Lepanto without considering if a defensive position or a few preliminary tactical manoeuvres might have suited them better. J. F. Guilmartin has argued that Ali Pasha hoped that his two wing squadrons and the small galleys would be able to use their superiority in manoeuvrability to turn the flanks of their opponents and attack the Christian formation from the side or the rear (where galleys were vulnerable), while his own centre squadron would fight a probably difficult defensive action. On the Christian side, the galeasses were placed as a vanguard (only four reached their place in the formation) to bring disorder to the advancing Turkish line with gunfire, while the reserve squadron was intended to be deployed at a decisive place at a crucial moment.

As the battle developed, the Christian inshore squadron – mainly a Venetian force – was able to make a difficult wheeling movement and press their Turkish opponent to the shore where it was nearly annihilated. The two centres fought an equally fierce battle where Christian firepower and heavy infantry finally won a crushing victory in which Ali Pasha was killed. The two offshore squadrons manoeuvred for a time until the Turks took an opportune moment to outflank the enemy centre. They began to capture Christian galleys but were halted by the Christian reserve squadron and finally attacked by the Christian offshore squadron.[27]

With the loss of around 180 Ottoman galleys and 60 small vessels against 12 Christian galleys, Lepanto ranks as a battle of annihilation. Galleys were easily replaced, however. The losses of men were more important. They were heavy and more equally distributed, but the figures reported in the literature are contradictory.[28] Guilmartin has argued that the Ottoman loss in skilled manpower was crippling for the efficiency of their navy.

During 1572 the Spanish-Italian galleys were as usual late in arriving in the Levant, but this time the delay can partly be explained by Philip II's orders. He was uncertain about the political and military situation in the Netherlands and France and wished to have his galleys available in the western Mediterranean as long as possible. During the summer the Venetian fleet repeatedly attempted to bring its weakened opponent to action, but the Ottomans skilfully avoided this and restricted the operations of the Venetians at the same time. When the Spanish-Italian fleet under Don John finally arrived, a half-hearted attempt to take the fortress of Modon in the Morea (Peloponese) was made. When that failed, Venice had had enough of the war and concluded peace with the Sultan in early 1573. In that year the Ottoman fleet did not leave the Levant, while Spain launched an amphibious expedition to retake Tunis, lost in 1570. It was lost again in 1574 when the Ottomans sent a large expedition with 280 galleys and 15 galeasses. This, however, was the last major long-distance expedition ever undertaken by a galley fleet and the last major operation of the Spanish-Ottoman war. The Spanish fleet was seriously weakened by financial problems and unable to intervene.

The war had reached stalemate and both sides were increasingly engaged outside the Mediterranean: Spain in the Netherlands and the Atlantic; and the Ottomans against Persia. A truce was concluded in 1580/81. It seemed as if the war was to be revived in 1593, when the Ottomans and the Austrian Habsburgs went to war but the two galley fleets mainly observed each other in the waters between Greece and Italy during 1594–96. On land, the war went on until 1606, but in the Mediterranean the two empires were finally at peace with each other.

It is obvious that galley warfare had reached a stage where it no longer could fulfil the ambitions of rulers with offensive long-distance operations in mind. The Spanish fleet was notoriously late in arriving in the Levant, the Ottomans were no longer effective in the western Mediterranean, and the Venetians could not act offensively outside the Adriatic. The three major galley powers lacked base systems for the forward deployment of large forces. At the same time, the size and cost of these short-range forces had increased dramatically. J. F. Guilmartin has argued that this was the result of technological, economic and social factors which made galleys less useful as offensive weapon systems than they had been in the first half of the sixteenth century. Guns had become less scarce, oarsmen less well fed, and modern fortresses took longer to capture. The Mediterranean way of warfare based on galleys and fortresses had reached a phase of stagnation.[29] Both the old maritime state of Venice and the two large Mediterranean empires had created huge and expensive armed forces which were barely able to fight each other. The next decades were to show that they were not even able to control the sea lines of communication within their hemispheres.

The triumph of private violence, 1580–1650

The return to peace around 1580 did not signal a revival of economic prosperity and a flourishing maritime economy in the Mediterranean. Instead, the period from 1580 to about 1615 saw the definite decline of this sea as the maritime centre of Europe. It could not survive the onslaught of private violence both from its own shores and from the dynamic maritime economy of north-western Europe. The old ship-owning centres, Venice and Genoa, left most of this business under the pressure of violence and superior economic competition, although Genoese investors could make profits from warfare as galley entrepreneurs. A new maritime structure developed where long-distance trade in the Levant was dominated by foreigners and where much of the trade between Asia and Europe, which earlier went through this area, had been diverted to the Cape of Good Hope route.[30]

Privateering in the form of coastal raids and trade warfare had been normal parts of the great wars up to 1580. This type of warfare continued after the end of the imperial wars and the private use of violence became an institutionalised part of Mediterranean behaviour at sea. The great centres of piracy and privateering were Algiers, Malta and Leghorn, the new maritime city of the Grand Duchy of Tuscany, ruled by the Medici family (formerly the Republic of Florence). Several other cities in North Africa and local communities in the Ottoman empire also became centres of piracy. This activity was part of a rise of political unrest and lack of central control which shook the empire from the 1580s and lasted for decades. Ottoman control over North Africa became largely nominal and the corsair cities in this area made their independent wars on the Christians. In the eastern part of the Ottoman empire, piracy was an aspect of local rebellions and banditry which the central government was unable to control. With the exception of North Africa, the Ottoman empire was more of a victim than an originator of piracy. One port under nominal Ottoman control, Ragusa (Dubrovnik), flourished as a ship-owning centre, probably because this city had adapted her fleet to modern technology. The Ragusans were even much in demand as leasers of warships to Spain.[31]

Another victim was Venice. This is interesting as the new conditions in the Mediterranean might have been favourable for a state which earlier had thrived under conditions of uncertainty and risk. In the Middle Ages, Venice had become dominant in the Levant in large part thanks to her ability to combine politics, trade and armed protection in a region of eternal conflicts. Her state-owned merchant galleys, largely abandoned before 1570, had been the cost-efficient armed merchantmen of this glorious epoch. By the 1580s the Levant was again a conflict-stricken region where the Ottomans had lost much of their control. The central government in Constantinople was markedly favourable to Venice. Since the peace of 1573 it acknowledged the Republic's claim that it had a monopoly on violence in the Adriatic and

Venetian merchants were treated with respect. But, instead of profiting from this situation, Venice lost most of its old Levantine trade to the English, French and Dutch merchants.

These foreigners, especially the English and Dutch, used sailing merchantmen of a new and more efficient type, armed with cheap cast-iron guns, the early-modern equivalent of the medieval merchant galleys. The western ships were faster, could sail closer to the wind, and could fight with many guns in proportion to their size and crew. Venetian galleys patrolled the Adriatic and the waters around Crete, but their ability to protect shipping proved insufficient. Foreigners soon found that they were not only able to defend themselves against Mediterranean galleys and local sailing ships but they were also able to attack local merchantmen, plunder at will along Levantine coasts, and circumvent the nominally very strict Ottoman control of trade.

For long periods, Westerners were even able to force their way in and out of the Mediterranean, although it meant sailing close to the coast of Spain. It is an interesting example of the inefficiency of empires that English and Dutch private shipping came to the Mediterranean during a period when these nations were at war with Spain, supposedly the most powerful state in Europe. They did so at high risk and often under various disguises. When Spain really tried to eliminate enemy shipping (1598–1607, 1621–45), they ran into trouble but the fact that this had not been the regular Spanish response from the beginning of the wars with the Netherlands and England says something about the lack of a consistent maritime policy in that empire.[32]

The efficient Christian powers at sea in this period were the small ones: the Orders of St John (Malta) and St Stephen (Tuscany). They sent out their official fleets as well as privateers not only to attack Muslim pirates but also Ottoman and Christian shipping. Venice was a chief object of these attacks as her ships traded with the Ottomans and the cargoes on Venetian ships might be described in one way or another as belonging to infidels. At least the Knights of Malta also attacked heretic English and Dutch shipping, although apparently not with much success. Tuscany sought co-operation with the west Europeans and Leghorn became an important port for their trade, including a convenient port for selling captured goods. The most important port for Western shipping in the Levant became Smyrna (Izmir), which in the early seventeenth century rose to be a centre for trade between east and west on the initiative of Western traders who sought a convenient entrepôt for their new informal trading empire.

Venice also suffered increasing hostility from the House of Habsburg. In the Adriatic her shipping was attacked by the Uskoks, a group of enterprising pirates living around Fiume in the narrow archipelago coast belonging to the Austrian Habsburgs. They acted as part of the warrior communities in the border zone between the Habsburg and Ottoman empires and they regarded Venetian trade with the enemy as free game.[33] More remarkably, Venice was under attack from Spanish viceroys in Naples and Sicily who supported and owned privateers. This activity reached its height during the reign of the Duke of Osuna in the 1610s. He created a veritable fleet of sailing ships (apparently owned by himself but probably using government funds) which acted against Venice, often together with the royal Italian galleys controlled by the viceroy.[34]

From 1616 to 1620, Venice and Naples (Osuna) were involved in a semi-official war. Venice finally hired about 20 to 30 Dutch and English armed merchantmen to fight Osuna's fleet. In November 1617 they even fought a battle in the Adriatic, the first Mediterranean contest where gun-armed sailing ships were the main combatants. Osuna was finally recalled and imprisoned in 1620, and his sailing warships were transferred to the Atlantic,[35] but the episode says something of the limited degree of control exercised by Spain in this period. Osuna's fleet was fairly efficient and seems to have discouraged North African raids as long as it existed. Its activity fits into a picture where efficient private violence at sea was closely intertwined with the use of gun-armed sailing ships. The Algerines began to adopt such ships in the first decades of the seventeenth century, when the technology was brought in by Dutch and English pirates who found Algiers to be a convenient port for their activities. Tuscany, Malta and France also began to use sailing warships, partly bought from the Netherlands. The truce between Spain and the Dutch in 1609 gave these two powers the possibility to send out squadrons of sailing warships to carry North African corsairs. Spain and France made a successful joint attack on the corsair fleet at Tunis in 1609 and the English navy sent a squadron against the Algerines in 1620/21. These efforts were sporadic and the results limited.[36]

In the 1620s and 1630s, small-scale warfare and piracy went on much as before between the North Africans, the Italian galley squadrons of Spain and minor powers, and Christian privateers. In the Levant, the Ottomans began to regain central control of their empire and became increasingly irritated by Venice's inability to control the Christian privateers in her waters which were used for attacks on Ottoman shipping. This was the main reason for the Ottoman invasion of Crete starting in 1645. The war lasted until 1669. The fact that Venice now – unlike the sixteenth century – was able to fight a very long war with the Ottomans was a somewhat paradoxical effect of the Republic no longer being a great maritime power. Venice was now a regional power in the Adriatic and much of the resources for the war came from taxes on landed wealth. Venice again hired a considerable fleet of armed merchant-men from the Netherlands (later also from England) including crews, officers and even admirals. With this the Venetians were able to blockade the Dardanelles and major ports in the Aegean, something they had been unable to do since the fifteenth century. The Turks also found themselves blockaded on Crete. Characteristically, they reacted like other Mediterranean people in search of counter-measures against northern European sailing ships: they began to hire Dutch and English armed merchantmen themselves, although with less success than Venice.[37]

Privately owned armed merchantmen from the Netherlands and England had achieved supremacy in the eastern half of the Mediterranean by 1650 – 150 years earlier, the home waters of the two largest fleets in the world. From 1636 the French–Spanish war had brought the two contenders' sailing-fleets from the Atlantic to the Mediterranean. But the permanent fleets of Spain, Venice and the Ottomans remained their galley forces up to 1650 and later, and even the re-established French Mediterranean fleet spent much on galleys. Such vessels certainly had a role to fulfil in a sea with archipelagos and much windless weather, but they were insufficient for serious warfare in the seventeenth century. Sailing ships had proved superior for offensive and defensive trade warfare and they had shown their ability to blockade enemy ports. In the Atlantic they had also proved useful as convoy escorts. The cost-efficiency of the northern armed merchantmen was easy to observe within the Mediterranean where they dominated the market for violence and protection as well as the long-distance carrying trade.

The inability of the established Mediterranean sea powers to change their technology is an important aspect of their failure as controllers of violence and protection selling. There were of course several other factors behind the decline of the Mediterranean as a political and economic centre, but growing backwardness in warfare and protection at sea was one of the most obvious signs of it. In the Mediterranean, the new maritime powers confronted the earlier leading maritime powers directly, sometimes with armed power, always with economic power. They won. The inability of Venice to adapt to the most recent maritime technology is instructive as it highlights the problems a once very successful system may have in innovating, even when failure to do so exposes it to loss of profit.

The maritime inertia of the two great territorial empires may have had other origins. The Ottomans had already encountered the Portuguese sailing warships in the Indian Ocean in the early sixteenth century and had been unable to defeat them. Spain took control of Portugal in 1580 and created her own sailing navy in the Atlantic in the 1580s. But in the Mediterranean this had little effect. The social and political composition of the two empires in the Mediterranean rendered them unresponsive to information not generated within their own neighbourhood. This probably reflects an inward-looking mentality which must be part of the explanation for the general decline of the region.

It seems as if the mentalities of the Spanish *reconquista* warriors and the Ottoman holy warriors (the *ghazis*) were very similar in the case of warfare at sea. The galley, with its fairly simple propulsion and manoeuvring technology, its ability to form into ordered battle lines and its usefulness in amphibious warfare and sieges has been a weapon system for true warriors. It had proved outstandingly successful in the period of imperial conquests. The galleys continued to provide the two empires with a force with which they could transfer the resources of the state (soldiers, money) and high-ranking passengers from one area to another with safety and predictability. But as protection-sellers and controllers of violence at sea, in the interest of their societies, the Spanish and Ottoman empires proved increasingly inefficient. The costs of protection were very high – a large number of galleys patrolled the Mediterranean even after 1580 – but those who paid for it received an increasingly obsolete form of protection.

The elite groups of these empires were unable to adapt to technical and organisational changes which would reduce the value of existing know-how. Those who did benefit most from change may have been distant from the conservative centres of power. The political systems of the hastily assembled empires may have been insufficiently integrated for a bargaining process where those who would have benefited most from improved protection could ask for it, pay for it and control the quality of service they paid for. These suggestions are hypothetical, but the Mediterranean is interesting precisely because it shows that the changes in warfare at sea which took place in the Atlantic and the Baltic were not a general European development. They were the results of interaction between dynamic change in technology, politics, economy and social conditions whereby one region of Europe prospered while others declined.

In the early sixteenth century, Spain and the Ottomans seemed to be on their way to becoming world powers.[38] Spain had linked Iberian military prowess with sophisticated Italian finance, technology and shipping and had added a new American empire with fascinating possibilities. The Habsburgs could complement these with the economic and maritime power in their Burgundian heritage in north-western Europe. The Ottoman empire was rapidly expanding in the Mediterranean and towards the Indian Ocean and could, reluctantly, have enjoyed the support of the old maritime power, Venice. The great entrepôts of Genoa, Seville, Antwerp, Constantinople, Alexandria/Cairo and Aleppo were under the control of Spain or the Turks. By adopting the most recent maritime technology, these empires might have continued to expand and control even wider territories. They failed. In the Mediterranean they created naval–military systems which effectively elimi-nated their ability to fight each other. By 1650 Spain was defeated at sea by the rebellious Dutch, while the Ottoman empire had lost all ability to expand through maritime policy. Since 1645, it had been involved in a war with the now relatively unimportant Venice where it had shown little ability to win. The maritime world had changed much more rapidly than the ability of Mediterranean societies and states to adapt to these changes.

7

MARITIME STATE FORMATION AND EMPIRE BUILDING IN THE BALTIC

From mercantile to monarchic sea power

This chapter is a brief description of the decline of the German Hanse as an economic, political and naval organisation as well as of maritime aspects of Danish and Swedish state formation. It also gives a violence-control orientated explanation of the rise of the Dutch trade hegemony in the Baltic. It describes how the new Nordic naval forces were used for territorial state building but also as instruments for selling protection where the increasingly centralised Nordic monarchies were able to enforce a practical joint monopoly of violence at sea in the Baltic. Denmark-Norway and Sweden became effective rulers of their own territories (thus making piracy impossible) and used their warships to discourage various Baltic interest groups from interfering with trade. The main loser was the city of Lübeck which lost its old position as middleman between the Baltic and Western Europe. The most obvious winners were the Dutch who could send large numbers of cheap and unarmed merchantmen to the Baltic without interference from competitors. But most towns around the Baltic as well as the territorial states also benefited from lowered transport costs and increased competition between merchants from the Baltic and Western Europe.[1]

In the late Middle Ages, the Baltic had been a region where political and military power had been strongly connected with trade and the control of markets. The role of territorial states had been very limited in comparison with the population and resources of the territorial societies. The states in the Baltic were the Nordic union (Denmark, Sweden and Norway), the Polish-Lithuanian union, the North German principalities (Pomerania, Mecklenburg and Holstein) and the German Order (the Teutonic knights) which controlled Estonia, Livonia, Courland and Prussia. The Nordic union, which for some decades in the early fifteenth century had been a strong political unity, was gradually developing into a single Danish-Norwegian state ruled by a king and the aristocracy, and a Swedish state ruled by various aristocratic factions. The Nordic states had long coasts and were dependent on maritime lines of communication both for trade and the transfer of resources and military power within their territories.

The central governments in these states as well as in the German principalities were often weak. Local power-holders could exercise strong power, they frequently started armed feuds with central governments and they were often tempted to use armed force against maritime trade in order to gain profit. For long periods the island of Gotland was controlled by groups beyond the control of central governments and they used it as a base for plunder of trade. Poland-Lithuania, a large and populous state, was only marginally a Baltic power and its kings only intermittently developed a maritime policy. The trading cities in North Germany (Lübeck, Hamburg, Bremen, Wismar, Rostock, Stralsund and others) and in the Eastern Baltic (Danzig, Riga, Reval, Narva and others), were practically independent and most of the territorial princes had little or no power on the sea.[2]

As the territorial states in the Baltic had only limited ability to mobilise the resources of their territories, the cities preferred to co-operate with each other for mutual protection. Their main instrument of co-operation was the German Hanse confederation. The Hanse was often divided on political and economic questions but, up to the early sixteenth century, it could organise the most powerful fleet in the Baltic. Essentially the Hanse was a trading cartel and a loose federation which enforced law and order along the trade routes. The trading cities controlled most of the major ships in the region and these could easily be converted to men-of-war. The cities also had easy access to cash and credit with which they could hire mercenaries. Armed merchantmen and mercenaries gave them an advantage in regional power struggles with territorial princes and competitors. Unlike Renaissance Italy, however, the German cities were not strong enough to take control over territories. Such a development was soon to take place in Holland and Zeeland, with interesting results on the naval scene.

The rich trading city of Lübeck often behaved as a major political and naval power and as the centre of an informal maritime empire around the Baltic. The key to this was its geographical position between the Baltic and Western Europe which enabled Lübeck to control the trade over land to Hamburg. In the Middle Ages this was a very profitable trade route and her economic strength gave Lübeck the ability to develop a network of trade with the Nordic countries based on privileges and the ability to protect trade with armed force. During the fourteenth and fifteenth centuries Dutch, and to some extent English, shipping expanded in the Baltic, primarily for the transport of cheap bulk cargo (salt, grain, timber). Lübeck retained its position as a middleman for the rich trades, but the Dutch penetration of the Baltic was a threat to her position as the central entrepôt for the Nordic countries. Direct contacts with the Dutch brought the Nordic and Baltic economies closer to the expanding markets of Western Europe. For Lübeck, limits on the trade through the Sound (Öresund) and the preservation of the old trading privileges in the Nordic countries, became burning political issues which guided its Baltic policy in the early sixteenth century.

The security condition for maritime trade in the Baltic in the medieval period was similar to that in other parts of Europe. Trade was vulnerable to local power-holders who might use violence. Foreign ships and their cargo might be captured in order to redeem real or alleged injuries and this might escalate into full-scale wars, usually fought at sea. Piracy (or peace-time privateering) was possible when territorial states were weak and the ruling elites often had the right to use violence. Small-scale violence was more or less perpetual, and numerous territories and ports were controlled by autonomous rulers who might make profit from plunder by protecting pirates. This made it easier for regionally powerful merchants to get access to the most profitable opportunities for trade, and for Lübeck and some other powerful trading cities, their ability to act as strong naval powers made it possible to get extensive trading privileges from the Nordic states. They were parts of political agreements, often concluded after successful interventions in power struggles between and within the Nordic countries.

During the sixteenth century the political situation in the Baltic drastically changed. The two Nordic kingdoms developed into centralised monarchies with strong gun-armed navies. The ability of German trading cities to intervene in Nordic politics was eliminated. The German Order was dissolved and its territories in the eastern Baltic (Estonia, Livonia, Ösel, Courland) became bones of contention between Sweden, Denmark, Poland-Lithuania and Russia. The decline of the Hanse as a sea power did not stimulate the princes in northern Germany to develop naval policies which might have integrated the interests of the trading towns with the surrounding territories. Brandenburg, Mecklenburg, Pomerania and Prussia did not seriously compete with the Nordic powers at sea. Except for a few convoy ships belonging to large cities and brief attempts to create a Brandenburgian navy in the seventeenth century, German sea power ceased to exist from 1570 to about 1850. Polish attempts to create a navy were actively suppressed by the two Nordic powers. Up to the advent of Russia as a naval power in the early eighteenth century, they had the only navies in the Baltic.

As the Nordic powers had small mercantile marines and weak merchant capital, their navies could not be financed from incomes derived from domestic trading interests. Instead, they were paid by taxes raised on landed interests and customs duties paid by foreigners. Both activities could be characterised as protection selling, and the most obvious example of this is the Sound Toll raised at Helsingör. It was based on the theory that the Danish kings protected shipping passing through the Skagerack, Kattegatt and the Baltic Sea, areas over which they claimed that they had a dominion (*dominium maris Baltici*). As the incomes from the Toll went to a state which spent much of its income on the navy the theory gradually turned into practical reality. In the sixteenth and early seventeenth centuries (before taxes on land increased) the Sound Toll was an important part of the state incomes in Denmark. For the kings, it was especially important that it flowed directly into their coffers without interference from the powerful aristocracy with which they had to share power in the Danish-Norwegian state up to 1660. It was paid by foreigners, not by Danes, and the kings could use it to support a navy which was their main instrument of power.[3] The Toll and the navy were interconnected instruments of centralisation and state building which made the Danish kings more powerful than most European rulers of territories with strong aristocracies.

The Swedish kings began to look for similar opportunities to increase their financial base for state building. This stimulated the creation of the Swedish Baltic empire where one aim was to gain control over the trade between Russia, Poland and Western Europe in order to raise customs duties.[4] As the empire building involved Sweden in wars with major territorial powers (Russia, Poland-Lithuania, finally the Holy Roman Empire and German territorial princes) it is normally treated as a military enterprise but it was based on Swedish control of the sea lines of communication. The Swedish navy was a pre-condition for the creation of what actually was the last maritime empire of Europe. It was the Swedish state which turned maritime – Swedish mercantile capital and long-distance shipping were weak up to 1650.

Nordic state formation interacted with the great increase in trade through the Baltic which was a major part of the transformation of European trade in the sixteenth and seventeenth centuries. Grain from Poland, exported through Prussia, became a major object of European trade and the Baltic also became the predominant export area for naval stores: timber, masts and spars, pitch, tar, hemp, linen, cast-iron guns and high-quality iron for shipbuilding. West European dominance in shipping and naval warfare was closely connected with easy access to the Baltic. From the early seventeenth century, Sweden became Europe's largest exporter of copper and iron which further increased the importance of Baltic trade. The most important carriers of this trade were the Dutch and, during the seventeenth century, Dutch capital also became predominant in the organisation and financing of the trade.[5] Trade and shipping were important objects of taxation, and states that developed efficient naval and military organisations for violence control might profit from this new major source of income.

From a maritime perspective, it is important to remember that the borders between the Nordic states were different from today up to 1645 and 1658. Finland was an integral part of Sweden while the provinces east of the Sound, which since 1658 have been southern Sweden (Scania, Halland and Blekinge) were eastern Denmark in this period. Denmark-Norway was in control of all territories bordering the Kattegatt, Skagerack and the Sound, except the Göta älv estuary (Gothenburg) where Sweden had its only western port. The island of Gotland was Danish until 1645. Swedish territories were centred around the central and northern Baltic Sea, the Gulf of Finland and the great lakes in Sweden while the Danish-Norwegian state controlled territories around the Skagerack, Kattegatt and the Danish straits with also a large but thinly populated Atlantic empire in the North: northern Norway, Iceland and the Färöes. Both states were built around maritime lines of communication.

The rise of Nordic sea power, 1500–70

The Nordic union had been formed by Denmark, Norway and Sweden in the late fourteenth century. Its first rulers had been able to create a strong monarchy which was able to fight the Hanse at sea on equal terms. However, from the 1430s aristocratic groups in Denmark and Sweden took control of the states. From 1448 the Oldenburg dynasty ruled in Denmark and Norway but various attempts to re-establish the union with Sweden failed. From 1470, Sweden was in practice an aristocratic republic. The Oldenburg kings of Denmark and Norway were formally elected kings also in Sweden but they were not allowed to govern there. During the 1480s and 1490s King Hans (r. 1481–1513) methodically accumulated power to himself in Denmark and Norway. He was one of the European pioneers in creating strong sailing navies as instruments of state power. In 1497 he was able to take control of Sweden with a combination of armed force and negotiation. But soon after, in 1501, a faction of the Swedish aristocracy again rebelled against the King. Nevertheless, King Hans retained control over the Baltic Sea with his powerful navy, using it for a trade blockade of Sweden as well as support of Swedish castles in his possession and attacks against Swedish towns and coasts.

In 1509 Lübeck went to war against Denmark, followed by the smaller Hanse cities of Rostock, Wismar and Stralsund in the next year. These cities had become increasingly dissatisfied with the king's policy which was intended to reduce their trade privileges in Denmark and Norway and to support Dutch trade with the Baltic. They were also hurt by the Danish blockade of Sweden which was one of their key markets. Lübeck sent a fleet to Stockholm which broke the blockade and during 1510/11 Danish and Lübeckian fleets operated against each other. Lübeck did its best to close the Sound to foreign shipping and both fleets raided enemy coasts. The Danish fleet could no longer support the remaining Danish positions in Sweden and in 1510 the Swedes took the castle in Kalmar and the island of Öland.[6]

In spring 1511 the Danish fleet escorted a convoy of more than 200 merchantmen from Holland to various Baltic ports. After that it attacked Wismar and captured its fleet. On 9 August 1511 20 Danish and 18 Lübeckian ships fought an intense action off the island of Bornholm in the southern Baltic. It was mainly, perhaps only, fought with guns and other missile weapons. The two fleets were finally separated by the night and by heavy weather, but three days later the Lübeck fleet sighted the Dutch merchantmen returning from Baltic ports escorted by four Dutch warships. Lübeck's fleet was able to capture, burn and drive ashore many ships before the Danish fleet arrived, the worst catastrophe ever suffered by Western European shipping in the Baltic. The naval operations in this year had been attempts to gain control of the sea lines of communication for strategic purposes. In 1512 peace was concluded. King Hans had for the time being given up the attempt to reconquer Sweden, but the Hanse had to give up the attempt to exclude the Dutch from the Baltic. It was Danish naval power which kept the Sound open for ships from outside the Baltic, although the Dutch catastrophe of 1511 showed that Lübeck might still be a powerful naval adversary.

King Hans' son, Christian II (r. 1513–23), continued his father's policy and made it into a more clear-cut programme for an early modern prince with radical ideas. Christian hoped to reconquer Sweden (where he had been elected heir to the throne in 1497), to create a centralised unified monarchy, to found a trading company based in Copenhagen and Stockholm in order to control trade between the Baltic and Western Europe and to eliminate the Hanse as a strong economic and political power. A strong and modern navy with large ships armed with heavy guns and an increased Sound Toll were corner-stones in this policy. He married a sister to Charles of Ghent, soon to become king of Spain and German emperor as Charles V. As Charles was the ruler of the Netherlands, this dynastic alliance was intended to create bonds of interest between Denmark and the rising mercantile centre in Western Europe. This Habsburg–Oldenburg connection became important in Nordic politics up to the 1540s. It was a complicated connection as Charles had to act as ruler of the Netherlands, as German emperor (as such the nominal protector of German Hanse cities), and as head of the House of Habsburg. These interests were often contradictory and usually made his support of his Danish brother-in-law ineffectual.

Christian II made new attempts to reconquer Sweden with amphibious attacks against Stockholm in 1517 and 1518 but his army was defeated on land. During 1520 a Danish mercenary army was able to occupy Sweden which was forced to accept Christian as king. The army, however, was too expensive to maintain and by 1521 rebellious Swedes under the young aristocrat Gustav Vasa were in control of most of the country. Christian could keep only Stockholm and some other coastal towns which could be supplied by his navy. Oldenburg empire-building efforts again proved to be essentially maritime: the kings could control fortified towns and enforce blockades, but their ability to control the vast rural areas of Sweden without the co-operation of local elites was limited.

Control over territory could, however, be converted into maritime resources and the future Vasa monarchy in Sweden was to prove this. In 1522 Gustav Vasa bought a substantial fleet of armed merchantmen in Lübeck and hired mercenaries in order to gain complete control over Sweden. Lübeck merchants provided the necessary credits which were to be paid by future taxes and trading privileges. Lübeck and other Hanse cities soon joined Sweden and the allied fleets began to assert control over the Baltic. Christian

II's regime in Denmark had become increasingly insecure and in early 1523 the Danish nobility sided with Lübeck. In spring 1523 Christian left Copenhagen with part of his fleet and sailed to the Netherlands. His uncle Frederik was elected king of Denmark and Norway, while Gustav Vasa was elected king of Sweden. The allied Hanse and (largely German-manned) Swedish fleets could blockade Stockholm, Copenhagen and other fortified towns into surrender.

Christian II had sailed to the Netherlands in order to organise a counter-attack on land and at sea. This failed, partly because of Dutch resistance towards a conflict which might damage Baltic trade, but his admiral Sören Norby, equally skilled in fighting and politics, continued the resistance in the Baltic by sea and on land up to 1526.[7] Lübeck played a major role in the fighting which gradually eliminated Norby's and Christian II's power base. The city was now in a position where it could get improved trade privileges from the Nordic kingdoms which were also in financial debt to it. The old mercantile metropolis on the Trave river seemed to have regained its former glory as the central Baltic entrepôt.

Christian II did finally sail to Norway with a Habsburg-sponsored army in 1531, but he was met by resistance from Sweden on land and by a Danish-Lübeckian fleet and was finally taken prisoner. Much had happened in his former Nordic kingdoms in his absence, especially in Sweden, where Gustav Vasa rapidly created a modern dynastic state, introduced Lutheranism, confiscated church property and used it to create a strong army and navy. In Denmark and Norway the power base of the junior branch of the Oldenburg dynasty was less secure. When King Frederik died in 1533 the majorities in the councils of the two kingdoms did not wish to elect his oldest son Christian (later Christian III) as king, partly because he was a sincere Lutheran. In 1534 a civil war started in Denmark. Lübeck intervened, occupied Copenhagen and the city of Malmö on the opposite side of the Sound and gained control over the Danish fleet. This was part of a radical programme, where the old Hanse city tried to close the Sound to the Dutch and regain favourable trading privileges in Scandinavia.

In Sweden, King Gustav had already begun to cancel these privileges and he regarded Lübeck's offensive actions as a serious threat. He chose to support Christian (III) in the Danish civil war.[8] Gustav sent his army to occupy eastern Denmark (Scania) and in spring 1535 his new fleet, including four major ships of about 500 to 1,700 tonnes displacement, was sent to the southern Baltic. The Swedes joined a Prussian fleet and a squadron of ships controlled by Christian (III), although most of these ships were small or simply armed merchantmen. A major part of the Swedish army sailed with the fleet which was further strengthened by Dutch merchantmen requisitioned for naval service. The allied fleet first defeated Lübeck's main fleet (whose major units were Danish warships) at Bornholm in a gunfire battle on 9 June and then destroyed or captured another enemy fleet which controlled the Danish straits. The allies were now in control of the sea lines of communication in the Baltic, the island of Zealand could be invaded, and Copenhagen and Malmö were surrounded by the allied army and fleet. In November 1535 Lübeck's fleet was able to land supplies close to Copenhagen, but early in the next year the city had to conclude peace. Its role as a power on the same level as the two Nordic kingdoms, with ambitions to intervene in their domestic politics, was finished.

Somewhat ironically, the defenders of Copenhagen and Malmö now sought and obtained support from the Habsburgs who began to prepare a large fleet with an army in Holland for intervention in Denmark and Norway in favour of Christian II and his relatives. It was, however, delayed by the reluctance of the Dutch towns to be involved in a war that might damage their Baltic trade, and the expedition was finally abandoned when the Habsburgs became involved in a war with France during 1536. Christian III could now send a fleet and an army to take control of Norway, where a powerful group under the leadership of the last Catholic archbishop had hoped for a Habsburg intervention. Protestantism now became firmly established in Denmark-Norway and confiscated church property increased the financial base of state power, not least the navy. From 1536, Denmark-Norway developed into a centralised monarchy, balanced by a strong but co-operative aristocratic council.

For some years, the Habsburgs continued to support Christian II's claim to the Nordic thrones and Sweden and Denmark-Norway felt compelled to form an alliance in 1541.[9] In these years there was much open and potential domestic insurrection against the still very recent creation of strong states and Protestant churches, but the opposition's traditional access to foreign support was cut off by sea power. Both kingdoms had given high priority to the creation of permanent royal navies of gun-armed ships, and this now gave them an edge over potentially much superior powers which had paid less attention to naval organisation and new technology. The two monarchies were now the dominant sea powers in the Baltic (the Prussian duke sold his navy in the 1540s) and this position made them fairly secure against invasion or infiltration (support to the opposition) from the House of Habsburg, Lübeck, the Dutch provinces and various power groups in northern Germany.

Geography, new technology and conscious state building rather suddenly made the Nordic powers into more powerful players on the international scene. In 1542 Denmark joined France in the war against Charles V. The Sound was closed to Dutch shipping and the Danish navy even took the offensive in the North Sea. It was planned to attack the strategically important island of Walcheren in the Netherlands in 1543, but severe gales in the North Sea made it impossible. Peace was concluded with the Habsburgs in 1544 where the emperor finally accepted that Christian III was king of Denmark, but the Danish navy had to continue to protect Danish-Norwegian waters from privateering and piracy during the almost continuous wars in Western Europe. From 1544 to the late 1550s the Baltic was a comparatively calm area where trade flourished and the new power structure began to settle. Sweden and Russia were involved in war from 1554. From 1540, Sweden had built a considerable galley fleet where its new army of state-controlled militia soldiers could be used as both oarsmen and landing force. This galley fleet was used in an attack along the river Neva in 1555 but without success against the unexpectedly strong Russian resistance.

The war ended in 1557 without any loss or gain, but in 1558 Russia took the important trading city of Narva in the Gulf of Finland. Thus started the final dissolution of the German Order when the towns and nobility of the eastern Baltic rapidly began to look for protectors against Russian expansion. The island of Ösel became a Danish protectorate in 1559, while Reval (Tallinn) and Estonia submitted to the Swedish crown, and Livonia and Courland to Poland-Lithuania in 1561. The three protecting powers immediately ran into a conflict about their spheres of interest. From a maritime point of view control of the trade to Narva, Reval, Pernau and Riga was at stake. Sweden began to claim a dominion over the Gulf of Finland, and its fleet began to capture ships from Lübeck and other towns which did not follow Swedish decrees that their Russian trade must be directed to Swedish-held Reval and that the profitable Narva trade should be left to the subjects of the Swedish king.

Sweden and Poland went to war in Livonia and tensions also rose rapidly between Sweden and Denmark-Norway, now ruled by two young, ambitious and naval-minded kings, Erik XIV (r. 1560–68) and Frederik II (r. 1559–88) respectively. Frederik found the new power assertions of Sweden intolerable and allied himself with Lübeck.[10] The tensions erupted in a naval battle off Bornholm on 30 May 1563. Swedish and Danish fleets met and the Danish admiral demanded that the Swedes offer the customary marks of respect to the Danish king in the waters under his *dominium*. These were denied and a four-hour battle followed in which the Danish flagship and two other ships were taken and two more damaged. The Danish fleet had attempted to board the Swedish ships which answered with gunfire, mainly from modern copper guns which could be fired with large powder charges. The Danish fleet was mainly armed with the older type of wrought-iron breech-loaders which could only be fired with small powder-charges and had less effect on major ships.

Tactically the battle was typical of the following years of war. The Swedes attempted to fight with gunfire and Erik XIV made a major effort to provide his rapidly increasing fleet with new copper guns from the royal foundries which could use Sweden's vast resources of copper ore. Denmark and Lübeck originally had to rely on boarding tactics, as their ordnance mainly consisted of wrought-iron breech-loaders. During the war they gradually renewed their armament, the Danes especially by purchase of English-made cast-iron guns – as the only guns which could be acquired quickly.[11] The contending navies also made large-scale investments in purpose-built gun-armed warships where Sweden initially had a superiority. Tactically the navies

120

developed new ideas. From 1564 the Danish admiral Herluf Trolle divided his and Lübeck's fleet into groups of three ships, one large and two smaller. The fleet was intended to form a wedge when it attacked from a windward position. If the fleet was attacked in a leeward position it was intended that it should form line ahead for mutual support. The Swedish fleet also used three-ship formations but here the tactical idea seems to have been that the major ships should form line abreast or line ahead, each with two smaller ships in a second line, ready to support the major units when they became engaged with the enemy. The contending fleets fought seven major battles in 38 months from 1563 to 1566. Technology, tactics and practical implementation of theories and lessons from earlier battles interacted as never before since the introduction of gunpowder in warfare between sailing ships.

During the summer of 1563 Denmark and Lübeck fitted out large fleets, mainly by buying and hiring merchantmen which were provided with guns and soldiers. The allied fleet sailed northwards in the Baltic Sea to blockade Stockholm and to force the Swedes to a battle. The Danes had around 20 major units of at least 300 tonnes displacement, while Lübeck had five.[12] Sweden met this fleet with a dozen major units of 300 tonnes or more, although most of these were purpose-built warships, and some smaller Swedish ships which took part in the battle probably had heavier armament than the allied merchantmen. The two fleets joined battle on 11 September, the allies to enforce the blockade, the Swedes probably to inflict so much damage on the enemy that he would have to return home for repairs. Tactically, the allies again attempted to board and the Swedish fleet was able to avoid that. It was, however, forced to retreat into the Swedish archipelago. The allies cruised in northern Baltic until late October in spite of the increasingly severe autumn weather, but it is doubtful if their blockade was effective. Baltic autumns were often too severe for effective naval operations in the sixteenth and seventeenth centuries.

In the next year, the alliance hoped to continue the trade blockade of Sweden while Erik XIV intended that his fleet should decisively defeat the enemy with gunfire in order to break the blockade and support offensive army operations in Scania. On 30 May 1564 a Swedish fleet of 16 major units (300 tonnes and more) met at least 15 Danish and ten Lübeck ship of the same size off the island of Öland. Most of the Swedish ships were purpose-built warships while all except the largest on the allied side were armed merchantmen. An intense gunfire battle followed in which the Swedes had the initiative as long as they had the weather gauge. On the following day, the wind turned, the allied fleet could attack, and gradually the Swedish ships left the battle, leaving the flagship, the giant *Mars* (c. 1,800 tonnes) to fight alone. This ship was finally destroyed by fire after her rudder had been damaged by gunfire. The attempt to win a naval battle with guns only had failed, although gunfire obviously had had significant effects. One of Lübeck's ships sank and some Danish ships suffered serious structural damage.

Apparently the battle caused the allies to underestimate the Swedish fleet. It was soon at sea again and at Bornholm it captured a large Lübeck convoy from Narva. The fleet returned to port with its prizes but was sent out once more by a dissatisfied Erik XIV who put it under the command of Klas Horn, an experienced soldier, in the hope that it would achieve what the king hoped for, a decisive defeat of the enemy battle fleet. The two fleets met once again in a series of fights between Öland and Gotland from 11 to 15 August 1564. The Danish admiral, Herluf Trolle, described the actions as an enervating chase of an enemy which consistently avoided close-range action and used the superiority in speed and weatherliness of his purpose-built warships to keep the distance. Apparently the Swedish fleet had learnt how to avoid close-range action, but not how to win a stand-off battle by gunfire. In the end, three Danish ships which probably mistook the positions of the fleets during the night were captured by the Swedes, but strategically the battle was a draw. The Swedes went to Kalmar and controlled the northern Baltic, while the allied fleet cruised in the southern Baltic, thus cutting off Swedish trade with Germany.

In 1565, Erik XIV was able to send a larger fleet to sea in early May, in itself an organisational achievement. It comprised around 25 major ships of 300 tonnes or more. Around ten allied ships cruising in the southern Baltic were surprised by the early appearance of the Swedes. Most of them were burnt by their own crews or interned by the Duke of Pomerania for the rest of the war. The blockade of Sweden was broken and the Swedes also took tolls from a large number of neutral (mainly Dutch) merchantmen which passed through the Sound. Apart from the income, it was a symbolic act to show that control of the southern Baltic had passed into new hands. When a hastily assembled fleet of 11 Danish and 10 Lübeckian major ships attacked the Swedes in the waters between Mecklenburg and the Danish isles on 4 June, it was beaten back by gunfire. Its commander Herluf Trolle, one of the most interesting admirals of the sixteenth century, was mortally wounded. On 7 July, the allies made a new and determined attempt to defeat the Swedish fleet off the island of Bornholm. In a fierce contest between around 27 major ships on each side, a close-range action was fought with heavy loss of life. It ended with an allied retreat after the Danish flagship had been taken and another Danish ship (possibly also a Lübeck ship) had been sunk by gunfire. The Swedes lost three ships.

In 1566 the Swedish fleet again started early, taking control of southern Baltic in June with a fleet of almost 30 major ships. Again tolls were levied at the southern end of the Sound and many merchantmen were forced to sail to Sweden to sell their cargoes there. The allies were able only slowly to gather a fleet of the same size which on 26 July fought an intense but indecisive action off Öland. Interestingly, both sides adhered to gunnery tactics in this battle. The allied fleet sailed to Gotland where it was caught on a lee shore when an unusually severe summer gale arose. Denmark lost nine and Lübeck three major ships (300 to perhaps 1,500 tonnes) wrecked off the town of Visby.

These losses could not be made good during the war. In 1567, the Swedish fleet dominated the Baltic, but in 1568 civil war (in which Erik XIV was deposed by his brothers) and financial exhaustion made it impossible to send the main fleet to sea. The situation on the allied side was much the same, although they were able to make a raid against Reval in 1569. Sweden and Denmark-Norway (allied with Lübeck and Poland) had fought a war on land and at sea on a much larger scale than ever before. The ability of the centralised state to mobilise resources for war had been proved but no victory was in sight on any side. In 1570 the three naval powers intended to make a final effort at sea but only the Swedish fleet finally appeared in full strength. No major battle took place and the three huge fleet flagships of at least 2,000 tonnes built in the middle of the war never met in combat. These three, the Swedish *Röde Draken* (originally called *Neptunus*), the Danish *Fortuna* and Lübeck's *Adler*, were the largest warships in the world at this time, and, together with other new purpose-built warships, they represented the lessons of the first 'modern' war between sailing fleets.

The least dramatic, but probably most important, lesson learned in this war was logistical and organisational. Both sides had attempted to keep their fleets at sea from spring to autumn. Earlier naval operations had often been concentrated in confined waters such as the Danish straits and the Swedish archipelago where the strain from the weather was less intense. The new type of naval operations required intense preparations during the winter and a well-planned supply of food and spare parts during the operations. The Swedish fleet was usually provisioned for about two months and continuously supplied with food from storeships. Ships damaged in combat and by heavy weather must quickly be repaired and seamen and soldiers must be found continuously to replace losses. Most officers were initially inexperienced in sea service and they had to learn how to solve these problems on a routine basis without returning to the main bases in Stockholm, Copenhagen and Lübeck which were often at a distance from the critical area of operation.

Tactically, it had become clear that gunfire could prevent boarding and even sink ships. Another lesson was that purpose-built warships were far superior to armed merchantmen due to their armament, speed, weatherliness and ability to resist gunfire. Armed merchantmen with infantry could no longer be the main force of a battle fleet. The large investments made in guns and warships by the three powers show that they drew the same lesson from the battles. However, the gun was not a wonder weapon that inevitably brought quick victory. The Swedish ammunition expenditure is known for the years 1564 and 1565. The ships which were engaged in most or all actions in these years fired on average 25 to 30 rounds for every gun during one year – major units usually more than the minor which suggests that they were more heavily engaged. This means that most ships did not fire more than a few shots from each gun every hour. As some ships are known to have fired more rapidly than this, the general slow firing rate cannot be explained only by slow loading procedures.[13] It must reflect the fact that the battle formations did not give many opportunities to fire, at least not full broadsides. In spite of that, ships were sunk or suffered considerable damage in hull and rigging and many men were killed and wounded by gunfire.

Strategically, both fleets consistently tried to defeat the enemy's main fleet in a decisive battle in order to take control of the sea lines of communication. Blockade, control of supply lines and power over neutral trade were important objects of naval operations. In earlier Baltic wars the main army had often been carried by the main fleet to a decisive area of operation, such as Copenhagen or Stockholm. In this war, the contending armies were much larger than in earlier wars and too large to be concentrated on the fleet. Erik XIV hoped to use his fleet for support of offensive army operations in areas close to the coast, but this was not achieved. As the fleets were no longer required to carry a very large number of soldiers their endurance and ability to stay at sea for extended periods increased. However, compared to later periods, the Baltic warships of this war still had very large crews and many soldiers.

The interaction between state formation, technology and naval and military organisation was also obvious. It was an initial Swedish advantage in modern gunnery and purpose-built warships that enabled that country to break the blockade which otherwise might have caused an early defeat. As the allies must have had an advantage in their number of experienced seamen – Lübeck was still a major shipping city – the Swedish advantage in technology was even more important as it neutralised this inferiority. The fact that Sweden, the power with the least developed maritime economy, was able to resist and defeat an alliance of the two powers which since the fifteenth century had fought over naval hegemony in the Baltic shows that the organisational power of the state had become decisive in naval warfare.

Protection selling and empire building, 1570–1650

The peace which was concluded in late 1570 was in practice only valid between the two Nordic kingdoms.[14] Lübeck had been promised that Sweden should open the Narva trade and pay an indemnity for captured ships. It was never paid and Sweden chose to ignore those parts of the peace treaty which Lübeck alone could never enforce. Sweden continued to fight Russia in Estonia and to blockade Russian-held Narva, although the blockade might be passed if ships bought a Swedish licence. Lübeck tried to force the blockade in the 1570s but was no longer powerful and many of her ships were captured. Finally Narva was taken by Sweden in 1581. Swedish hopes that this port, and Reval, would develop into large and profitable centres for Russian trade with Western Europe proved illusory however. War between Sweden and Russia continued up to 1595, but on the naval scene it was one-sided as only Sweden had a navy, which she used to support the army in coastal areas and on the lakes of Ladoga and Peipus.[15]

While the Swedish navy was mainly engaged in the Gulf of Finland, the Danish navy in the 1570s definitely secured the Baltic as an area where neutral ships might sail unharmed as long as they followed the rules set by the two Nordic sea powers. Outside the Sound, intense privateering and piracy went on in connection with the civil wars in the Netherlands and France. Frederik II sent out warships which patrolled the Skagerack, Kattegatt and the Norwegian coast in order to discourage this type of violence. Similarly he sent out ships to patrol the Baltic where ships with Russian commissions as privateers attempted to profit from violence while Polish privateers captured ships sailing to Russia. He also discouraged Polish attempts to create a navy in order to gain better control over Prussia and Danzig. Captured pirates were brought to Helsingör at the northern end of the Sound for public execution in order to show foreign seafarers that they got something for the protection money they paid. In 1580 the two Nordic powers negotiated an agreement on various old conflicts, including how their warships should behave when they met at sea, thus avoiding events like that which caused the war in 1563. This détente made it possible for the Nordic powers to reduce their navies which in the 1570s had been maintained by large shipbuilding programmes.[16]

By the 1580s the Baltic was pacified and the Danish king began to think in terms of an extended maritime dominion over the North Atlantic and the Arctic, a *dominium maris septentrionalis*. The trade route to Archangel had first been used in 1553 and it had become increasingly important for Dutch and English trade with Russia. This was the result of a Russian desire to trade from a port of their own, Western interest in avoiding the Sound Toll and improved shipbuilding technology which allowed merchantmen to sail a route often in inclement Arctic weather. Danish attempts to raise customs on the northern trade proved illusory. There were no natural choking point where a custom might be raised and no threats from piracy which could motivate protection.[17]

The pacification of the Baltic was very important. The German towns largely abolished their own organisation for convoys and trade protection inside the Baltic, thus making the Hanse obsolete. The Dutch used the opportunity to develop peaceful shipping and trade in the Baltic. They began to make large-scale investment in this trade and in the Nordic countries (especially Swedish industry), and Dutch shipping interests began to develop cheap cargo-carriers, the *fluits*, specialised for the non-violent Baltic trade. They were largely unarmed and designed to sail with small crews, thus making profit from the fact that ships no longer required large crews for defence. Just as the maritime interests in Western Europe developed efficient armed merchantmen for dangerous waters (such as the Mediterranean) the Dutch responded to the new market conditions in the Baltic by innovative combinations. By the 1570s and 1580s the Baltic had become a unique haven for seaborne trade in a Europe where civil wars, piracy, loosely controlled privateering and unpredictable royal actions causing high protection costs for shipping were the norm. The Baltic, only a few decades earlier a rather backward area, suddenly enjoyed the benefits of unhindered peaceful trade.

In 1587 the Swedish crown prince Sigismund, a keen Catholic with counter-Reformation ambitions and twice married to Habsburg princesses, was elected king of Poland-Lithuania. When he inherited the Swedish throne in 1592, he nominally became the most powerful ruler in the Baltic. Actually, he was quickly challenged by his Protestant and power-hungry uncle, Duke Karl, who had created his own power base in Sweden, including his own (nominally mercantile) navy. The crisis developed into a civil war, in which Karl gained full control of Sweden by 1599. Both sides built many ships during the war (Karl in Sweden and Sigismund in Finland) and the Swedish navy was permanently increased. From 1600, Karl (IX) started a war of conquest in Polish Livonia. On land it did not go well for Sweden, but the navy began to blockade Riga, one of the largest ports in the Baltic. By 1610, this had caused a crisis with Denmark where the naval-minded King Christian IV (r. 1588–1648) regarded the blockade as an infringement of his dominion. He sent out his fleet which broke the blockade.[18] Karl IX also had territorial ambitions in northern Norway and in early 1611 Christian persuaded his council to support an attack against Sweden. That country was by then heavily engaged militarily in Russia, in order to 'protect' Russian allies during the civil war there, and not in the best position to fight a defensive war against its western neighbour.

The war revealed that the Danish navy was in a better shape than the Swedish. On paper the latter was stronger with a total displacement of around 24,000 tonnes against 15,000 tonnes. But the war began with an excellently led Danish surprise attack on Kalmar, an important fortress city and naval base in southern Sweden. It was blockaded from land and sea and, when it fell, Swedish warships totalling around 7,000 tonnes had to be sunk to avoid capture. In 1612 the Danes could also take Älvsborg (Gothenburg) – Sweden's only port to the West – with its naval squadron. The remaining Swedish fleet had no inspired leadership, some ships could not be fitted out for sea service, and the Danish fleet gradually got the upper hand in the Baltic. The war was clearly a Danish victory, but the Danish aristocracy was not interested in its continuation when Sweden made concessions on the original points of conflict. Peace was concluded in 1613. No major battles took place at sea.[19]

In 1617 Sweden and Russia concluded a peace in which Russia lost her coastline in the innermost part of the Gulf of Finland – the area which Peter I retook a century later when he founded St Petersburg and Kronstadt. In 1621 Sweden, now ruled by Gustav II Adolf (r. 1611–32), began to use its increasingly efficient armed forces for ambitious offensives.[20] An amphibious operation was launched against Riga, one of the largest cities in the Baltic. 13,000 soldiers were transported across the Baltic and took the city after a siege. In the following years the navy supported the army in further campaigns in which Livonia was conquered. These conquests gradually undermined the Danish dominion of the Baltic and created a case for an enlarged Swedish *dominium maris Baltici*, as it was difficult for Denmark to deny Sweden the control of the sea lines of communication to Swedish ports. Christian IV attempted to balance the Swedish expansion with an expansionistic policy in Germany.[21]

In Poland, Sigismund III Vasa attempted to create a navy in the 1620s. He hoped that it might be joined by a major Spanish fleet which should give him the strength to return to Sweden. The 1620s was a period of Spanish naval revival which made this idea fairly realistic. The dynastic power struggle within the Vasa family and its Habsburg connections with the great wars on the continent was one factor behind the great expansion and modernisation of the Swedish armed forces. In 1626 another major amphibious expedition of around 13,000 men sailed to Prussia. Here, the Polish fleet could be blockaded and Sweden gain control over the Vistula estuary, the main artery for east–west trade with Polish grain. The Poles increased their fleet but, with the exception of a successful late autumn attack in 1627 against a small Swedish squadron, it could not achieve much.[22] When a truce was concluded with Poland in 1629 Sweden kept ports in Prussia and the right to sell licences to trade for six years, a major source of income to the Swedish state. It was mainly the Dutch merchantmen which paid for these licences and as Dutch trade now was under serious threat from a Habsburg fleet in the Baltic the Prussian licences became a kind of Swedish protection selling to the Dutch.

The background was that the Thirty Years War in Germany had spread to the Baltic. The Danish king had been defeated on land in 1626 when he led the Protestant army, and the combined forces of the German Catholic League and the Habsburgs reached the Baltic coast where the emperor attempted to create a navy. The Danish fleet easily protected the Danish islands, but the main purpose of the Habsburg fleet was not invasion. It was actually funded by Spain, which hoped to attack Dutch trade in the Baltic, and it was joined by the small Polish fleet.[23] This was the first serious challenge to Nordic seapower for nearly a century and one of several causes of the Swedish intervention in the Thirty Years War when Denmark was forced to conclude peace in 1629.

The Swedish invasion of Germany was a major operation against enemy-held territory. In late June 1630 the initial assault force landed on the island of Usedom in the Oder estuary. By 10 July, 20,000 soldiers had been landed and their strength was gradually built up by additional troops shipped to the area. In the early months of the invasion the army relied on seaborne supplies. The Habsburg fleet was captured in early 1632 when Wismar capitulated. By then, Sweden was deeply involved in the German war and the German Baltic coast had been secured for Sweden. It remained so for the rest of the Thirty Years War when naval operations became the routine tasks of supply and sea control.

Swedish successes on the continent worried the Danish king who in the late 1630s raised the Sound Toll to finance armaments, interfered with Swedish export trade through the Sound (especially the important weapon trade), and put out political feelers to the Habsburgs. This annoyed Sweden, the Dutch merchants and the powerful Dutch-Swedish arms trader, Louis De Geer. In late 1643 the main Swedish army in Germany suddenly marched into Jutland and the Swedish home army attacked Scania. The plan was that the two armies should join in an attack on the Danish islands and Copenhagen. This required command of the sea. The whole Swedish fleet was mobilised and in order to increase its strength further, Louis De Geer was commissioned to hire a fleet of armed merchantmen in the Netherlands. Dutch and English armed merchantmen and their crews enjoyed much prestige. Such ships had defeated the Portuguese in the Indian Ocean, they had been hired by Venice, France and (in 1641) even by Portugal as warships and in 1639 they had provided a valuable addition to the Dutch warships when the Spanish main fleet was totally defeated in the Channel.[24]

In May 1644, a fleet of 21 hired Dutch armed merchantmen sailed to Lister Dyb on the west coast of Jutland to receive instructions from the Swedish army commander. They were twice attacked by Danish squadrons of warships, the first time with king Christian IV in personal command. In terms of total displacement the armed merchantmen were roughly equal to the Danish force in the first battle, and had a superiority of about 50 per cent in the second, but in spite of that they suffered badly. Mainly armed with 12-, 8- and 6-pounders and lightly built, the merchantmen were severely damaged by the heavy-calibre guns on the purpose-built warships. Dutch seamanship saved the ships but they quickly returned to the Netherlands. This was an unexpected setback for a type of armed force which had been a successful instrument of warfare for decades. As the Dutch had been used to fighting Spanish and Portuguese purpose-built warships with armed merchantmen, these failures indicate that northern warships were now superior to the types of warship used in southern Europe – they probably had heavier armament, possibly stronger hulls and more manoeuvrability. The actions at Lister Dyb foreshadow the demise of hired ships in battles against major warships which was one of the main lessons of the first Anglo-Dutch war of 1652-4.[25]

The Danes were able to engage the enemy before his forces were united. In June 1644 the Swedish main fleet sailed to the southern Baltic. On 1 July the Swedish and main Danish battle fleets fought their first full-scale battle since 1566. Thirty Danish ships of 300 to 1,300 tonnes (total displacement around 18,000 tonnes) met 34 Swedish ships of 300 to 1,700 tonnes (total around 24,500 tonnes) and fought an indecisive action off Kolberger Heide between Germany and the Danish isles.[26] The Swedes had the windward position and made four attacks but many ships failed to close the enemy. Losses were slight – the Danish *rigsadmiral* (Lord High Admiral) was one of the few killed and king Christian one of the few wounded. This failure to turn quantitative superiority into victory made it impossible to invade the Danish islands and developments in Germany forced the main Swedish army to turn south. In early

August the Swedish fleet returned to Stockholm. It sailed at the same time as the hired Dutch ships made a successful passage through the Sound and reached Kalmar.

Christian IV thought that the worst was over. He decommissioned most of the fleet and concentrated the army against the Swedes in Scania. In earlier wars the Swedish navy had not operated in the southern Baltic during the autumn, but now it could use Swedish-controlled German ports as bases to return to for the winter. In October, a Swedish fleet of 14 warships (c. 8,500 tonnes) and 19 hired Dutch ships (c. 9,000 tonnes) arrived in Danish waters. It was met by 15 Danish warships (total c. 8,000 tonnes).[27] The Danes may have thought that this was an invasion, and the fleet was their only defence as the troops had left the islands. They decided to fight the much superior enemy, and at the battle of Femern on 13 October their fleet was almost annihilated: 10 ships were captured and two burnt by fireships. The Swedish warships concentrated on the major Danish ships, while the minor units were attacked by the armed merchantmen. The vulnerability of the merchantmen was shown once more when one of them was sunk by a large Danish ship. No Swedish invasion took place in this year or the next but the Danish–Norwegian navy was no longer in control of its home waters.

The consequences were disastrous. The Dutch merchants decided that the time had come to show their dissatisfaction with the increased Danish Sound Toll. Many in the Dutch Republic wanted to join forces with the Swedes and inflict a decisive defeat on the Danish king, but they could not get a majority for this hard line. Sea power might, however, be used in flexible ways and, as a compromise, a Dutch fleet of 49 ships (partly armed merchantmen) was sent to the Sound. Under its protection, 300 Dutch merchantmen sailed through the Sound without paying the Toll. The Dutch intended to use Danish resistance as a pretext for joining Sweden but the Danes carefully avoided being provoked.[28] Instead, they concentrated on blocking the southern end of the Sound to the Swedish fleet. This was successful, but Denmark–Norway had to sign a disadvantageous peace in which important territories, including the islands of Gotland and Ösel and province of Halland, were lost. The traditional Swedish freedom from the Sound Toll was extended to ships from all Baltic and German provinces conquered by Sweden. The Dutch obtained a lowered Sound Toll. The Danish role as protection-seller to Dutch trade seemed to be close to an end, as much of the Baltic was now controlled by the Swedish empire. However, in a few years, the Dutch and the Danes formed an alliance, and during the Anglo-Dutch wars of 1652–4 and 1665–7 the Danish fleet was mobilised to protect Dutch trade in the Baltic in exchange for Dutch subsidises.

The war of 1643–5 and the peace of Westphalia in 1648 (where Sweden gained large territories in northern Germany) settled the power struggle in the Baltic in Swedish favour. In the next war in the 1650s, Sweden made further major territorial gains from Denmark–Norway, but, in these years, the new balance of power at sea in Western Europe began to show its effects in the Baltic. During the first Anglo–Dutch war of 1652–4 both sides built large battle fleets. These could also be used for interventions in the Baltic and in the 1650s the Dutch navy began to support Denmark, and to limit Swedish ambitions in Prussia. After that, the Dutch and the English realised that they might influence Baltic power politics and trade by threatening to use their battle fleets not only against an already defeated power, as in 1645, but also against the strongest power in the Baltic.

After more than a century of Nordic dominance of the Baltic Sea, the great entrepôts for Baltic trade were back on the naval scene. In the Middle Ages, Lübeck had been the great entrepôt and also the leading sea power in the region. After 1650, Amsterdam could use the Dutch navy to protect her trading interests, and later the English merchants could also rely on the English navy to keep the Baltic open for their trade. Just as Lübeck had once done, these western entrepôts could influence Nordic power politics through control of the sea lines of communication. This was mainly due to a new type of state formation in Western Europe where territorial power and merchant capital had joined forces in a way that the north German cities and territories never managed. Nordic naval power, based on efficient organisation of territorial resources and protection selling to foreign shipping, had dominated the Baltic Sea from the early sixteenth century to the mid-seventeenth century. From then on the Baltic was integrated into the European state system where control of the European seas belonged to the strongest battle fleet or combination of battle fleets.

8

WAR IN WESTERN EUROPE
UNTIL 1560

Opportunities for state formation and trade

Geographically, Europe's Atlantic coast and the British Isles may in the year 1500 seem to have been destined to become the centre of a new maritime economic order. Situated between the Baltic and the Mediterranean and conveniently placed at the end of the new trade routes between Europe and Africa, Asia and America, it was an area with a rapidly growing population and an economy favoured by cheap maritime communications. It was hardly a wonder that entrepôts for global and interregional trade, large shipowning centres and dynamic capitalism developed in this region. The opportunities for formation and expansion of economic centres were unusually favourable.

The economic development was not spreading from just one centre to various parts of the Atlantic seaboard. On the contrary, it gained momentum at several places during the fifteenth and early sixteenth centuries: in Lisbon and Seville; on the eastern side of the Biscayan coast of Castile; in Brittany, Normandy and the Netherlands; in London and Hamburg. The growth of maritime trade was a late medieval phenomenon throughout Western and Northern Europe which preceded the expansion of European influence overseas. However, by the early seventeenth century dynamic development and economic power had been concentrated in a small area in the southern North Sea. Holland, Zeeland and later southern England became the centres of the dynamic Atlantic economy, France took part in the development on a more limited scale, while the Iberian powers dramatically declined from their favourable position as pioneers in trans-oceanic trade. The new centre was ahead of the rest of Western Europe (and the Mediterranean) in prosperity, technology and a wide array of skills connected with maritime trade, shipping and finance. One of these skills was the ability to use violence at sea.

In Chapters 8 to 10 two main lines of development will be followed. One of these is warfare at sea as a part of the power struggle between the states. These struggles had often little to do with maritime trade but trade was affected by them. The other line of development is the increasing concentration of economic power and dynamic capitalism in a small area in the southern North Sea. Why was the originally broad development of several Atlantic and North Sea regions transformed into a situation where most regions stagnated or declined while one region achieved supremacy? It is of course not possible to provide any definite answer, but the question is one of the most challenging problems in the role of conflict at sea for the transformation of early modern Europe. Political, naval and economic aspects are intertwined but traditionally they have been treated separately. Which institutions, organisations and interest aggregations grew and which stagnated when Western European conflict at sea spread from Europe (Chapter 8) to the Atlantic (Chapter 9) and finally became global (Chapter 10)?

Around 1500, the Atlantic nations in Western Europe shared the same maritime and military technology, they had many political institutions in common, and they were involved in an increasingly dynamic maritime trade with each other, with the Mediterranean and with the Baltic. Fishing had also become a major maritime enterprise in this region. Wool, textiles, salt, wine, fish, grain and other kinds of food, metals and manufactured products, naval stores, spices and luxuries were exchanged in a network of West European trade. The fifteenth-century development of maritime technology (three-masted ships, carvel hulls, etc.) had made it easier, safer and cheaper to transport goods in the nautically demanding Atlantic/North Sea region. Reduced transaction costs increased the possibility for international and inter-regional trade to fulfil its basic task of promoting economic growth by allowing different regions to specialise in production for which they had comparative advantages and providing all regions with the cheapest and best products available on the market. Up to the 1560s there are no signs that any region in Western Europe (or any other part of Europe) was negatively affected by this development.[1]

With a remarkable co-ordination in time, all nations along the Atlantic seaboard also saw a rapid consolidation of territorial and centralised state power in the late fifteenth century. Long periods of civil wars or weak central power came to an end in France, England and Castile. In the Netherlands, the new Habsburg rulers were able to stabilise an initially insecure position and continue a slow process of centralisation and elimination of regional conflicts. On the Iberian peninsula, Castile and Aragon were unified. Portugal and the new Spanish monarchy were able to end various conflicts and even to agree on a division of their future seaborne empires in the treaty of Tordesillas in 1494. Before the 1560s, rebellions against rulers were rare (except in England), local and quickly suppressed. Aristocrats and mercantile cities practically ceased to use violence in conflicts with each other and with their sovereign. For the first time since the fall of the Roman empire, all rulers of Western Europe were simultaneously able to achieve a practical monopoly of violence in their territories.[2]

Much of this was achieved by consent and compromise rather than by coercion and a large central bureaucracy. Traditional instruments for political dialogue and compromise – parliaments, estates and formal bonds of allegiance between rulers and elite groups – were used. The role of modern military technology, primarily heavy guns, in the stabilisation of Western Europe has been much debated. As the development towards centralisation was far from universal in Europe – it did not affect Germany and Poland – it seems too simple to explain it by arguing that heavy guns controlled by princes could now break the formerly impregnable walls of feudal castles and autonomous cities. That would be technological determinism, which gives the supply of new technology a decisive role. On the other hand, it would be surprising if the use of new military technology had had no effects at all on the power structure of Europe. Heavy guns on land and at sea gave new options for ter-ritorial rulers. They could be used for increased control over territories, for power projection, and for protection. As we have seen, heavy guns on ships were important instruments for empire builders in the Mediterranean and for Nordic kings who were able to establish themselves as monopolistic power sellers in the Baltic Sea.[3]

It did, however, require entrepreneurial efforts (efforts to achieve new com-binations) to develop heavy guns, warships and permanent armed forces as effective instruments of power and state building. As outlined earlier in Chapter 2, technology might develop in situations where supply and demand closely interact with each other within networks or organisations. We must presume that there was a broad demand for protection from violence and plunder which favoured those who could enforce a monopoly of violence. This demand could be expressed through estates, parliaments and trading communities, and the rulers could use new instruments of warfare to fulfil their traditional role as protectors more efficiently than before.

The military and naval contributions to the growth of centralised states in this period were probably primarily questions of interaction between new technology, the organisational abilities of rulers and the opportunities created by this demand for protection from elite groups. Much basic and comparative research is lacking but that which exists gives a strong impression that modern artillery and specialised gun-armed warships at least up to the 1560s were developed by princes and the artisans in their service. Some rulers were able to use new technology to satisfy the demand for protection and in that process they gained a broad acceptance for their claim that violence ought to be a state monopoly. Normally, such acceptance was the result of bargaining processes between rulers and elite groups where the result was a stronger state. The new ability of the territorial state to control violence also made this state into a more useful partner for elite groups, who might be more interested in gaining control over it without trying to emasculate it in favour of local interests.

Up to the 1560s a surprisingly 'modern' Western Europe took form. Politically, it was dominated by non-absolutist princes who were able to develop a state monopoly on violence in co-operation with aristocrats, whose political and military ambitions became connected with the states, and with rising cities which used the new opportunities for increased trade and profitable investments in a growing economy protected by the rising states. It was not a period of peace but the wars were, much more than in earlier and later decades, fought between states and not within states. War affected trade and economy but not disastrously, and maritime trade in itself was not an important issue in the wars. The cause of the wars was frequently the power struggle over Italy rather than conflicts in Western Europe – the period 1494–1559 in European history is often referred to as the 'Age of the Italian Wars'.

The new strong states were able to formulate and enforce a more ambitious maritime policy than earlier rulers. This policy was based on the rulers' ambition to control violence and as far as possible achieve a monopoly on it at sea as well as on land. A monopoly of violence at sea is necessary for coastal and seafaring states which claim a monopoly of violence on their lands as they cannot allow their territory to become a base for private violence against foreign interests which the state is not in conflict with. Furthermore, in coastal regions and on islands (where the sea was often the best or only transport route) it was difficult to uphold a monopoly of violence on land without practical control of violence off the coast. Ambitious rulers also claimed a responsibility to protect their subjects at sea against violence from foreigners as well as from other subjects. This responsibility was often the legal and political justification for taxes and customs – that is, it was a form of protection selling.[4]

In order to enforce a monopoly of violence at sea, the states followed three main lines. They introduced laws and courts-of-law which controlled the legal aspects of violence at sea, primarily in order to distinguish piracy from lawful privateering and private protection against violence. The state also had to enforce these laws by punishing pirates and denying those who disobeyed them the right to use the territory of the state as a base for attacks on shipping. In practice, this required that the state, or local elite groups co-operating with the state, should have means of violence on land as well as at sea and that these were used within a legal framework.[5] Second, states could co-ordinate the private maritime resources of their country in order to make them useful for warfare: protection of trade and fishery as well as power projection and defence against invasion. The state might organise convoys (armed merchantmen sailing together for mutual protection) and create systems of taxation to pay for protection. It might also regulate shipbuilding in order to create a fleet of large merchantmen suitable for warfare and it might hire or requisition merchantmen for national war efforts. Third, the states could create operational naval forces of their own: permanently organised navies. This gave the state an opportunity to make full use of a new technology by the development of specialised, gun-armed warships. It was also an important step in the state formation process as it created organisational structures which might be controlled by a central state.

In France and the Habsburg Netherlands, legal aspects of violence at sea as

well as the organisation of maritime resources for war were left to high officers of the state, admirals, and to special maritime courts and authorities, admiralties. In France these institutions were provincial (Normandy/Picardy,
Brittany, Guienne and Provence) and they were also entrusted with the
administration of the more or less permanent state navies.[6] In the duchy of
Brittany the admiralty had in the late fifteenth century provided the state with
almost half its incomes through the selling of protection to shipping: charges
on convoys, safe-conducts, etc. This also made it possible for the duchy to create a permanent navy, which became the backbone of the French sailing fleet
when the duchy formed a dynastic union with France in the early 1490s. In
the Netherlands, the Habsburgs had centralised three provincial admiralties
(those of Flanders, Zeeland and Holland) into one in 1488 but the provinces
continued to have much influence in maritime policy and organised much of
the trade protection in their own way. It was only by the mid-sixteenth century that the maritime groups in Holland had become seriously interested in
co-operation with the ruler in trade and fishery protection. As the admirals
and the members of the admiralties were normally strong regional power-
holders their co-operation with the central states could not be taken for
granted, but in this period mutual co-operation and control from the centres
gradually increased. Admirals were normally aristocrats who were supposed to
command fleets. The English Admiralty courts were legal institutions, much
concerned with privateering and piracy, but they had nothing to do with naval
administration. The permanent Tudor navy was directly administered by the
monarchs with the help of professional specialists, just as in Portugal and the
Nordic states. In Scotland the state was less successful in gaining control of
violence at sea and Scottish privateering often operated in a twilight zone
between piracy and legal warfare.[7]

In Castile, the northern trading cities traditionally co-operated with each
other in the protection of maritime trade, as also did the Hanse cities in
Germany and the Baltic Sea. The new strong Castilian state began to regulate
this in a more systematic way in order to use the maritime resources of the
country for warfare when the state required it. A similar and even more centralised institution, the *Casa de Contratación*, was created in Seville from 1503
for the new trade with America. The Spanish state wanted shipowners to build
large ships, an interest that often conflicted with the economic interests of the
traders and shipowners who preferred smaller and more flexible ships. On the
other hand they benefited from the trading privileges and monopoly rights
granted by the state as a part of the bargaining system between rulers and local
elites. Before the 1560s, Spanish kings believed that their viable and state-
regulated maritime communities provided them with sufficient naval force in
times of war, and they refrained from creating a permanent Atlantic fleet of
sailing warships.[8]

Sixteenth-century maritime policy in Western Europe was a middle-way
between what happened in the Baltic and the Mediterranean. In the former

area the Nordic monarchs took control of violence at sea and they also became reluctant to authorise privateering. In the Mediterranean, the two great empires and Venice failed in enforcing any control of violence and there was no effective distinction between legal privateering and piracy. In Western Europe the states were able to curb piracy although, from the 1560s, civil wars and rebellions made it difficult to draw a line between legal and illegal violence acceptable to all contenders. Privateering within a legal framework remained an important part of warfare at sea and uncontrolled West European violence at sea found new areas of operations in the Iberian colonies in America and in the Mediterranean. Guns and improved sailing ships made such long-distance expeditions by pirates and armed traders possible and profitable.

In Western Europe, the limited state power could also employ safe-conducts as a reasonably efficient way of protecting trade and fishery. This was based on the fact that both sides in a conflict often had a mutual interest in not disturbing such economic activities or leaving profitable trade to the neutrals. Consequently, rulers and admiralties often issued safe-conducts which protected enemy (and neutral) merchantmen from capture and embargo and allowed their own merchantmen to trade with the enemy. Safe-conducts or licences were normally sold to provide incomes for the states. Today, the archives created by the bureaucracy surrounding the provision of safe-conducts and adjudication about captured ships are important sources for research on maritime trade.

Strategically, the Channel was the key area in Western Europe. Trade between Northern and Southern Europe and between England and the continent passed through this waterway and for military operations between England and the continent control of the Channel was obviously important. For the maritime centres in Spain, the Netherlands, the Mediterranean and the Baltic control of or safe passage through the Channel were necessary for profitable international trade. The dynastic connection between the Netherlands and Spain which developed in the early sixteenth century also made the Channel into a politically important route for the transfer of resources (men, money, weapons) within the Habsburg empire. Even the voyages of members of the ruling house between the Netherlands and Spain became major naval expeditions.

In the latter half of the fifteenth century the French crown took effective control of the southern coast of the Channel by conquering Normandy from the English in 1450, Picardy from the Burgundians (Habsburg) in 1477 and Brittany (through marriage and a war with England) in 1492. For the English, only Calais remained as a bridgehead on the Continent until it was lost in 1558. This consolidation of French control over territories which for centuries had been connected or allied with England drastically changed English relations with the Continent.[9] Medieval English foreign and military policy had been moulded by ambitions to control large parts of France. From the seventeenth century England began to make large territorial conquests on all continents except Europe. Our period covers the transitional phase, when the last attempts at a Continental come-back failed and England gradually acquired the means to create a seaborne empire. For the defence of the British Isles the Channel remained important. France and the Habsburgs in the Netherlands had the potential to gather larger armies than England in the Channel area, and control of the sea might be decisive for invasion or counter invasion plans.

Naval warfare with few battles

When did early modern warfare at sea begin in Western Europe? Traditional historiography (not only in Britain) has often made the year 1588 into the decisive turning-point for naval warfare in Europe. This view, abandoned by naval historians but still strong among the general public, is, as we have seen, far from correct. Permanent navies, sailing warships, heavy guns and stand-off fights had been in use for a century by 1588, in the Mediterranean, the Indian Ocean and the Baltic. They had also been important in Western Europe long before the Armada campaign, but, for naval historians who have limited their view to the Atlantic seaboard, there had been a disappointing lack of decisive naval battles before 1588. We should ask whether naval operations had been important in sixteenth-century wars in Western Europe before the Armada.

Up to 1560, France, Spain, England, Scotland and the Habsburg Netherlands (from 1504/1516 unified with Spain) fought several wars over territory and political power. Spain and the Netherlands were usually allied with England and Scotland with France. The causes of the wars were normally the power struggle in Italy and conflicts along the hazy French-German border. Portugal was part of the trade network in Western Europe, but this state, with its permanent navy, stayed outside the European wars. It concentrated resources on the creation of a maritime empire from the South Atlantic to the China Seas. Two other sea powers, Denmark-Norway and the German Hanse, also normally avoided taking active part in these wars. At sea, the important problems for the contending nations were the connection between Spain and the Netherlands, the Channel as a frontier zone between France and England, and control of the east coast of England and Scotland which was important during conflicts between these two states.[10]

The Spanish-Dutch trade was protected by convoys organised by the shipping and merchant communities in both countries and co-ordinated by the Habsburg rulers. The efforts of these maritime communities – among the most important in Europe – were normally sufficient to keep the trade route open, although at a cost. The fact that the Habsburgs normally were allied with England during wars against France naturally made the passage through the Channel safer for their shipping. On the Habsburg side it was only during the 1550s that the ruler organised a state-owned navy. From 1550 the Dutch

admiralty purchased merchantmen and converted them into gun-armed warships for convoy protection. Partly they were used for protection of important
transfers of American silver from Spain to the north-western war zone. After
the peace in 1559 these ships were sold.[11]

The Channel was the most eventful scene of large-scale naval operations.
Traditionally, the literature has more or less taken for granted that the English
navy was the pioneer of warfare with heavy guns and that this type of warfare
was introduced, with other innovations, in the early years of the reign of
Henry VIII (r. 1509–47). The *Mary Rose* of 1509 (raised in 1982) is still often
given the distinction of being a warship of revolutionary design with heavy
guns firing through ports low in the hull.[12] Actually, such guns were introduced earlier in Western Europe and probably not by the English. The
Normandy admiralty built a great ship (*la Louise*) in the late 1480s which at
least carried heavy guns later and in the 1490s Brittany and several French
cities built large ships for the French war effort in Italy. The largest of these was
la Cordelière which was armed with 16 heavy guns mounted on the lower
deck. Fourteen heavy guns are mentioned on another very large ship from the
1490s, *la Charente*. These and other large French ships (which probably also
had some heavy guns) saw much service in the Mediterranean during the
Italian Wars and they were also deployed to Greek waters during the war
between Venice and the Ottomans in 1499–1502. The French Atlantic navy
thus gained considerable experience in long-distance expeditions and the use
of guns against ships and targets on land.[13]

In the British Isles, Scotland appears to have been the first state to imitate
this. In the early sixteenth century, James IV built at least two gun-armed
ships, of which *Michael* (1511) was armed with 27 heavy guns.[14] Henry VII of
England had built two large ships, *Regent* and *Sovereign*, in the late 1480s, but
after that he invested little in his navy. In the later years of his reign these ships
may have carried some heavy guns and from 1509 England undoubtedly had
specialised warships with such guns on the lower deck. From 1492 to the end
of his reign Henry VII cautiously avoided being involved in continental warfare and the fact that the new French gun-armed warships were mainly
deployed to the Mediterranean probably made them less threatening than if
they had been based close to England. However, Henry VIII's decision in 1511
to join the Habsburgs and Spain in a war against France brought about a dramatic expansion and change in the English navy. A large number of ships were
hired, built or bought, and several of these were armed with heavy guns.[15]

The allies had agreed that the English fleet should operate in the Channel
while the Spanish took control of the Bay of Biscay.[16] They first escorted an
English army to Guienne in south-western France without interference from
the French. It helped Spain to conquer Navarre but achieved nothing for
England. In the Channel the English made raids on the coast of Normandy,
captured merchantmen and protected trade. The French and the Bretons
(Brittany was still a separate state in union with France) were slower to

mobilise their fleets, and when the English fleet approached Brest on 10 August they retreated. The French overestimated the strength of the enemy fleet which was accompanied by several recently captured prizes. A few French ships, especially the great *la Louise* and *la Cordelière*, covered the retreat and became involved in a gun-fight with some English ships, including *Mary Rose*, *Sovereign* and *Regent*. The latter and *la Cordelière* boarded each other and after a long fight the French ship caught fire – if by design to avoid capture, or accident, is unclear. Both ships, two of the largest in Western Europe, were destroyed with heavy loss of life.[17]

During the autumn of 1512 six French galleys armed with heavy guns arrived from the Mediterranean. In spite of their limited number they made a great impression on the English fleet which in April 1513 arrived off Brest. In an attack they sank one English ship and severely damaged another with gun-fire. The English Lord Admiral, Edward Howard, was killed when he led an attack with small craft which attempted to eliminate the galleys in their base. Discouraged, the English fleet sailed home. The galley threat and logistical difficulties caused Henry VIII to give up further fleet operations around Brittany and instead the fleet was used to cover the transport of a large English army to northern France. In October the combined French-Breton-Scottish fleet attempted to capture Henry VIII when he returned to England, but it was dispersed by a gale. Apart from mutual coastal raids, little more happened at sea before peace was concluded in 1514. England and Scotland were both financially exhausted – Scotland to such an extent that she sold the great *Michael* to Brittany. Scotland never again became a naval power of any importance.

In 1521, war broke out between France and the Emperor Charles V, who now ruled Spain and the Netherlands.[18] Italy was the main scene of operations until 1529. During 1521 the Breton fleet took part in the siege and capture of the Spanish border fortress, Fuenterrabía. During 1522 England again went to war with France as an ally of Charles V, and Scotland joined France. The English fleet attacked Scotland and cruised in the Channel, but the main effort was again a land invasion of France from Calais. During 1523 the English fleet again landed an army on the Continent, while the French fleet was able to sail along the western coast of England with reinforcements for Scotland. Both fleets failed to prevent their adversary's power projection. This was the final English attempt to invade France and recreate a Continental empire. The results of Henry VIII's first two French wars were disappointing for him. He had been useful to his allies, as his army could threaten Paris and his navy keep the Channel open for Dutch-Spanish trade, but England had gained nothing. By the early 1520s both England and France ceased to invest more in major gun-armed warships. There had been a considerable enthusiasm for such ships from the 1490s, first in the Mediterranean (Venice and the Ottomans) and in Brittany and France. After 1500 interest had spread to the British Isles but by the 1520s the results of several wars had not proved that such ships were of decisive importance in Europe. Typically, Emperor Charles V did not build such warships.

The Habsburg states and France again went to war over Italy in 1536–38 but no important operations took place in the Atlantic. In 1542 the war started again, with Denmark-Norway in alliance with France.[19] During 1543 La Rochelle was threatened by both Spanish and Dutch fleets. A French fleet (apparently privateers and ships armed by the admiralty of Guienne), fitted out in the Bayonne region was surprised and defeated by a Spanish fleet on 25 July 1543 when it levied a ransom on the town of Muros, close to Cape Finisterre. French ships began to attack Habsburg merchantmen and an ambitious plan was prepared to form a joint French–Scottish–Danish fleet for attacks on Habsburg merchantmen in the North Sea. When England joined the war during August 1543 this had to be abandoned. The war efforts in 1542–43 seem rather unco-ordinated and partly controlled by regional interests.

The English navy expanded rapidly during the first half of the 1540s, an expansion which Henry VIII could finance by confiscated Church property as a result of his break with the Papacy. During 1544 his fleet had the initiative at sea. It escorted an army to Scotland (largely carried by Dutch and Baltic merchantmen), and brought an army to Boulogne which was taken after a siege helped by a naval bombardment. This time Henry VIII refrained from grandiose invasion plans and focused his efforts on a strategic coastal port, important for the control of the Narrows. But this limited war effort made his ally, Charles V, dissatisfied and in the autumn of 1544 Charles concluded a separate peace with France and turned his attention to his Protestant antagonists in Germany. The equally heretic Englishmen were left to fight for themselves. For the first time in the sixteenth century England had to face France and Scotland without any allies. It was the first time that the Channel served as a moat patrolled by warships against a possible full-scale invasion of England. Francis I decided to make a major effort against England for the first time in his reign (1515–47).

The French permanent navy of sailing-ships had declined since the 1510s and 1520s. In 1545 only a few large warships existed, and the largest of these was accidentally burnt before operations began. But France had a considerable galley fleet in the Mediterranean and 20 galleys as well as 28 sailing ships were ordered to proceed to the Channel during spring 1545. The galleys duly arrived but many of the sailing ships, carrying much equipment and weapons, were lost or delayed. A large number of merchantmen were mobilised in Normandy, especially from Dieppe where the great shipowner and pioneer in French transatlantic trade, Jean Ango, ruined himself by loaning large sums to the king to make the ships ready. Many ships came from south-western France and 30 Dutch merchantmen (hulks) were also hired or requisitioned in the Biscay region. An English attempt to defeat the ships gathering on the Biscay coast before they arrived in the Channel failed. So did a fireship attack against the French fleet in the Seine estuary and an attack against other ports which was fought off by French galleys. The Breton fleet, which in the early spring had made a successful expedition to Scotland, returned in time for the big event in the Channel.

The size and composition of the French invasion fleet is obscure, but there were about 25 galleys and at least 150 sailing ships in the Seine estuary in early July 1545.[20] Higher numbers (up to 300) are also mentioned and may have included ships gathering in other ports or small vessels. The number of purpose-built warships in this fleet is unknown as is the armament and the size of the crews. A French army of 50,000 men was at least planned to gather in the Channel ports, but it is not known how many of these actually embarked in the fleet. Although this was the closest England ever came to an invasion after the Middle Ages[21] and although the French forces were at least as large as the Spanish in 1588, research on this episode is limited. Many questions about the events in the Channel in 1545 remain unanswered. It is far from certain that Francis I really intended to make a full-scale invasion of England. He may have aimed at defeating the English fleet as a preparation for the capture of Boulogne and Calais, or he may have intended to take Portsmouth and the Isle of Wight in order to negotiate from a position of strength.

The French fleet, commanded by the Admiral of France, Claude d'Annebault, arrived off the English coast east of the Isle of Wight on 18 July. Soldiers were landed at Brighton which was burnt and the fleet proceeded to the eastern entrance of the sound between the Isle of Wight and the mainland. The English fleet was gathered here with the main army close to the shore outside Portsmouth. Henry VIII was present and in direct command of his armed forces. The English realised that they were up against a superior enemy (probably much superior in number of men) and had decided to fight cautiously and defensively in the confined and treacherous waters behind the Isle of Wight where the enemy fleet lacked space to develop more than a fraction of his full strength. During 18 and 19 July, the French attacked mainly with gunfire from their galleys which were at an advantage in this area, especially as the weather was calm. When the wind freshened and the English sailing ships counter-attacked, *Mary Rose* heeled over and sank when water entered her open gunports. The French galleys retreated, but the English did not follow them. Active skirmishing by small English row-barges made a certain impression on the French side.

The French now tried to induce their enemy to come out and fight by landing soldiers at various places on the Isle of Wight. Henry VIII sent considerable militia forces to the island which offered effective resistance. The French realised that they would have to make a full-scale landing and commit large parts of their army to major siege operations against local forts if anything was to be achieved. This would have seriously weakened the fighting capacity of the fleet. That was exactly what the English hoped for and they discussed the possibility of attacking the enemy fleet if a large part of the French army was sent ashore.

The French decided to leave the Isle of Wight area and sailed to Boulogne where some of their troops were landed to increase the force committed to the siege there. The English fleet was hastily strengthened with requisitioned merchantmen (many of them German) and proceeded to sea. A total force of 114 vessels with almost 14,000 men is reported, nearly the same number of men as the English fleet had in 1588. On 15 August the two fleets sighted each other in the Channel but the winds were very light and only skirmishes between oared forces – French galleys and English galeasses and row-barges – took place. The French were by now apparently crippled by disease and inadequate logistics and by 17 August they returned to Le Havre. The English were again in control of the Channel and in September they made a successful raid on Normandy, but this fleet too was severely hit by the outbreak of disease. England and France concluded peace in 1546.

The operations of 1545 showed how difficult it might be for a superior force to achieve a successful landing when an inferior but undefeated gun-armed fleet was in the vicinity. The fortifications around the English base area were also important as the French believed that it required major siege operations to reduce them. Similar problems were usual during major operations in the Mediterranean and there are striking similarities between the Channel operations in 1545 and the Prevesa operation seven years earlier.[22] The operations once more showed that galleys might be useful and versatile warships in the Channel; the capabilities of sailing warships were not tested in this unusually calm summer. The result of a battle between two major sailing fleets which apparently intended to fight in one or more lines abreast would have been interesting, but we are left to speculate about how it would have been fought. French logistics seem to have been a vital weakness. The large forces of ships and soldiers gathered in the Channel were used for offensive operations for only about five weeks and probably could not have lasted much more. The general impression is that the French hoped that Henry VIII would commit some major blunder and send out his fleet in a premature counter-attack.

The versatility of the French galley fleet under its able Florentine commanders Leone and Pietro Strozzi was again demonstrated in 1547–8 when it intervened in Scotland where a civil war was in progress.[23] It was partly an Anglo-French war with proxies during a period when both England and Scotland were ruled by minors, Edward VI and Mary Stuart respectively, and the prospective marriage of the young Scottish queen might determine the power balance. The French fleet was able to support their Scottish allies effectively and during 1548 it brought queen Mary to France where she was betrothed to the French heir to the throne, Francis (II). French sea power had made Scotland into a French satellite state.

The new French king Henry II (r. 1547–59) inaugurated an ambitious naval policy and rapidly strengthened his permanent navy during 1547–50. The fleet was raised to at least 11 major sailing warships and 40 galleys, but the most interesting feature of the rearmament programme was the construction of about 20 *roberges*, light and medium-sized oared warships with guns fore and aft. The English navy had built or converted 14 galeasses during 1544–6 as a counter-measure to the French galleys. The French had found their Mediterranean galleys highly useful even in northern waters – they did much of the actual fighting – but evidently they found that a more seaworthy type of oared vessel would be useful too. Anglo-French technical development in the 1540s obviously reflects operational experience. After 1550 something evidently happened which made it less necessary for them to build hybrid warships – we may guess that sailing-ship technology progressed rapidly.[24]

Anglo-French disputes caused a brief war in 1549–50 which ended when England agreed to sell back Boulogne to France. Naval operations had been limited and French galleys had again been important. During 1551 war between France and the Habsburgs began again. This time England was neutral and in Western Europe the war at sea became mainly convoy battles. The French navy and privateers attacked Dutch and Spanish shipping and the Habsburgs organised large and well-protected convoys of armed merchantmen sailing from both Spain and the Netherlands. The two Atlantic parts of the Habsburg empire (soon to become arch-enemies) were by now well co-ordinated in their protection of trade, and the French on their side had a reinvigorated navy. Habsburg losses were considerable, but trade was not interrupted.[25]

A brief interlude of peace in 1556–7 was only nominal and the war started once again.[26] This time England joined it as ally of the new Habsburg ruler of the Netherlands and Spain, Philip II, who also happened to be the nominal English king as husband of Queen Mary. In spite of co-operation between the three fleets the war was no success for the allies at sea. The French took Calais from England in a surprise attack on land and at sea in early 1558. In summer 1558 an Anglo-Dutch amphibious attack against Brest failed, while an English squadron proved useful when it supported an Habsburg army with gunfire in a battle against the French on the shore at Gravelines between Calais and Dunkirk. General peace was concluded in 1559. The epoch when Spain (Castile), the Netherlands (formerly Burgundy) and England were normally allied against France was close to an end.

Was sea power important and efficient in Western Europe up to 1560? This brief survey has provided several examples showing control of the sea lines of communication was important for long-distance trade, for military operations and for political alliances. But the naval operations connected with these activities were surprisingly uneventful which may give the impression that they were unimportant. Major army forces were taken from one area to another without interference from substantial enemy fleets, and armed merchantmen sailing in convoys were often able to put up much resistance against warships. Sailing battle-fleets armed with heavy guns had begun to take shape in France and England, but they had not met in a full scale battle. The reason was partly that such battles were not absolutely essential for the strategy of any of the contending states, but the ability of sailing warships and – especially – temporarily armed merchantmen to reach decisive areas of action was also far from certain. With little ability to sail close to the wind, sailing ships were best suited when enjoying favourable winds to reach a predetermined area. They were less suited to interfere with an enemy using winds favourable to *his* operational aims.

Efficient use of heavy guns at sea in Western Europe had in this period been exercised by galleys and modified types of oared warships. They were able to fight each other, to attack sailing warships in calms and moderate winds, to bombard fortress walls, and to carry out amphibious operations independently of the wind, even at such long distances as from France to Scotland. They could hardly defeat major gun-armed sailing fleets, but they could often avoid actions with them and fight only under favourable conditions. In the Mediterranean these qualities had convinced the navies that galleys were the only viable warships and that sailing ships were best used as defensively armed transports. In Western Europe, gun-armed sailing warships continued to be used but after having met considerable enthusiasm in the decades around 1500 they were, by 1550, regarded as part of a more complicated naval system where oared warships were still important too. Clearly it was the heavy guns which had made oared warships important again as they could combine the mobility and manoeuvrability that sailing warships still lacked.

The strength of contending fleets was still reckoned in terms of armed men, and large ships with many soldiers were regarded as important. An army at sea in a galley fleet or a sailing fleet might still have been regarded as invincible if not met by a fleet carrying a superior army. Both types of warship now carried heavy guns which were useful against fortifications, during long-range battles and as a preliminary weapon in close-range combats. There was, however, still no instance of a fleet with superior gunpower defeating a fleet with a superior army. The Portuguese in the Indian Ocean had, in fact, already demonstrated this in the early sixteenth century, but their experience was apparently not regarded as relevant in wars between European states. The Portuguese themselves did not take part in the European wars. When they finally did so in the 1580s they represented an established but stagnating technology. It was to be in north-western Europe that the sailing gun-armed ship concept was to be driven to its maturity.

9

ATLANTIC WARFARE
UNTIL 1603

Crisis and change in Western Europe

France and the Habsburgs had by 1559 reached agreement over Italy and the balance of power in Western Europe which seemed to have a chance to be lasting. A few years earlier the Habsburg dynasty had also separated into two branches. Philip II ruled Spain, large parts of Italy, the Netherlands and Spain's American colonies. The Austrian land-locked lands and the imperial crown were transferred to the junior branch of the House of Habsburg and this made the economically dynamic Netherlands into a northern outpost in a maritime empire centred in Southern Europe. Philip's empire faced both the Mediterranean and the Atlantic and it was dependent on sea lines of communication for defence, trade and transfer of money, weapons and soldiers. France was a compact territorial state with a huge population and an important maritime economy. England, the third party in the peace of 1559, was a medium-sized power traditionally connected with the Habsburgs which now faced Europe's two great powers as close neighbours. The Tudor dynasty had created a permanent navy for home-water operations which had become the first line of defence of an island state but also a key to the European sea lines of communication within the Spanish Habsburg empire. Up to 1560 England had shown very limited Atlantic ambitions and its maritime trade had increasingly been concentrated on the Netherlands and the great entrepôt, Antwerp.[1]

Portugal had its own far-flung maritime empire and an agreement with Spain about how European control of the global sea lines of communication should be divided. The two Iberian powers claimed that they had a monopoly on trade and colonial settlement in the Atlantic hemisphere outside Europe. This was based on a combination of violence and an advantage in know-how about maritime enterprise and geography outside Europe, and the monopoly came increasingly under attack when other European maritime groups began to gather the same know-how. The Portuguese Atlantic empire had started in the fifteenth century with ambitions of conquest in North Africa and control of the trade to West Africa, and it was here the Portuguese had begun to use guns at sea in order to keep other Europeans out. In the sixteenth century

Brazil and its sugar plantations became the most dynamic part of this empire and, together with the Spanish colonies, it became an important market for the Portuguese slave trade from Africa.

Spain, Portugal, England and France were the contenders in the next decades of maritime power struggle in the new Atlantic hemisphere, an economic and political area largely unknown before the late fifteenth century. Western Europe began to experience the effects of being part of a new seaborne economy where maritime innovations and geographical explorations created new opportunities and new sources of conflict. During the peace negotiations in 1559 France and Spain had been unable to reach an agreement about French ambitions to develop settlements and trade in America. Potentially this was the source of a new major conflict, the first clash over trans-oceanic interests between two European powers. France looked like the realistic challenger to Iberian Atlantic hegemony. It had a huge population which might provide a surplus for emigration and by 1560 French seamen had gained much experience of trans-Atlantic enterprises. Furthermore, France was a unified monarchy – a form of statehood which seemed to be better suited for concentrating resources for national efforts than the conglomerate of territories with different traditions and languages ruled by the Habsburgs. In the 1550s English seafarers had begun to join the French in their overseas ventures, but the traditional English friendship with the Habsburgs made it uncertain if their government would allow such activities on a larger scale. In 1559 the political future of England, recently inherited by Elizabeth Tudor of doubtful legitimacy, looked like a problem which might cause a European crisis.[2]

Events were to take a very different turn. After many decades of increased political integration, few revolts and gradual consolidation of centralised power, large parts of Western Europe saw a sudden political collapse. In France, a series of civil wars began in 1562, and lasted until 1598. In the Netherlands, political and religious conflicts turned into armed revolt in 1565/66. Philip II tried to end it with military force, but the consequence was that the civil war increasingly became a national conflict between Spain and his Dutch subjects. In this situation of political chaos and conflicts close to her coasts, England surprisingly became the main challenger to Iberian power in the Atlantic. English security interests required that no single power should have a dominating military position in the Channel and the Low Countries, and English economic interests demanded expansion in the Atlantic. Both security and economic interests meant conflict with Spain. The Channel/North Sea region became the centre of effectively organised challenges to Spanish supremacy in Western Europe and the Atlantic hemisphere. These challenges from the Dutch rebels and the English – motivated by a coalition of royal security policy and economic interests in trade and plunder – were more effective than the huge resources of France which French rulers proved unable to control or organise.[3]

Many of these conflicts had strong religious dimensions and it has been usual to label the period as the 'Age of the Wars of Religion'. In a maritime perspective it is obvious that the French, English and Dutch seamen who challenged the two Iberian powers around the world were also overwhelmingly Protestant, sometimes even religious militants. The established European power structure overseas was Iberian and Catholic, and attacks against it might serve religious as well as economic purposes. However, in a longer perspective, it must be remembered that stability, *not* internal conflict, was unusual in Western Europe. It had been the 70 or 80 years of internal peace and efficient state control of violence from the 1480s to the 1560s which had been exceptional, not that elites and regions used violence to achieve political and economic aims. The increased power of the state had been based on compromises between rulers and elites rather than on strong organisations controlled by the state, such as permanent armies and navies, but it had allowed such structures to develop. The long period of civil wars and revolts saw both further state formation and the breakdown of existing organisations. The Spanish army grew stronger, a permanent Spanish sailing fleet was created, the English navy developed as an important and flexible instrument of state policy in co-operation with private maritime interests, the Netherlands became a major military and naval power, while the French army and navy were destroyed as permanent forces.

Whatever the original reasons for the Dutch revolt (they were hardly maritime) it released forces which rapidly made north-western Europe into the maritime centre of the Continent. Together with England, the Dutch developed superior maritime technology and organisation for war and trade with which they were able to challenge the Iberian powers. The opportunities opened up by European, Atlantic and Asian trade and politics stimulated economic and technological innovations, but it was the challengers, rather than the defenders, who were able to innovate more quickly and successfully. The political power structure and its capacity for producing men with new ideas and competence for new tasks must have been important. In this chapter the rise of England as a successful maritime power is given a certain emphasis. In Chapter 10 the more spectacular rise of the Dutch will be analysed.

Challenges to the Spanish monopoly in America until 1585

The Spanish conquest of the Caribbean after Columbus' first voyage in 1492 is normally not regarded as warfare at sea. The conquistadors did not meet any maritime resistance from the indigenous population. The invaders' maritime skills and the fact that Columbus stumbled into the only large agglomeration of islands in the New World are nevertheless important ingredients in the early Spanish penetration of America. It became to a large extent a maritime enterprise where the conquest of Caribbean islands was followed by scattered coast settlements in Central America, on the north coast of South America and on the western coasts of the Americas. The conquests of Mexico and Peru added large continental territories to the empire but the maritime character of the enterprise remained.[4]

The rapid spread of Spanish power and the fairly strong control which the Spanish state was able to exercise on a distant continent are difficult to explain if the close connection between settlements and seaborne trade controlled from Seville is not taken into account. The islands and the coastal settlements were easy to defend against attacks from the indigenous population for a power which was supreme at sea. The same supremacy made central control from Spain conceivable as the settlements would be isolated without seaborne communications. Even Peru was connected with the rest of the empire by a sea route to Panama. In the 1560s, Spanish expansion westward continued, with a small settlement on the Philippines and a monopoly on trade between Asia and America. Even if the control of this ocean was extremely limited, the Pacific became a 'Spanish lake' where other Europeans were not welcome and no other power regularly sailed across it from one side to the other.[5]

An empire built around maritime lines of communication was also vulnerable to attack from powers which shared the same maritime skills. In the long run, experience was to show that only Europeans who decided to settle in America were a serious threat to sovereignty over colonies. Fleets and armies sent out from Europe were often struck down by tropical diseases to which the local inhabitants had become immune and major expeditions of conquest were difficult to undertake without a local base of food production.[6] But even small-scale attacks against local shipping and scattered settlements might be resource-consuming for the defender as it was difficult to predict where seaborne raiders might strike. Modern fortifications might delay an attacker long enough to give mosquitos and disease time to defeat him, but such fortifications were expensive.

The French, English and later Dutch penetration of America had three aims: plunder, interloping trade and settlements. These aims were partially overlapping and based on violence. Piracy and privateering were naturally based on armed force. Interloping trade had to be carried out with well-protected ships and with at least symbolic amounts of violence as the Spanish settlers had to show that they had been forced to trade against their will. It was often not very difficult to force them to do so as small Spanish settlements were badly served by the monopoly traders. The interlopers could offer products of good quality at better prices. Finally, the establishment of alien settlements in defiance of Iberian claims of a monopoly – based on their 'discovery' and their investments in the conquest – had to be protected with armed force. Even if an alien colony was established far from any existing settlement, Spain and Portugal feared that it might serve as a base for piracy and illegal trade. The Spanish authorities were also restrictive in selling licences for foreigners to trade, except sometimes to the Portuguese who could supply

148

slaves from Africa. Foreign capital, especially Genoese, was also important in financing the Seville merchants.

Up to 1560 the threat against Spanish Atlantic trade and American settlements came from France. Most of it was normal privateering activities during the numerous French-Spanish wars. They gradually increased in intensity and spread westward. In the period 1536–45 privateering attacks mainly took place on the European side of the trade route, in the 'Atlantic triangle' between the Azores, Madeira, the Canary Islands and the Iberian peninsula. It was in this area, also threatened by attacks from North Africa, that in the 1520s Spain began to organise convoys for its trans-Atlantic trade. Portugal (to which the Azores and Madeira belonged) also had naval patrols in the area to protect its in- and out-bound shipping to the Indian Ocean, Africa and Brazil. On some occasions warships of the Portuguese navy (Spain had no navy) also protected Spanish shipping. In 1548–50 Portugal and France were involved in informal armed conflicts as Frenchmen attempted to create settlements in Brazil and French ships also acted as interlopers in the Portuguese-controlled trade with West Africa where English interlopers also began to appear in the 1550s. Portugal resisted the intrusions with armed force.[7]

During the 1550s the French attacks against Spanish interests in America intensified, especially in the eastern part of the Caribbean where they were able periodically to cut the communications to Spain. In 1555 French privateers even conquered Havana. The French also developed a flourishing interloping trade, partly by selling goods they had captured from Spanish ships to local Spanish settlers who during wars must often have had to trade with those Europeans of any nationality who actually came to them with goods. The fact that the French usually traded with the settlements, rather than plundering them, indicates that they were thinking in a longer perspective and hoped to create trade relations. Spain sent weapons and small forces of soldiers to America and the crown organised local militias as well as patrols with armed ships in the Atlantic triangle and the Antilles. The merchants of Seville preferred convoys with merchantmen of a minimum size. This system favoured their interest in controlling the trade as a monopoly system.

The classical Spanish convoy system found its definite form by 1564 and was in use beyond 1650. Each year two convoys sailed from Seville and its outports in Cadiz Bay, one in April for Vera Cruz in New Spain (Mexico), Cuba, Santo Domingo (Haiti), and Honduras, and one in August for the *Tierra Firme* (the north coast of South America) and the Panama Isthmus. Both convoys were to leave for Havana early in the following year and from there return to Spain in March. In practice, war, weather and economic factors often changed the convoy schedule but the basic pattern remained. Westbound convoys took a southerly course, passed the Canaries and entered the southern half of the Caribbean, while eastbound convoys sailed north of Cuba and through the Bahamas, often calling at the Azores for reorganisation before the final and dangerous passage to Seville.[8]

This system was developed to make best possible use of the prevailing winds and to avoid sailing in the Caribbean during the hurricane season in late summer. The eastbound convoys carried large amounts of American silver which in the sixteenth century gained crucial importance for Spanish power and the European economy. The silver from Peru was sent by ship to Panama, brought over the Isthmus by mule-trains and loaded on to the *Tierra Firme* convoy. Each convoy had at least two large armed merchantmen as escort. When the threat to the convoys grew, squadrons of purpose-built warships were added as extra escorts and as carriers of silver. The convoys were strong enough to resist anything except attacks from major enemy fleets and before 1650 it only happened once (Matanzas 1628) that an entire convoy with its silver was captured.

In the 1560s the most spectacular confrontations were an attempt to establish a French Huguenot colony in Florida and the ambition of the Plymouth merchant John Hawkins to become a supplier of slaves from Africa to the Spanish settlements. The French colony was ideally placed as a corsair base for attacks against Spanish shipping but it was eliminated in 1565 by soldiers sent with a fleet from Spain. Hawkins' expeditions were financed by merchants in London and leading men in the navy. They came to an end in 1568 on his third voyage. Hawkins had the misfortune to be at San Juan de Ulúa, the roadstead of Vera Cruz in Mexico, when the heavily armed New Spain convoy arrived at its destination. His fleet – which included two major warships hired from the queen – was to a large extent annihilated by the Spanish force.

Many smaller French and English attempts to penetrate the Spanish monopoly in the 1560s and 1570s were more successful. Spain continued to lose ships to raiders, and interlopers returned year after year. The evidence is vague, but it is probable that the armed ships which attacked Spanish shipping and settlements were sometimes the same as those who traded with the Spaniards. Attacking Spanish ships was one way of getting goods to trade with, but also a method for eliminating competition. Some interlopers also fought each other, another way to reduce competition with violence. The Spanish patrol squadrons sent out to eliminate raiders and traders were also a problem for the mercantilist Spanish system, as they often took part in the illegal trade themselves. Some privateers showed a high degree of skill in commanding daring enterprises. Francis Drake gained both fame and fortune when in 1573 in co-operation with runaway slaves, he attacked a trans-Isthmus shipment of Peruvian silver. As late as 1568 he had been master on one of John Hawkins' slave-ships – flexibility in European behaviour might be profitable overseas.

The crown of Castile organised the defence of shipping and settlements in much the same way as it organised protection of trade in Western Europe. Merchants and settlers had to pay for much of it themselves, and convoy escorts and patrol ships were often armed merchantmen, The state provided some money, weapons, military and naval leaders and specialists, a legal and institutional framework, and rules of behaviour. In the Atlantic triangle, where

Portugal and Spain had a joint interest in protecting their shipping, the two powers often co-operated. Portugal appears to have deployed a considerable part of its royal navy in this area.

The first major attempt to protect the Caribbean and trans-Atlantic trades with specialised warships belonging to the crown were made in 1567/68 when 12 small galleons with auxiliary oars were built. This force, the first real royal sailing navy of Castile, served for about a decade as convoy escort and patrol force. It was not able to be everywhere and Pedro Menéndez de Avilés, since the 1550s the strategist behind the defence of Spanish trade and colonies, intended it to intercept raiders and interlopers when they were homeward bound in the north-eastern Caribbean. The prevailing wind and currents system made it relatively easy to predict their route and to concentrate the Spanish warships in its narrowest part. Intense demands for local defence and convoy escorting made it impossible to fulfil this ideal. From 1577 the galleons were replaced by galleys and small vessels in the Caribbean, making the system of defence strikingly similar to the Mediterranean system with forts and local patrol forces. For a time galleys were a successful deterrent against small corsair ships as they could defeat them in calm weather and in shallow waters. A new squadron of larger galleons was ready by 1583/84, but by then it was no longer small privateers that were the main threat. Full-scale war with major fleets operating in the Atlantic hemisphere was imminent.

The European civil wars at sea, 1559–85

After the general peace of 1559 international politics in Western Europe was dominated by the effects of revolts and civil wars, while the states officially remained at peace with each other until 1585.[9] The first of these crises occurred in Scotland where a Protestant revolt against the regent, the French-born dowager queen Marie de Guise, broke out. The regent, who ruled in the absence of her daughter, Mary Stuart (who until 1560 was in France as consort to King Francis II), kept it under control with her French troops. In late 1559 the French decided to send a fleet with more troops to Scotland. The situation was especially dangerous for England, as the legitimacy of Queen Elizabeth was not beyond doubt and Mary Stuart was a claimant to the English throne. Elizabeth reacted by sending a fleet to the north. Winter expeditions in these waters were risky and the French fleet was dispersed by gales and had to return home. The English fleet persisted in its mission and arrived in the Firth of Forth in January 1560. This limited the operational freedom of the French troops and reduced their hope of relief. By the summer they had been forced to leave Scotland and Mary Stuart had to accept Elizabeth as Queen of England. The almost eternal Anglo-Scottish conflict had reached a settlement which proved to be lasting and French influence in the British Isles was eliminated.[10]

In 1562 the first French civil war began. The English decided to intervene on the Protestant side by taking control of Le Havre and a major fleet was mobilised to support the operation. It ended with a costly failure, as Le Havre had to be evacuated when it was attacked by superior forces after the truce in France in 1563.[11] For more than two decades the English refrained from getting involved in continental embroilments during the French and Dutch civil wars, but they were active in them at sea through private warfare. From her position on an island Elizabeth could refine the use of limited and, often, even profitable violence at sea as an instrument of policy and at the same time keep the increasingly aggressive English seafaring community occupied with overseas ventures in plunder, trade and settlements. Elizabeth could permit, redirect or prohibit such ventures but they were hardly part of a central plan, least of all of a plan for empire building.

Especially in works written during the culmination of British seaborne imperialism, this has sometimes been regarded as a faulty strategy or the result of a capricious policy of a woman. It should, instead, be regarded as an efficient way of co-ordinating very different kinds of information: the government's knowledge about the complicated and volatile political situation on the continent and the seafarer's superior and rapidly increasing know-how about how to explore opportunities for trade and violence in parts of the world where few Europeans had ever been. The private investors and the enterprising seamen acted at their own risk which might have made them eager to develop technology and skills on their own initiative. They were allowed to do so, and the government co-operated with them, invested in the enterprises and integrated the new know-how with the permanent navy – a number of investors in private warfare were also naval administrators.

However, the crown concentrated its own efforts on English security policy in Europe. When that policy forced England to go to war with Spain, a much stronger power, the joint development of private and state-controlled sea power had forged an instrument that technologically had a decided advantage over Iberian sea power, in spite of Spain's long sea-faring traditions. This had been achieved without any dramatic increase in taxation or state formation. In a world with men of many and often irresponsible and destructive ambitions, Elizabeth might appear as the mistress of well-controlled ambitions, aiming at increasing security, power and reputation all at the same time. She was not, in fact, a state builder or an empire builder, but a ruler who allowed her subjects to gather power and wealth by developing new competencies, without fearing that she might lose control over them. In the Western Europe she lived in, this was unusual behaviour.

After 1563, civil wars and revolts continued in France and the Huguenots were especially strong on the Atlantic coast. Much of the seafaring population turned Protestant and the great port of La Rochelle became the most important stronghold for the Huguenots. They also controlled much of the legal framework of French activities at sea as the Huguenot leader Gaspard de Coligny was admiral of France and the Huguenot king of Navarre (later

Henry IV of France) was admiral of Guienne. As such they could commission privateers with papers that were legally acceptable to friendly powers. For the politician Coligny a war in the Atlantic against the Spanish arch-enemy might unite France behind an expansionist and profitable policy and also give the Protestant groups increased influence. He shared this interest with many in the French maritime communities who during the civil wars attacked Spanish and Portuguese shipping, to get both financial support for the Protestant side and to hit the religious enemy. These attacks intensified from the mid-1560s and were the main cause behind the strengthened Spanish naval presence along the trans-Atlantic trade route. The French crown vacillated between lukewarm support for a maritime policy that might strengthen the country and fear that it might strengthen groups which undermined the authority of the central state. In practice it exercised no control over overseas ventures or the groups which undertook them.[12]

In these same years the political situation in the Netherlands reached a crisis when the authority of Philip II was undermined by popular Calvinist revolts and elite resistance against attempts to strengthen the power of the central Habsburg government in Brussels. To break this resistance Philip sent a large army under his most experienced general, the Duke of Alba. The Army of Flanders, for nearly a century ahead a centre of gravity in European power politics, had been created.[13] In 1568, William of Nassau (the Prince of Orange) and his brothers organised an attempt to raise a revolt with the help of German mercenaries, but it was defeated by Alba's army. The Netherlands, a conglomerate of provinces and cities with a strong tradition of self-rule, seemed to be on its way to becoming a centralised territorial state and a mere appendage to Spanish power. Philip II had no intention of giving his industrious subjects in the north free rein for a development that might undermine his own power.

Philip II had sold his Dutch navy after the peace in 1559. His lack of permanent armed force at sea became immediately apparent when the Dutch rebels in 1568 began to organise a force of privateers which sailed under commissions from the Prince of Orange in his capacity as sovereign prince in a small city-state in southern France. These privateers, the Sea Beggars (*geux de mer* or *watergeuzen*), were often successful but were also notoriously undisciplined.[14] They co-operated with French Huguenot privateers and English privateers with French letters of marque and together they could use English and French ports, as well as Emden in Germany, as bases. During the years 1568 to 1572 this coalition of privateers cruised from the North Sea to the Azores and Canaries and made Western Europe into a war zone where no seafarers, Spanish, Dutch, French or neutral were safe if they were Catholics, loyal to Philip II or carried enemy goods.[15]

The attacks were extended to the Caribbean and rumours of a great Protestant attack against the Iberian and Catholic empires circulated. It became impossible for Philip II to send men and money by sea to the

Netherlands, especially since Queen Elizabeth in 1568 had made a forced loan of money on Spanish ships which had sought protection from the privateers in Plymouth. In the future, Spain sent galleys with silver to Genoa where the bankers organised the payment of Spanish troops in the Netherlands through their financial network. This increased the financial power of Genoa. The Army of Flanders was logistically connected with Spain and Italy through the famous 'Spanish Road' over the Alps, in itself a proof of Spain's inability to control the sea route between Spain and the Netherlands.

The Huguenots were successful in controlling the Bay of Biscay during the French civil war of 1568–70. The Sea Beggars were able to blockade Dutch ports to such an extent that grain shipments from the Baltic were reduced. Food prices rose and this increased the dissatisfaction with Alba's rule, preparing opinion for a renewed revolt. Alba made no attempt to create a Habsburg navy in the Netherlands. He relied on the mobilisation of private ships for war, primarily from Amsterdam, and he concentrated his army to resist a possible invasion from France, leaving the coastal provinces of Holland and Zeeland more or less without soldiers.

In early 1572 the English asked the Sea Beggars to leave English ports. The result was unexpected. On 1 April the Sea Beggars took the town of Brielle (Brill) in southern Holland. In a few months, internal revolutionaries and Sea Beggars had taken control of a large number of cities, especially in the north. The Protestant Dutch sea forces rapidly switched from privateering to becoming a provisional navy in the struggle for inland waterways and the coastal regions.[16] In 1572/73 the Zeelanders and South Hollanders gained control over the Rhine/Maas and Scheldt estuaries which also meant that they could control trade to the great port of Antwerp. The North Hollanders and the Frisians gained command over the Zuiderzee, finally confirmed in a naval battle on 13 October 1573. By 1574 Habsburg naval power in the Netherlands was practically eliminated, although Amsterdam remained loyal to Philip II until 1578 and could, for some time, maintain control over some internal waterways. The Dutch began to make money for their navy from their control of the sea routes in the Netherlands. They sold licences to trade with the enemy to their own ships and to neutral shipping, a source of income that was to be important for the Dutch navy.[17]

Philip II was slow to react by sending major naval forces from Spain to regain control of the sea in the north. He was engaged in the great struggle with the Ottomans in the Mediterranean and, apart from the already overstrained guard fleet for the American trade, he had no permanent Atlantic navy. However, early in 1574 he began to mobilise a large fleet in northern Spain through the traditional method of requisitioning armed merchantmen. The first intention was to use it to relieve Middelburg, Philip's last outpost in Zeeland, but this city fell in early 1574. The new plan was to send the fleet to the Channel and, if possible, to base it on Ireland or the Scilly islands in order to gain control of both English and Dutch trade. It seems doubtful if a fleet of this size could have been successful as it would have resulted in a total mobilisation of the English navy. However, the plan is interesting as early evidence of the great Spanish optimism about what they might achieve in the Channel. The plan had to be abandoned as the fleet was severely struck by illness.[18]

In 1575 Spain suffered one of its recurring financial crises and further offensive operations on land and at sea were impossible for a time. A truce was concluded in the Netherlands in 1576. In France the civil wars ended for a time in 1577. Spanish plans for major offensives in the Atlantic were made, however – among them a somewhat imaginative project of 1578/79 to hire 30 warships, several of them large, from Sweden.[19] Anglo–Spanish relations became less tense, but English attacks continued outside Europe. The most spectacular was that of Francis Drake who in 1578 sailed around Cape Horn and attacked Spanish interest in the Pacific. His great success was the capture of a silver-laden ship on its way from Peru to Panama.[20] Spain knew of only one place where the English were vulnerable to retaliation for such activities: Ireland. In 1580 a small Spanish force landed at Smerwick to support Catholic rebels, but it was quickly eliminated by a force brought to the scene by an English squadron.

In 1580 a decisive change took place. A lasting truce in the Mediterranean was reached with the Ottoman empire and Philip II of Spain became king of Portugal too. As the son of a Portuguese princess he had a legitimate claim to the throne when the last king of the House of Aviz died and he was the only person who could support his claim with overwhelming military and naval power. The resistance organised by Dom Antonio, an illegitimate son of a Portuguese prince, was crushed by Spanish military and naval power and Portugal became a Habsburg kingdom. It was agreed that the Spanish and Portuguese empires were to be kept separate, but that the two powers should co-operate in the defence of their transoceanic interests, something they in fact already did. For the Habsburgs, the acquisition of Portugal meant that they obtained a permanent sailing navy, an excellent naval base in Lisbon, and a seaborne empire which stretched across the world. The two Iberian empires met each other in the East Indies archipelago (the Moluccas/the Philippines) and in South America.

Dom Antonio went to France and England to get help. He promised to open the Portuguese Atlantic empire to those who supported him and, as nominal king of Portugal, he became a convenient legal source of letters of marque for privateers who wished to attack Iberian interests. Initially he had an important asset as one part of Portugal remained loyal to him after 1580: the Azores. A small Spanish fleet attempted to take control of the islands in 1581, but it failed. The Azores were of great strategic importance for the Spanish convoy system and for Portugal's communications with her empire. They were also an excellent base for a European power who wished to challenge Philip II and penetrate the Iberian empires. The influential dowager queen of France, Catherine de Medici, became interested and decided to resume the Atlantic policy of admiral Coligny, murdered in 1572, possibly on Catherine's initiative. Her ultimate aims are not clear but as an experienced negotiator she probably intended to use Dom Antonio, the Azores and further conquests in the Portuguese empire in order to extract concessions from Philip II. Queen Elizabeth was less interested in the project than some of her privateers and only a small English force took part in the expedition to the Azores which left France with Dom Antonio on board early in 1582.[21]

The size of the French fleet – which formally was a private venture – is not known in detail but various reports indicate a size of around 60 ships (about half of them large) and around 6,000 to 7,000 soldiers. This was the largest French force sent overseas before the age of Louis XIV. It met an Iberian fleet of two large Portuguese warships, 19 armed merchantmen and ten transports with 7,000 men of which 4,500 were soldiers. This force was smaller than planned as part of the fleet was delayed, but the Spanish commander, the Marquis of Santa Cruz (Don Alvaro de Bazan Jr) decided to fight. After an indecisive gunfight on 24 July 1582 the fleets met two days later in a fierce close battle south of the island of St Miguel.[22] The French initially had the advantage of the wind and attacked the Spanish rear with superior forces but that gave the Spanish commander the opportunity to gain the wind for the Spanish van, which in its turn attacked the French. Several French ships took flight. The magnitude of French losses is uncertain but they were heavy and decisive.[23]

An improvised French fleet had not been sufficient to challenge the Spanish in the Atlantic triangle. In 1583 a Spanish fleet with about 16,000 men systematically conquered the Azores. It comprised five large sailing warships, 31 armed merchantmen, two galleasses, 12 galleys and 48 small vessels. This was the largest force any European power had sent out in the Atlantic up to then, and it indicates both the rising Spanish ability to organise large sailing battle fleets and the importance of the Azores in their Atlantic strategy.

The conquest of Portugal was the start of a general Spanish offensive in the Atlantic and Western Europe which lasted until 1588. Peace in the Mediterranean and massively increased shipping of American silver were two preconditions. The galley fleet remained strong to secure the former and the convoys from America were the lifeline which secured the latter. The Army of Flanders was reinvigorated and became again a highly efficient force under the Duke of Parma, who, unlike his predecessor Alba, was also a skilled politician. In 1582–85 Parma retook most of the rebellious provinces in a series of offensives, sieges and political compromises with the elite groups. In 1579–81, the seven provinces in Northern Netherlands had formed a union and declared themselves independent, but their situation became increasingly desperate. Dunkirk and Nieupoort on the coast of Flanders were taken in 1583 giving Parma ports where he began to create a force of light ships for attacks on trade and an invasion of England. However, the supply lines for his army remained the 'Spanish Road' as the shallow coast outside the Flanders ports was closed to ships from Spain by the small Dutch warships. William of Orange was assassinated in 1584 and the great port of Antwerp fell to Parma's army in 1585. By 1585 the new Dutch Republic had lost much of its territory. Holland, Zeeland and Utrecht, protected by the small ships of the new navy and the Rhine–Maas delta were still beyond Parma's control, but, if no help were to arrive, the future looked bleak.

The Anglo-Spanish struggle 1585–1603

In May 1585 the Spanish government seized northern shipping, including English merchantmen, in Spanish ports. The intention was almost certainly not to start a war with England, but the event came as an unusually convenient pretext for an English government which had already decided to take fateful steps towards war with Spain. England sent a small army to the Netherlands to stem Parma's offensive. At sea an English fleet of privateers and two of the Queen's ships sailed to the West Indies under Francis Drake. It carried 2,300 soldiers and early in 1586 took and ransomed Santo Domingo and Cartagena, two of the most important Spanish cities in the region. Spanish vulnerability was demonstrated and the threat against the supply of silver damaged Spanish credit in Europe.[24]

During 1586, Philip II decided to make a decisive strike against his enemies in north-western Europe. A successful invasion of England would destroy the base of attacks against his empire and stop foreign support to the Dutch. As Philip also became involved in the renewed French civil war, it began to look like a gigantic effort to create Spanish hegemony in Western Europe. The old man in the Escorial might have believed that he only defended his inheritance and the traditional religion, but, for his enemies, he looked like a contender for a universal Christian empire.[25]

This was the background to the drama that unfolded at sea during 1587/88. Philip II and his admiral Santa Cruz began to concentrate a great fleet in Lisbon, his new Atlantic naval base. During the spring and early summer of 1587 an English fleet under Drake made a cruise to the Iberian coast, attacked Cadiz and destroyed or captured 24 ships, some of them large. It later captured a large and richly-laden Portuguese ship from the East Indies. At Cadiz, the English fleet was attacked by galleys which were repulsed with greater ease than in earlier actions during the sixteenth century. The attack delayed the Spanish preparations as they had to search for Drake's fleet and protect the Atlantic convoys with their own. Plans to send it to the Channel during 1587 had finally to be cancelled. In early 1588 Santa Cruz died and the Duke of Medina Sidonia was appointed as his successor. Like many other events connected with 1588 this appointment, perfectly natural in its own time, has raised much controversy. Medina Sidonia was an able administrator who coordinated the final preparations of the fleet in an efficient way and his hesitation to sail may have been based on good judgement rather than lack of self-confidence. For good reasons he doubted if he had the right instrument for the planned operation in the Channel.[26]

The Portuguese navy was the nucleus of the great Armada, but most of it was mobilised in the traditional Spanish way, with armed merchantmen hired from Castile's Biscay provinces and from Andalucia, Italy, Ragusa and Venice. From Philip's kingdom of Naples came four large galleasses and a late decision to cancel the westbound *Tierra Firme* convoy in 1588 made the Castilian galleons available. The total force included 20 sailing warships (*galeones*) with a total displacement of around 12,000 tonnes, 47 armed merchantmen (*naos*) of around 32,000 tonnes, four galleasses (possibly around 1,000 tonnes each), four galleys, 21 transports (*urcas*) and 31 small vessels for scouting and dispatch-carrying, nearly all smaller than 100 tonnes. The fighting ships in the Armada had a total displacement of around 50,000 tonnes. The three largest of the *galeones* were of around 1,000 tonnes, but, among the armed merchantmen, there were no less than 11 with a displacement of around 1,000–1,200 tonnes.[27] There were about 8,000 seamen, 19,000 soldiers and 2,000 oarsmen on the fleet when it left Lisbon in May 1588.[28]

This huge fleet, known to posterity as the Invincible Armada, is usually regarded as the greatest sailing fleet ever assembled in Europe up to then. This is possible, although we know too little about the French Channel fleet of 1545 to be certain. The English had commissioned 23 major royal warships of about 250 to 1,500 tonnes displacement, a total of about 18,000 tonnes, ten minor royal warships, one galley and no less than 192 private vessels. However, most of the latter were small and far from all took part in the fighting. Thirty private ships had a displacement of (probably) around 300 to 600 tonnes (total around 11,000 tonnes) and may be regarded as front-line warships. About 30 others were of around 200 to 250 tonnes displacement (total around 7,000 tonnes) while the majority of the private ships were of little importance. The fleet may have had around 16,000 men, of which only 1,500 were soldiers, although these figures are uncertain.[29]

The purpose-built royal warships represented a much larger part of the English fighting power than on the Spanish side and some of the private English ships were real warships, built for privateering. The gun armament of the two contending fleets gave the English a marked quantitative advantage and this seems to have been increased by a qualitative advantage in gun-handling and in the ability of the ships to manoeuvre into a favourable position for a gun-fight.[30] The Spanish fleet could only win a battle if it came to close combat and boarding and, with inferior armament and a fleet of slow and unweatherly merchantmen, it could not force the English to such a battle. Medina Sidonia did not act as if he intended to defeat the English fleet in a major battle to gain command of the sea. His strategy was based on the idea that the Armada should sail through the Channel to its narrowest part. There it would protect the transport of an invasion army of elite solders from the Army of Flanders. The plan made sense if it was based on the assumption that

English gunnery was not numerous and efficient enough to sink or disable a substantial number of his huge fleet where the sheer size of the ships enabled them to survive a number of hits. Losses might be expected, but, if they could be kept within acceptable bounds the Armada might be successful.

Such an assumption was not unrealistic. The effect of English gunnery in 1588 was indeed not devastating although we will never know if the Armada really would have been able to protect an invasion flotilla in the open sea where the more manoeuvrable English ships probably would have concentrated their attacks on the transport vessels. But the problem was how these vessels should come out to the open sea. The Duke of Parma had created a large invasion flotilla in the Flanders ports, but the coast outside these ports was shallow and inaccessible for the large ships of the Armada.[31] Light Spanish naval forces available in July 1588 were inferior to the light forces of the Dutch and English fleets which would have sunk or captured much of the invasion flotilla before it could reach the deep water where the Armada would have a chance to protect it. The enigma with the Spanish planning is why they brought with them only four galleys when they actually had at least 80 galleys available in the Mediterranean. The French had shown that it was possible to transfer a Mediterranean galley fleet to the Channel in 1512 and 1545, and galleys with heavy guns were the obvious answer to English and Dutch shallow-water forces.[32]

The summer of 1588 seems to have been unusually stormy and the Armada was seriously delayed by heavy weather. The four galleys actually never reached the Channel. The fleet finally entered the Channel on 20/30 July (Julian/Gregorian calendars). The English fleet was divided. Most of it was in Plymouth, guarding the entrance of the Channel, while a smaller force was in the Narrows, guarding Parma's invasion flotilla in company with the Dutch. The English, under the command of the Lord Admiral, Lord Howard of Effingham, with the privateering veterans Francis Drake, John Hawkins and Martin Frobisher as sub-commanders, easily gained the wind from the Spanish and followed the Armada when it proceeded east along the English coast. From a distance they attacked the Spanish fleet with gunfire but, with the exception of two ships which suffered accidents, Spanish losses were small. The main effect of the English shadowing of the Spanish fleet was that it made it impossible for it to make a landing on the English coast or anchor in the protected water inside the Isle of Wight.

On 27 July/6 August, the Spanish fleet anchored on the open roadstead off Calais and the English western fleet joined the squadron in the Narrows. Nothing had happened to solve the problem of how Parma's invasion army would pass the sand-banks guarded by light Dutch ships. The alternative, that the Armada might land its own army, could not be executed in the presence of an undefeated English fleet which effectively might interfere with such a landing or defeat the Spanish ships if the soldiers were landed. Both lack of light forces and inferiority in gunpower had doomed the enterprise to failure. No explanation for this failure other than Philip II's wishful thinking has ever been found – no Spanish admiral or general had assured him that the plan was feasible.

Failure did not in itself mean catastrophe. That phase began on the night of 29 July/8 August when the English made a fireship attack on the Armada. The Spanish ships cut their cables and escaped (except one galleass which ran aground), but in that process many ships sailed far to leeward and the fleet lost its earlier cohesion. Medina Sidonia was able to form a defensive line with several of the best ships but, with many of the troop-carrying Spanish ships in a leeward position, the English felt free to close for a fight with guns at decisive ranges. English gunnery proved superior. During the battle off Gravelines one Spanish merchantman sank, two galleons ran ashore and were lost and other Spanish ships suffered considerable damage.

The Spanish fleet was now in a critical situation. Ammunition and supplies were running out, ships were damaged and there was no friendly deep-water harbour in the North Sea or the Channel. To sail back through the Channel meant fighting both the English and the prevailing westerly winds, and the Spanish fleet had to make the long return journey to Spain northward around Scotland and Ireland. Many ships were damaged and 28 ships sank at sea or were wrecked on the coasts, often when trying to take on fresh water. The large Mediterranean merchantmen were particularly unsuited to Atlantic weather and suffered badly, eight of ten being lost.[33] The losses of men were very high, although, in that respect, the English also suffered large losses in the months after the battle. Epidemic disease and bad logistics caused the death of thousands of seamen in a fleet where the losses in action were minimal.

The Armada campaign of 1588 has perhaps more than any other naval event become part of mainstream historiography. Maybe the battle of Salamis 480 BC is comparable and for the same reason: it was a decisive battle between a huge empire (Persia) and an upstart sea power (Athens). Fifteen eighty-eight has often been seen as a watershed – the year when Spanish expansion was changed into English and Dutch expansion. There is nothing fundamentally wrong with this interpretation, although Spain did remain the strongest power in Europe for several decades. Spain was never more so close to hegemony in Europe and the Atlantic as in 1588 and a different outcome might have had far-reaching consequences in England, the Netherlands and France. After 1588 Philip II ordered the Army of Flanders to support the Catholic League in France with the predictable result that the Dutch in the 1590s were able to recover much lost territory. The support of the League proved to be without lasting result as Henry IV was able to gain control over France and end the civil wars.

The events in the Channel undoubtedly had a psychological effect as a blow to the Spanish reputation for invincibility, a reputation which seems to have misled Philip when he drew up the strategy before 1588. From a naval perspective the outcome was not sensational as it confirmed a century of technical, tactical and strategic change in warfare at sea, demonstrated in the

160

Indian Ocean, in the Baltic and already in 1545 in the Channel. It revealed growing north-western technical superiority at sea and made it clear that modern technology had made it more difficult to invade a power which defended itself at sea. A century earlier an invading army required only sufficient transport capacity. Now it required a superior gun-armed fleet as well. For an island state like England this meant that national defence could be organised more cheaply around a fleet which could also be used for offensive operations at long distance.

The first English post-1588 attempt to carry out a seaborne offensive was not a success. A fleet under Drake with a strong army was sent to the Iberian peninsula. It had orders to attack the remaining Armada ships at Santander, to support Dom Antonio in his attempt to raise the Portuguese against Spain and if possible intercept the silver fleet at the Azores. Drake did not even sail to Santander and the Portuguese showed no interest in supporting the pretender. By 1590 it was clear that no side could win a decisive victory and that it had become a war of attrition between two coalitions, Philip II's empire and the French Catholic League against the French king, England and the Dutch Republic. From a maritime point of view it was primarily an Anglo-Spanish war where the Channel, the Atlantic triangle and the Caribbean were the main theatres of operations. The English as before operated with a royal navy in co-operation with private investors in privateering and with small-scale privateers who acted independently. After the failure in 1589 the government did, however, take firmer control over the joint venture operations. Spain radically changed her naval policy after 1588 and built a large state-controlled navy, the largest battle fleet which had existed in Europe up to then. This fleet has received little attention from historians.[34]

The Channel was controlled by the English fleet which could support limited English army interventions in northern France. These were of urgent importance for England as the Catholic League and Spain periodically were close to achieving full control over the French Channel coast. Neither of the two French sides in their civil war had a real navy, only small and improvised forces which supported military operations along the coast.[35] By 1595 the Spanish threat in the Channel was reduced although Brittany remained under pro-Spanish control until France and Spain concluded peace in 1598. The Dutch navy was as before mainly occupied in home waters.

In the Caribbean intense but usually small-scale trade warfare continued throughout the war. Primarily it was a war of attrition where Spain was forced to increase expenditure on convoys, fortifications and garrisons, while the English seldom gained the fabulous wealth they hoped for. The English privateers were normally operating with small ships and attacked only local trade, not the great convoys. An exception was the large squadron of royal warships and privateers which Drake and Hawkins led in 1595/96 – their last voyage as both died in the Caribbean. The fleet failed in its main purpose, attacks on San Juan on Puerto Rico and Panama. In 1598 a private fleet led by the Earl of

Cumberland, one of the most important English investors in privateering, was able to take San Juan, but there was no possibility of keeping it permanently.

In the Atlantic triangle between the Azores, the Canary islands and the Iberian peninsula the English began to implement a more systematic strategy where the Spanish silver fleets and the Portuguese East Indiamen were the main objective. Squadrons of English ships patrolled the Portuguese-Spanish coast or the waters around the Azores. An early attempt with a three-month cruise had already been made in 1586. Another attempt was made in the autumn of 1589 and during 1590 one squadron was sent to the Iberian coast and another to the Azores. In 1591 another squadron sent to the Azores was surprised by a superior Spanish force and one ship, *Revenge*, was taken in a famous fight. These English fleets took few prizes, but they delayed enemy shipping and silver shipments and forced them to sail during seasons with bad weather. The Caribbean convoys had to be protected by large fleets of warships, a system which proved efficient but expensive for Spain. The huge and richly-laden Portuguese East India carracks were more vulnerable targets and a few were captured.

In June 1596 a considerable part of the English fleet, joined by a Dutch squadron of armed merchantmen launched a surprise attack on Cadiz. The fleet attacked and defeated a Spanish squadron in a battle where English gunnery seems to have been more destructive than in 1588. *San Felipe*, one of the largest warships in the world, and another large Spanish warship were destroyed and two large warships were taken. Later two Portuguese warships and 40 merchantmen, including a westbound Caribbean convoy with its rich cargo, were burnt to avoid capture. An army was landed and took Cadiz which was partly destroyed. The raid was executed with skill and must be seen as the apogee of English efficiency in maritime warfare in the pre-1650 period. It cast doubt on Spain's ability to protect her trans-Atlantic trade and contributed to the financial crisis of 1596, but Queen Elizabeth was upset by the lack of booty for the royal treasury. Spain quickly organised a counterstroke with a large fleet which sailed to the Channel in the autumn. It was dispersed by gales and no fewer than 25 ships, mainly transports, were wrecked on the Spanish coast close to Ferrol.

In 1597, the English fleet attempted to take Ferrol where much of the Spanish fleet was based. When that failed owing to severe weather a large part of the English fleet went to the Azores where it again failed to take a silver fleet. In its absence, the Spanish fleet in Ferrol made a new autumn attack in the Channel. One hundread and thirty-six ships, most of them rather small, with crews of 4,000 seamen and 8,600 soldiers (less than half of the Armada of 1588) set sail for a surprise attack on Falmouth. This port, close to the tip of the Cornwall peninsula and close to Spanish-controlled Brittany, was to be made into a bridgehead to which further reinforcements would be sent in the following spring in order to establish Spanish power on both sides of the western entrance of the Channel. This time the Spanish reached the Channel undetected, only to be dispersed by another autumn gale. Twenty-eight ships were lost. The Spanish armadas of 1596/97 were attempted in defiance of the Atlantic climate. Not even in the twentieth century have invasions in the Channel been attempted in the autumn when the equinoctial gales are a normal phenomenon. Spain was, however, forced into this gamble as surprise offered the only chance of invading England successfully. The last attack was made only because the old and dying Philip II insisted on it.

The new king Philip III (r. 1598–1621), or his advisers, began to try new ideas. One was an embargo on Dutch shipping to Spanish ports. Up to then the Dutch had traded with their enemies, but Spain now began to wage a trade war on the Republic in the belief that the trade had been more profitable to the Dutch than to them. In retaliation, the Dutch sent a fleet to the Spanish and Portuguese coast in 1599. They searched for suitable forms of attack and finally divided their forces for attacks against Guinea and Brazil. It was the largest Dutch naval expedition up to then, but it ended in a failure due to disease. The Spanish fleet which was sent out to find the Dutch was again struck by a gale and suffered severe losses.[36] The English, by now deeply committed against rebels in Ireland, feared that Spain planned a new invasion and mobilised the fleet. Actually, their intelligence reports had magnified a minor Spanish plan into a new Armada (The 'Invisible' Armada). Spain only intended to transfer six galleys to the Netherlands. It succeeded and for some years they showed that galleys had value as special forces in coastal waters.[37] Spain also had plans against Ireland, although it took them a long time to assemble a force. When it sailed in September 1601 the English were on their way to defeating the rebels. Some of the Spanish ships were again forced back by heavy weather and the 3,400 Spanish soldiers that landed at Kinsale could not achieve anything. In early 1602 they surrendered on condition they were allowed to return to Spain.[38]

In 1602 the English, assisted by the Dutch, decided to try to maintain a blockading fleet continuously on Portugal's and Spain's western coast in order to damage trade and check further offensive movements by the Spanish fleet. The blockade started in March and the fleet did not finally return until November, but there had been a break in the summer when a captured Portuguese East Indiaman was escorted to England. Only a limited number of ships could be on station at the same time and when they once sighted a convoy from the Caribbean they found that its escort was too strong for an attack. Nevertheless, the operation showed that the English had made progress in their ability to maintain a fleet in distant waters and early in 1603 they were preparing to repeat the operation. The death of Queen Elizabeth and the truce concluded by her successor James I made it unnecessary. England had, however, repeatedly shown that her fleet might cruise unhindered for long periods in the Atlantic triangle, a strategic area for Spain's Atlantic policy and communications. Technically and logistically they had begun to master the problems inherent in long-distance deployments of battle fleets, but their fleet was too small to achieve supremacy outside home waters.

Unfortunately we know little about Spanish sea power in the period 1589–1603.[39] There were great ambitions, but also great problems. There seems to have been technical difficulties with the ships, lack of seamen and logistical obstacles against the concentration of the large number of ships into an efficient battle fleet which could have defeated the English in the Atlantic triangle. The interaction of logistics, administration and strategy is unknown on the Spanish side. The failure to create a concentrated and mature battle fleet which could project Spanish power to north-western Europe and support Spanish policy in the Netherlands, northern France, England and Ireland is obvious. Spain could not protect her sea lines of communication to Northern Europe, nor seriously disturb the lines of communication of her northern enemies. As Spain had gained experience from the same war as England and the Netherlands, we must suspect that the Spanish institutional framework for learning, adaptation and change was deficient. But Spain had shown that she was able to defend her trade and the very important transfer of silver from America with such efficiency that English attacks against them became unprofitable. By 1603 both sides were ready to conclude peace. The first war in the Atlantic was at an end but another was soon to follow. It was a part of the first global war at sea.

10

THE FIRST GLOBAL WAR AT
SEA, 1600–1650

Empires, embargoes and entrepôts

From around 1600 Europeans began to fight their maritime wars on a global scale. The conflict between the new Dutch Republic and the two Iberian powers spread to America, Africa and Asia. It was not the first global war. The major non-European powers: China, Japan, the Mughal empire in India, Persia and the Ottoman empire were not involved except as trading partners to the contenders. It was a maritime war between Europeans which affected trade, islands and coastal areas around the world, and as such it was a telling demonstration of how much Europe differed from the rest of the world. Some Europeans now had both the ambition and the ability to connect the world in a maritime network of trade and power. Future generations were to turn this into a network in which non-European powers became dependent on the western peninsula of the Eurasian continent.

The Dutch-Iberian power struggle outside Europe was a part of their long conflict in Europe (1568–1648). Its origin was the Dutch revolt against their Habsburg ruler, but by the early seventeenth century it had become a war between an increasingly powerful Dutch Republic and the Spanish-Portuguese empire. When a 12–year truce was concluded in 1609 the armed conflict continued in Asia and the Dutch expansion there was a main cause behind the renewal of the war in 1621.[1]

The confrontation at sea was economic as much as naval. Efficiency in trade and shipping was intertwined with efficiency in fighting, and naval strategy was co-ordinated with mercantile strategy. By the 1580s the Spanish Habsburgs ruled the largest maritime empire the world had ever seen. It had been created by dynastic alliances, proficiency in arms, ventures in maritime exploration, and trade protected by monopoly claims and naval power in the Mediterranean and the Indian Ocean. Dynamic Iberian and Italian maritime economies had every chance of creating a Habsburg primacy in world trade if their shipping could be protected and promoted with efficiency. In the entrepôts of Seville, Lisbon, Antwerp and Genoa (aligned with Spain) trade in Western Europe and the Mediterranean might have been linked with the

Habsburg-controlled network of trans-oceanic trade in a coherent system of world trade.

The Habsburg rulers and the military-political elite in Spain had other ideas. To them, control of maritime trade might be used as an instrument of political power, rather than for economic transformation. Some aristocrats, especially Olivares, the leading Spanish minister from 1622 to 1643, understood that thriving merchants were useful as objects of taxation and a source of credits. But the idea that capitalism in itself – if it was allowed to act with dynamic force – might create technical, naval, mercantile and even political structures that might give the empire strength was alien to most members of the ruling elite. Having brought much of the world trade under its control, the main question for the Habsburg regime became how to use this power in order to *deny* much of Europe the possibility of normal trade with Spain and Portugal. Enemies and rivals of the Iberian powers were not to be allowed to trade in ports controlled by these powers. The instrument of this policy became embargoes on trade with the enemy, a policy that was introduced with much determination in 1598 and again in an even more systematic form from 1621 when the war with the Dutch Republic was resumed after the truce ended.

The Spanish embargo policy was confronted with a totally different Dutch policy, where 'trading with the enemy' (*handel op den vijand*) was officially approved. Such trade was allowed in order to give Dutch maritime interests incomes and profits but also in order to provide the Dutch state, and particularly its navy, with income through the sale of licences (*licenten*) for trade with the enemy. Such licences might be sold to Dutch as well as to foreign shipping and the price might be adapted to suit Dutch economic and political interests. The enemy, in this case the Spanish-controlled southern Netherlands, Spain, Portugal and Habsburg-controlled Italy, got most of the products they wanted, but their trade was increasingly brought under the control of their Dutch enemy. The Spanish embargoes were based on the idea that the Dutch were more vulnerable to economic warfare than Spain. Dutch trading with the enemy policy expressed the idea that an economy with low barriers favoured them more than total blockade would have done. It was a policy based on the belief that economic activity which gave Dutch capital opportunity to gain profits also gave the Dutch state financial muscle to wage war.[2]

The efficiency of the Spanish embargo policy has been evaluated differently by historians. It has been common to minimise its importance and put the emphasis on the Dutch ability to circumvent it with contraband trade. Jonathan Israel, who has made detailed investigations of the problem, claims that the embargoes were efficient in denying the Dutch access to Iberian ports. Trade might continue with the help of neutral shipping or through more or less clandestine contraband trade, but that made transaction and transportation costs markedly higher. However, he also underlines that the Dutch reacted with innovations. When they were denied the right to trade with Asia, Africa and America through Iberian ports, they sailed to these parts of the world themselves in order to trade, often in armed conflict with the Iberian powers. The Dutch lost trade with Habsburg-controlled ports in Europe, but gained trade with the rest of the world. The Iberian powers on their side were damaged economically by their self-imposed embargoes. They were further damaged by their loss of monopoly trade with the rest of the world and their increased protection costs for that trade.[3]

The combined effect of Dutch efficiency in trade, shipping and warfare at sea, the Spanish embargoes and Spain's inability to protect her own European shipping was that Holland and Zeeland became the first central entrepôt for world trade. The Dutch were able to retain control over trade between Northern and Western Europe (except Spain and Portugal) and they gradually gained control over much of the trade from the Indian Ocean, as well as a substantial part of the trade with Africa and America. Spain was more efficient in denying the Dutch access to the Mediterranean, but that stimulated Dutch attempts to divert the traditional Levant trade with Asia to the Cape of Good Hope route, thus contributing to the economic decline of the Mediterranean. Both the Spanish empire and the Dutch in the late sixteenth century had the opportunity to create world supremacy in trade. As the established imperial power with around ten times as many inhabitants in its many dependencies in Europe, Spain seemed to have every advantage, especially during the periods when they had no enemies except the Dutch (1603–25, 1631–35). But the global struggle ended with undoubted Dutch supremacy in world trade, a considerable Dutch empire and Spain and Portugal at war with each other.[4]

It seems obvious that the methods used in this struggle and its outcome reflect two different types of state formation. The federal Dutch Republic, its navy and its advanced maritime technology, the Dutch supremacy in world trade, the world entrepôt and the empire, were all created as parts of efforts to win an economic and political war with the huge Spanish empire. The state was created by an elite of capitalist entrepreneurs in trade and industry who looked upon Europe and the world as a series of opportunities for commercial investments. Increasing control of the sea opened even more opportunities for investment and, in a process that has striking similarities with entrepreneurial efforts to exploit unexpected opportunities, the Dutch gradually created the maritime instruments suited to the different types of war they fought – in home waters, along the European trade routes, and in trans-oceanic areas. Spain and Portugal were territorial states where landowning elite groups were thinking in terms of European power politics and where seaborne trade was a source from which resources might be extracted. To capitalist groups in the Habsburg empire, their own state increasingly became a burden which made demands and enforced embargoes without encouraging entrepreneurial skills in seaborne trade under conditions of uncertainty and risk.[5]

These different perceptions of the sea by the two types of ruling elite are probably our most important explanation for the different maritime and naval strategies adopted in this global war. To the Iberian rulers the sea was primarily a means of communication with their European and trans-oceanic empires and on land as well as by sea they based their actions on the logic of coercion. The transfer of troops, silver and spices (controlled by the Portuguese state monopoly) was a prime concern. Attacks against Dutch trade got high priority from the 1620s as an important part of the economic war against the Dutch. Protection of Iberian commercial interests was lower on the agenda and the ruling elite had few members who had gained their fortunes through entrepreneurial efforts in maritime trade or shipping. Many members of the elite had indeed gained from trade opportunities received as rewards for service to the state or through their power to circumvent monopoly restrictions, but such behaviour did not promote entrepreneurship. The elite in the Dutch Republic was the very opposite of this. Those who were successful at sea joined the elite and reinforced its ability to lead a maritime war. Opportunities connected with the sea were easily perceived by this elite and perception was rapidly transformed into action whenever the Dutch were able to gain advantage over the Iberians in technology, trade and warfare. The result was a new European and global network of trade centred in the Dutch entrepôt, and a new European great power based on resources organised according to a capitalist logic.[6]

Dutch maritime policy aimed at control and development of trade as the economic base of the society and the state. Trade had to be protected but also promoted, taxed but not to the extent that it lost its attraction for investors. The opportunities for profitable trade created by changing political, economic and technical circumstances had to be used quickly and ruthlessly, and the state had to adjust its policy to that. Technology and competence for warfare at sea was intertwined with the promotion of trade. Alliances were concluded in order to protect Dutch commercial interests and the basic security of Dutch territory – not for profitless prestige, territorial ambition or religious ideals. The contrast with Spanish obsession with reputation, religion and European-wide political systems promoted by American silver and dynastic ties is obvious.

The Dutch attitude is typified by her allowing trade with the enemy, and the state made this into an important base for taxes. The Dutch state was also involved in the creation of two monopoly companies for overseas trade and warfare in the Indian Ocean and the Atlantic, the *Verenigde Oostindische Compagnie* (VOC) in 1602 and the *Westindische Compagnie* (WIC) in 1621. Both were owned by many shareholders and the success of these combined naval, military and economic activities could be seen in the stock market value of the shares. These monopoly companies were innovative successful organisations for overseas warfare which attempted both to attack the enemy and protect and promote the companies' own economic activities. The Iberian powers had no comparable system for measuring the efficiency of their overseas activities and various attempts in the 1620s to imitate the Dutch companies failed.

The decentralisation of the navy into five provincial admiralties was also a reflection of the Dutch attitude to warfare at sea. It has often been regarded as a weakness but if seen as a part of the mechanism by which the Dutch society mobilised resources and monitored how the state used them it may have been efficient. It was a way for the powerful trading interests to ensure that the navy was used for trade protection in a way that suited these interests, which after all were responsible for financing the war through taxes and loans. Whatever the shortcomings of the Dutch system it compares favourably with the Iberian system where the state taxed the trade and protected it in a way that suited the non-mercantile elite groups. The result was that Iberian maritime and mercantile power declined dramatically.

Basic facts about the events of the global Dutch-Iberian confrontation are known from a rather large but uneven literature, and many articles which normally concentrate on one country, one area or one problem. There are however also great gaps in our knowledge of these events. The size, armament and crews of the fleets that operated against each other have not been the subject of much analysis. Many of the combatants were armed merchantmen, not specialised warships, which complicates comparisons of strength. The logistical aspects of these very long-distance operations have never been systematically studied. How were ships maintained very far from their bases, how were their crews kept alive and how were the Dutch able to establish themselves in areas where Spain and Portugal already had advantages in bases? Fleets which operated outside Europe were normally small but the presence of small forces at the right place and the right moment was often decisive. Only the more important operations can be covered in this brief text. It is also not possible to cover the war of attrition against trade which was the crux of the conflict both in Europe and overseas. It was also a rather special type of trade warfare as the Dutch and the Iberians were economic competitors in the same trades. It was equally as important for them to delay the enemy's trade and increase its protection costs as it was to capture enemy shipping. This interaction between economy and warfare may have been the most significant part of the struggle.

War overseas, 1598–1650

The rapid Dutch rise to primacy in European trade began around 1590 when the Spanish Army of Flanders ceased offensive operations in northern Netherlands in order to support the Catholic League in France. In the same year Philip II lifted the embargo on trade with the Dutch Republic. The Dutch army, supported by Dutch control of coastal waters and internal waterways, began to reconquer the landward provinces and Dutch shipping around the coasts of Europe increased rapidly. Dutch ships continued to sail to Portugal, Spain and the Mediterranean until 1598 when Spain declared a new embargo on trade with the Dutch. The effect was the opposite to Spanish intentions. Unlike the English and French, the Dutch had up to then showed little interest in plunder and interloping trade against Spanish and Portuguese interests overseas. This may have given Spain the idea that the rebellious merchants were unwilling to take risks and fight overseas. But from 1598/99 the Dutch began to sail to the East and West Indies and Africa on a large scale to obtain the products they needed for trade and production in Europe and which they had earlier bought in Spain and Portugal. These overseas ventures, based on interest in trade, soon developed into the most efficient naval, military and economic attacks which had been launched against Spain's and Portugal's empires up to that time.[7]

By 1600 trade in pepper and other valuable commodities in the Indian Ocean had been controlled by the Portuguese for almost a century. This control had been far from perfect and from the mid-sixteenth century much spices also went along the traditional route through the Red Sea and the Levant.[8] But Portugal's mercantile and naval presence in the East Indies was still impressive and represented great potential for future development. The strategic bases were Goa, Diu, Hormuz and Malacca and the most effective naval presence was maintained along the west coast of India and in the straits close to Malacca. From America Spain had established an entrepôt in Manila to which Chinese ships came for trade. In order to protect this trade, Spanish warships were based in the Philippines and Spain monopolised the trans-Pacific trade with armed merchantmen sailing between Manila and Acapulco in Mexico.

The Dutch penetration of the East Indies started in the Moluccas, the famous Spice Islands, rich in cloves and nutmeg. Fleets of armed merchantmen of the type that had been developed in north-western Europe began to cruise and trade in the area. The large archipelago of present-day Indonesia was dependent on sea lines of communication. Any power which controlled them with armed ships could force the local rulers to trade on conditions set by themselves. Blockade and armed force were often used to establish a Dutch monopoly on this spice trade. Just like Spain and Portugal the Dutch also found it expedient to admit Chinese merchants and ships to trade under their protection as these were often very efficient and there were few Europeans who actually wished to settle in that part of the world. The islands were far from the Portuguese centre of power in India and far from any major Asian power and therefore not vulnerable to attack. The Dutch could also operate in this area without being dependent on the monsoon winds which in the Indian Ocean made it impossible for the superior sea power to take the initiative during certain parts of the year. Indonesia was windward of the Indian Ocean which made it easy for Dutch ships to project power into this area.[9]

The unification of various Dutch trading interests into the VOC in 1602 focused these efforts and increased the use of violence. In 1605 Amboina, Ternate and Tidore in the Moluccas were conquered by the Dutch. Spain counter-attacked on the latter two islands but the Dutch had gained control over some of the richest sources of spices in Asia. They continued with blockades of Malacca in 1606–8 and the foundation of a factory at Pulicat in south-east India where they bought Indian textiles on a large scale for export to Indonesia in exchange for spices. A system of Dutch-controlled intra-Asian trade had been founded and under the protection of armed force it developed into an important source of income.

The Portuguese reaction to the Dutch intrusions came in 1605–7 when unusually large fleets were sent from Lisbon to the east for trade and warfare. The results were disastrous. The number of ships *returning* to Lisbon with spices actually fell and their incomes declined.[10] The contest revealed both institutional and technical weaknesses in the well-established Portuguese trading system. The very large ships (*naus*) used in the trade with India were vulnerable to the weather if they sailed in the wrong season. Their large size, intended as a protection against Asian attacks with a large number of men, was no advantage when they were attacked by smaller but well-armed Dutch East Indiamen. Events during the war often forced the *naus* to sail in the wrong season and they often turned back damaged or suffered total wreck. The loss of income from trade caused further delays and further sailings in the wrong season in a vicious circle. Meanwhile the Dutch with their more moderately-sized and well-armed East Indiamen established a fairly safe shipping service between the Indian Ocean and Europe which appeared almost invulnerable to Portuguese counter-measures.[11] This set the pattern for several decades of Dutch–Portuguese stuggles. Portuguese inability to modernise their shipping technology is an interesting case of inertia in an established organisation.[12]

The truce of 1609 was short in the Indies. The Portuguese attacked Pulicat in 1612 and in retaliation a Dutch squadron took two Spanish forts on Tidore in 1613. The war continued with raids and counter-raids in the Moluccas and the Philippines and both sides sent reinforcements. A Dutch squadron of four warships sailed for south-east Asia via the Straits of Magellan and met two Spanish warships and around five armed merchantmen off Canete in Peru on 17 and 18 July 1615. The action was a decisive Dutch victory where their superior gunfire defeated a superior number of men. It was the first fleet action ever in the Pacific and Spain was forced to improve its defence system along the American coast.[13]

Meanwhile, in 1615/16 Spain and Portugal attempted to concentrate their Asian fleets in order to drive the Dutch out of south-east Asia. The Portuguese squadron of four large ships from Goa first met a fleet from Muslim Aceh on northern Sumatra which burnt one of their ships. The remaining three were destroyed by the Dutch off Malacca in December 1615. The expedition was the culmination of a series of Portuguese naval disasters which in large part reflected mismanagement.[14] The Spanish fleet was blockaded in Manila from late 1616 but on 15 and 16 April 1617 it defeated a scattered Dutch fleet in a hard-fought battle at Playa Honda. One effect of the Dutch presence in south-east Asia was that Portugal had to cease sending the huge yearly *nau* to Macao and Japan ('the great ship from Amacon') where it had made great profits from trade between China and Japan. It was replaced by smaller and swifter ships which appear to have been successful. This makes one wonder why the Portuguese did not reform their shipping to Europe in a similar way.[15]

In 1619 the Dutch founded Batavia on Java as their capital and main base in Asia. This was part of a new grand imperial strategy outlined by the governor-general Jan Pieterszoon Coen. Ultimately he hoped to make the VOC the dominating force in Asian trade by creating fortified trading factories from Hormuz and Aden to Nagasaki, conquering Portuguese and Spanish positions and making Batavia the central entrepôt for trade between Europe and Asia. In the early 1620s the Dutch also briefly co-operated with the English East India Company, EIC (founded in 1600), in actions against Spain and Portugal. Most of the offensives were joint operations although the Dutch had much larger resources. In 1621/22 Manila was blockaded, interrupting the trade in silk between China and America. Another fleet cruised between Goa and Mocambique in 1621/22 and a third fleet blockaded Malacca. A fourth fleet was sent to Macao in 1622 in an operation which aimed at controlling China's foreign trade and especially denying Spain and Portugal access to it. Macao repulsed an attack and the Dutch fleet began to harass Chinese shipping instead. After an attempt to establish a fortified island base on the Pescadores the Dutch settled in 1624 on Taiwan where they created a successful base for Chinese trade at Fort Zeelandia on the west coast. In the same year, a Dutch fleet arrived on the other side of the Pacific with the intention of establishing a base on the west coast of America. It was the largest naval expedition to the Pacific in the sixteenth and seventeenth centuries but it found Spanish defence much improved since 1615 and achieved little.[16]

The Portuguese began to build up their naval strength in the Indian Ocean from 1619 with the dispatch of several warships (galeaos) in addition to the large merchantmen (naus). The results were disappointing. A Portuguese squadron of five warships began to blockade the Persian Gulf against intrusions from the EIC in 1620. It was twice defeated by four English armed merchantmen which must have been markedly superior in gunnery. The Shah of Persia was thus encouraged to co-operate with the EIC fleet in besieging and taking Hormuz. This and the destruction of the Portuguese warships were accomplished in the spring of 1622. One of the key fortresses in the Portuguese system designed by Afonso de Albuquerque had been lost. In July 1622 three Portuguese naus from Europe were intercepted by the Dutch and English and destroyed off the Mocambique coast with much silver on board. A galeao carrying the new viceroy, a great-grandson of Vasco da Gama, escaped. A major Portuguese fleet which arrived during 1624 was partly able to restore Portuguese prestige in the western Indian Ocean. It fought an even battle with a joint EIC-VOC force at Hormuz in February 1625 and later in the year it had some successes against EIC ships. But it was only able to force the English and Dutch to sail in convoys, not to seriously disturb their activities.[17]

172

The Dutch seaborne offensives in Asia during 1621–23 were expensive and not universally successful. They had, however, imposed great costs and losses on the enemy and they were the most spectacular example of Dutch warfare in any part of the world in these years. Madrid had restarted the war under the illusion that the Dutch could be forced out of the Indies. Instead, the Iberians faced a ruthless offensive and had to fight for survival. From 1626 to 1635 the East Indies was a comparative calm area where the VOC, EIC, Portugal and Spain concentrated on defending their own trade and exploring their commercial abilities. The Dutch came out best in that competition. They were able to halt the Muslim trade in spices from south-east Asia to the Red Sea and the Levant and they established themselves in the trade with Japan and China. The English EIC, which had been ousted from south-east Asia in 1623 after a conflict with the Dutch, concentrated on peaceful trade with western India and Persia. They concluded peace with the Portuguese in 1635.

In the 1590s Dutch merchants had begun to penetrate the Caribbean where they traded hides, brazilwood, tobacco, sugar, cacao and indigo in exchange for cloth and other manufactured products much in demand among the Spanish settlers. But the main impetus for expansion came with the Spanish embargo in 1598 which cut off the Dutch from Iberian salt for their herring industry and export trade to the Baltic. In order to get salt, fleets of Dutch merchantmen sailed from 1599 to the large salt pan at Punta de Araya in Venezuela. This had not been exploited by Spain and in the following years it became a major source of salt, especially for ships from northern Holland. At the same time the Dutch began to discover opportunities for trade and settlement in the Caribbean and northern Brazil. Spain responded with depopulation of the area, restrictions on crops that might interest the Dutch, and in September 1605 sent a large fleet that attacked the Dutch salt-ships at Punta de Araya. These counter-measures were effective for a time but also self-destructive. The alternative of competing economically with the Dutch by developing a more efficient trade with their own colonies seems not to have been considered. The Dutch also penetrated Guinea and other parts of Africa where the Portuguese claimed control over trade. These conflicts continued during the years of truce (1609–21) when the Dutch argued that they only settled and traded in areas where Iberians were absent while the latter held firmly to the belief that all American and African trade belonged to them.[18]

The idea of forming a West India Company for large-scale trade and conquest in the Caribbean and South Atlantic had appeared early, but the Dutch state shelved the project during the truce. In 1621 it was implemented on a grand scale and attracted capital which had found that trade in Europe had become less profitable when the war started again. Early in 1624 it was ready to launch its first major expedition, an attack against Bahia (Salvador), the capital of Brazil, with 26 ships and 3,300 men. Bahia quickly fell but the Iberian reaction was prompt and truly imperial. A joint Spanish-Portuguese force of 56 ships and 12,500 men – the largest European expedition to the New World up to then – was sent to Bahia which was retaken in May 1625.[19] The Dutch garrison was demoralised by the unexpectedly large counter-attack and did not await the relief expedition sent by the WIC which arrived a month later. Most of this force sailed to the Caribbean where it cruised until mid-1626. It made a serious attempt to take San Juan de Puerto Rico but failed due to determined resistance. Another part of the force sailed to Guinea where it suffered a serious defeat by Africans and Portuguese when it attempted to take the fortress Elmina. These and other setbacks showed that Iberian power in the south Atlantic was more deeply entrenched than the Dutch had hoped but they had at least forced their enemy to spend large sums which could not then be used against the Dutch in Europe or the East Indies. But for the private investors in the WIC it was not much consolation that their losses had helped the national effort and profited the shareholders of the VOC.

The WIC changed its strategy from conquest to trade warfare. This had its most spectacular result on 8 September 1628 when the homebound convoy of New Spain was captured by a Dutch squadron under Piet Hein in the Bay of Matanzas on the northern coast of Cuba where it had sought protection. In a fashion which was probably common in these convoys the four warships loaded with silver were also crammed with merchandise in such a way that they were unable to use many of their guns. The crews panicked, ran the ships aground but failed to burn them.[20] The silver, at least 11.5 million guilders, represented a considerable part of the yearly income of the Spanish state and the consequences for the Spanish war effort in Europe were serious. Matanzas was one of the most spectacular events at sea during the sailing-ship epoch. In 1630, with improved finances the WIC could launch an invasion of northern Brazil. Sixty-seven ships with 7,000 men took Pernambuco and its capital, Recife. The Dutch began a colonising project which was successful for 15 years.[21]

Spain and Portugal were only able to send limited reinforcements to Brazil to stem the Dutch expansion. For once a major fleet action took place. On 12 September 1631, 16 WIC warships met the Spanish-Portuguese relief force of 20 warships off Abrolhos, half-way between Bahia and Rio de Janeiro. It was a hard-fought battle, partly at very close quarters, although the fleets lost coherence and several ships on both sides did not seriously engage each other. The Dutch lost the flagship and another ship, the Iberians three ships and the losses in men were heavy on both sides. Strategically, it was a Spanish-Portuguese victory, as the Dutch failed to hinder them in their mission to land the relief force, but the Iberians had not been able to force the Dutch fleet to leave the Americas.[22]

In the 1630s the WIC launched a series of attacks against Spanish islands and settlements in the Caribbean and under the protection of their fleets, English and French settlers began to colonise the Lesser Antilles.[23] The Caribbean also began to be infested with outright piracy by groups of more or less outlaw buccaneers who settled on islands beyond effective control of any

European power. Spain fought back with warships and soldiers sent from Europe or detached from the yearly convoys; they strengthened fortifications and local initiatives in Mexico financed a Caribbean squadron, the *Armada de Barlovento*. Islands were taken and lost and the WIC did not make much profit, but they drained the Spanish resources and sometimes delayed the vital silver convoys.[24]

During 1638-40 both sides tried to achieve something decisive in America. The WIC sent a major fleet to capture the silver fleet off Cuba in 1638 but this time the convoy was efficiently protected. After a series of battles and manoeuvres in August and September, the Spanish convoy returned to Mexico – the silver was delayed for a year. Another WIC fleet sent out in 1640 caused Spain to delay the convoy but no silver was captured. In spring 1638 the Dutch sent a fleet with an army from Pernambuco to Bahia but failed to take the city. Later in the year a Spanish-Portuguese fleet of 46 ships, 26 of them major warships, sailed to Brazil in order to retake Pernambuco. Disease and weak leadership caused it to sail to Bahia (south of Pernambuco) to collect reinforcements before the attack was made. Reinforced to 30 warships, 34 armed merchantmen and 23 small units with around 5,000 soldiers the fleet left Bahia in November 1639. The Dutch decided to fight them at sea and their own fleet of 41 ships with 1,600 seamen and 1,200 soldiers was sent out. After an indecisive five-day battle off Itamaracá in January 1640, the Spanish-Portuguese force gave up the attempt to attack the Dutch colony, although part of the army was landed north of it. The Iberian fleet was dispersed in a way that indicates a total breakdown of central control. It was the last joint Spanish-Portuguese operation. Less than a year later Portugal revolted against Spain.

From the mid-1630s, the Dutch began a new series of offensives in the East Indies, mainly against the Portuguese, who were finally eliminated as a major sea power in Asia. The governor-general, Antonie van Diemen, followed a battle fleet strategy. Goa was blockaded almost continuously from 1636, thus reducing the Portuguese main fleet to inactivity and leaving Portuguese shipping and fortresses in Asia without relief. The blockade was possible because the Dutch fleet could be based in a nearby port controlled by a friendly Indian ruler. Two major battles took place at Goa. On 4 January 1638, six warships attempted to break the blockade. The blockading fleet was superior in gunpower but inferior in manpower and the Portuguese naturally tried to board. The fight ended when the Portuguese flagship took fire, also setting one Dutch ship afire. The Portuguese fleet returned to Goa. On 30 September 1639 the Dutch fleet attacked the port and burnt three large Portuguese warships after a fierce fight.[25] Repeated blockades of Malacca from 1633 on ended when this city, the eastern corner-stone of the Portuguese empire, fell in January 1641 after a siege. Ceylon, important as a producer of cinnamon, was partially conquered from the Portuguese through yearly expeditions against various parts of the island in 1638-40. Portuguese shipping to Europe was reduced to a small fraction of its earlier strength. In turn, the VOC was able to act with much superior forces, thanks to funds from their increasingly profitable trade.

When Portugal revolted against Spain in late 1640, the Dutch and the Portuguese became allies. However, their truce in Brazil was not concluded until 1642 and in the East it had to wait until 1644. The Dutch used their sea power to gain as much as possible before hostilities ended and Portugal had no possibility of resisting. Goa was blockaded until 1644 and Dutch conquest continued in Ceylon. From 1645 to 1648 Dutch fleets repeatedly attacked the Philippines and blockaded Manila. The blockade caused the Chinese to trade with the VOC on Taiwan rather than with the Spaniards. In the Caribbean the Dutch and Spanish continued with fighting over islands until peace was concluded in 1648 but the forces involved were limited.

In mid-1645 the Portuguese rose in revolt against the Dutch in Brazil. The Dutch colony was reduced to a few fortified places along the coast and with the loss of the sugar plantations the WIC became unprofitable. A Dutch fleet with reinforcements was sent out in 1646 but a force which might have been strong enough to retake the colony was delayed until the end of 1647. Meanwhile, the Lisbon government sent its fleet with about 3,000 soldiers to Brazil in the autumn of 1647, even though the Portuguese wished to avoid war with the Dutch. The Dutch were defeated on land during 1648/49. The Dutch fleet was superior in strength but unable to bring the Portuguese main fleet to action as it sheltered in Bahia. However, Dutch privateers were successful in capturing Portuguese ships carrying sugar from Brazil, thus to some extent recapturing the lost sugar trade.

During 1648/49 the Portuguese government, in co-operation with the New Christian (crypto-Jewish) merchant elite of Lisbon, created a privately financed company which fitted out a considerable fleet for the protection of trade with Brazil. It left Portugal in November 1649. At the same time the WIC was in financial distress and the Dutch political system was in conflict over the extent to which the state should support the colony. No reinforcements were sent and the fleet returned home during 1649/50 when the ships were in urgent need of repairs and the crews demanded payment. In spring 1650 the Portuguese were in naval control of Brazilian waters and had the resources for effective protection of the trans-Atlantic trade. The Lisbon government, not officially at war with the Dutch, avoided using this force for a final attack against the surviving Dutch garrisons. They were obliged to surrender early in 1654 when the Dutch were preoccupied with their first war with England (1652–54). The Portuguese had been successful in imitating the Dutch in mobilising private capital for overseas investments in trade and protection. Spain had never been able to achieve that in the long global conflict.[26]

The global war at sea showed that European fleets were able to operate anywhere in the world. It was in Brazilian and Caribbean waters, not in Europe, that the Dutch and the Iberians used concentrated battle fleet strategies against each other in a way that gave a foretaste of the great Anglo-French-Spanish confrontations in America in 1739 to 1783. The really large overseas expeditions did not proceed further than Brazil and the considerable forces which the two contenders kept there could be supported by local bases. In Asia the forces were more limited and their size and efficiency were dependent on the trade which financed this warfare. Success in trade in its turn depended to a large extent on superior technology in sailing and protection.

Warfare in Western Europe, 1603–35

When the war between England and Spain ended in 1603 (peace was concluded in 1604) naval activities in Europe were reduced. Piracy from the British Isles remained a problem for several years and the French state had only limited control of its coasts. The Dutch navy was in active service. It kept local control of their home waters, escorted convoys, cruised in the Channel and the North Sea and blockaded the coast of Flanders. The Dutch were only marginally challenged by Spanish attacks on trade from Dunkirk.[27] The large Spanish battle fleet of the 1590s rapidly shrank in size and made no further offensive operations in north-western Europe. Dutch attempts to raid the Spanish coasts in 1606 failed but a fleet sent to Andalucia early in 1607 was able to destroy ten Spanish warships at the battle of Gibraltar on 25 April. It was the first major Dutch victory in a fleet action and it showed the remarkable rise of the young republic which two decades earlier had been fighting for its very existence.[28]

At the outbreak of the war in 1621, the Dutch and the Spanish-Portuguese navies were both rapidly expanding. The Dutch organised a vast convoy system for its shipping in the North Sea, to France, the Mediterranean and northern Russia and for the North Sea fishery. The blockade of the ports of Flanders was resumed in order both to hinder Spanish warships from attacking Dutch trade and to channel trade with the enemy through the Scheldt estuary where it was taxed by the Dutch. Spain reorganised the Armada of Flanders and formed an armada for the blockade of the straits of Gibraltar. The latter fought two convoy actions against heavily armed Dutch merchantmen in 1621/22 after which it was reduced in strength. The Armada of Flanders was given additional strength in 1624 when Spain decided to reduce the Army of Flanders in order to concentrate offensive operations at sea. In Europe the Dutch were almost totally absorbed with defensive actions. They had to protect much of Europe's seaborne trade (i.e. their own) and they refrained from actions against the Iberian peninsula and the 'Atlantic triangle'. Offensive actions were concentrated in the Indian Ocean and Brazil. Only in 1621–23 did squadrons cruise off Portugal and in the Atlantic triangle probing the new and much improved Spanish defence system.

In England anti-Catholic sentiment rose and demanded that the king

(Charles I from 1625) should act in support of threatened Protestants in Germany, preferably in a way that would not cost the English tax-payer anything. The most convenient way seemed to be to attack Spain and its convoys as their American silver was used to finance the wars in Germany and the Netherlands. During 1625 the king and his chief minister, the Duke of Buckingham who was also Lord Admiral, attacked Spain but only very limited funds were voted by Parliament for this activity. The only major operation was launched in autumn 1625 when a fleet of English and Dutch warships and armed merchantmen, a total of around 100 ships, attacked Cadiz. The result was a total failure. Spanish defence was efficient and English amphibious competence had declined markedly. The war continued until 1630 with attacks against trade in which England suffered at least as much as Spain.[29]

Remarkably, English policy also managed to involve the country in war with France. The old conflict between the Huguenots and the French central government had erupted in a new civil war in 1620–22 when both sides improvised fleets of about equal strength. As in earlier civil wars La Rochelle was the centre of Huguenot maritime power and also the most important centre of Huguenot resistance against the central government. In 1625 a small group of Huguenot rebels achieved such strength at sea that the French government had to hire Dutch armed merchantmen and borrow English warships to suppress it. Cardinal Richelieu, leader of the French government from 1624, saw the creation of a permanent navy and control of the French coast as central to his plans for strengthened royal authority and he took personal control of naval administration and maritime policy in general. In 1627/28 the army and the new fleet were concentrated off La Rochelle in order to eliminate this port as a centre of Huguenot autonomy.

Buckingham decided to help the city with two major expeditions, one in 1627 when fighting was concentrated to the island of Ré outside La Rochelle, and another in 1628. Both failed, La Rochelle fell and the autonomous position of the Huguenots in France came to an end. The Anglo-French war of 1627–9 was mainly maritime and part of a crisis in the state formation process on both sides of the Channel. English war policy against France and Spain was strongly driven by a royal desire to secure Parliamentary funds for a stronger and better navy. While Parliament and the king became involved in a conflict of naval financing that ultimately (1642) would end in civil war, Richelieu used the war as an opportunity for creating a new navy which was almost as large as the English by 1630. The new French corps of sea officers and the naval administration was much influenced by Richelieu's patronage and was also used as a mean of integrating Huguenots with a maritime background into the French state.[30]

Like his counterpart first ministers in England and France, the Spanish Count-Duke of Olivares was interested in maritime innovation. During 1625–8 he intensified the war against Dutch trade and worked for a programme where private capital would finance four companies for organising armed convoys for Iberian trade. The Spanish and Portuguese trade with the West and East Indies would have one company each; a company for trade between Spain and Northern Europe should be organised together with the Hanseatics; and a company for Mediterranean trade would be created in Barcelona. The aim was to defeat the Dutch by a combination of successful Iberian shipborne trading and ruthless attacks against the Dutch trade. The private capital failed to materialise although a short-lived Portuguese company was created in 1628. Like many of Olivares' ideas, this project was interesting in theory but remote from the realities of the Habsburg empire.[31]

The attacks on Dutch trade and fisheries, especially by the royal Armada of Flanders and the privateers based in Dunkirk, Mardyck, Ostend and Nieupoort started on a large scale in 1625 with a destructive autumn raid against the fishing fleet. They became very effective from 1627 on. From 1631 the Armada of Flanders also began to transfer troops and money from Spain to the Netherlands, something the Spanish fleet had been unable to do since 1572. This was important, as the 'Spanish Road' became insecure in the 1630s and was blockaded for long periods by Habsburg's enemies in Germany. From 1633 the Dutch navy regained some of the initiative and the number of ships lost declined but this had been achieved by increased and expensive convoying. The Flanders ports were notoriously difficult to blockade efficiently, a fact which also made Dunkirk very useful as a base for French trade warfare during the war period 1689–1713. Warships with skilled crews might enter or leave during heavy weather, fog, dark nights and early spring or late autumn when the blockading force was absent, dispersed or unable to observe what was happening. But, despite the losses, the Dutch trade continued in all areas where it was not prohibited by Spanish embargoes. The Dutch navy was the only navy in Europe which was primarily deployed for trade protection. The Dutch Republic triumphantly survived the war period 1621–48 as the supreme shipping nation, a fact which shows that its system for trade protection was robust enough to handle even a determined general assault from the Iberian superpower.

The Spanish royal warships and privateers based in Flanders were better designed and better manned than ships built in Spain and Portugal. As in the Dutch navy the officers were recruited among men with long seafaring experience which made the Armada of Flanders unique in the Spanish navy.[32] During the 1620s shipbuilders in this region developed the frigate, a light but well-armed warship with higher speed under sail than any earlier type of naval vessel. The Dutch quickly imitated the type and it later spread to the English navy. It seems never to have been built in Spain where warship design lagged behind. This is interesting as it shows that north-western Europe was a regional centre for technical development where ideas spread rapidly without being limited by national or religious borders.[33] The Spanish Dunkirkers were to a large extent the cutting edge of Habsburg sea power and the most offensively-minded force in the Habsburg war machine in the 1620s and 1630s.

It was an elite force upon which much was spent and it increasingly gained a central position in Madrid's strategic thinking.

Battle fleets opposed, 1635–50

France declared war on Spain in 1635. The causes of the war were continental, not maritime. French maritime interest had revived a little but, unlike the sixteenth century, France was now a small player overseas compared to the Dutch or even the English. During the war years 1635–59 France made practically no attempt to attack Spain overseas, an interesting contrast to the Dutch achievement which illustrates how special the republic was. France and Spain were by their geography and size 'natural' contenders for supremacy in Europe, but in the 1630s they were both colossi on feet of clay. Both states were to suffer deep internal crisis in the 1640s. However, France in 1635 had a permanent battle fleet for the first time since the 1560s. Allied with the Dutch it had the potential to sever Spanish communications with both the Netherlands and Italy, thus cutting the Spanish European empire into three pieces. With the French and Spanish armies fighting each other on several fronts, both fleets became much occupied in flank support and logistical operations along the coasts of France, Spain and Italy.[34]

Spain quickly used its superior galley fleet and took the initiative in the Mediterranean. The Lerins islands off Cannes were occupied in September 1635 and fortified as a base in the conventional style of galley warfare where local bases were important for control of the sea lines of communication. The French shelved possible offensive plans for its Atlantic battle fleet and in June 1636 it sailed for the Mediterranean. During 1636/37 this fleet, the Spanish and French galley fleets and an increasing number of Spanish sailing warships operated cautiously against each other. The Lerins were retaken in May 1637. In spring 1638 about half of the French fleet went back to the Atlantic in order to support the army's offensive in northern Spain. It joined several ships recently added to the French Atlantic fleet. The Spanish navy, which on paper was larger than the French, was unprepared and in haste could send only 14 major warships to the combat zone. On 22 August 1638 this force was annihilated by a much superior French fleet at Guetaria on the Basque cost. The French made good use of their recent improvement in fireship technology and the Spanish losses of life were heavy, variously reported from 1,500 to 4,000 men. It was the first major victory of the French navy in the early modern period but its strategic effect was small – the fleet could only protect the evacuation of the French army which was defeated two weeks later.

During 1639 Spain attempted a full-scale mobilisation of its fleet for two major expeditions. One was sent to Brazil in order to retake Pernambuco. The other was sent to the Channel with soldiers and silver for the Army of Flanders which was in a critical situation. But this operation was not intended simply as one more of the blockade-evading operations in which Spain had been successful several times since 1631. It was deliberately planned with the intention that the Dutch – and possibly also the French – fleet should be brought to action and defeated in a decisive battle. Olivares and Philip IV had discussed the idea since autumn 1637. The high quality of the Armada of Flanders was one feature of the plan. If this fleet was strengthened with a large number of Spanish-Portuguese warships a combination of quality, quantity and knowledge of the Channel might achieve a major victory.[35]

Admiral Antonio de Oquendo, the son of one of the Armada admirals of 1588 and the commander of the fleet which successfully fought the Dutch off Brazil in 1631, was appointed captain-general of the fleet which left La Coruna on 5 September 1639.[36] It was late in the season for a major operation but the experience of sea warfare from 1621 on indicated that the Spanish fleet was now better suited for operations in northern waters than in the years 1588–1601 when every major operation had ended with many ship-wrecks. The fleet had 67 units of which at least 24 seem to have been armed merchantmen. The total displacement was probably around 40,000 tonnes of which about a third were armed merchantmen. There were also around 30 transports. On board were about 23,000 men of whom 8,500 were soldiers for the Army of Flanders. Both in tonnage and men, the famous Armada of 1588 had been about a quarter larger, but it had been composed mainly of armed merchantmen.[37]

From early June the French fleet had operated with some success along Spain's northern coast and had also prepared fireship attacks against La Coruna. The gradual concentration of Spanish strength at this port made the French cautious and in late August they retired to their bases, leaving the route to the Channel free for Oquendo. This decision may seem surprising but the French had probably exhausted much of their stores during the summer cruise. On 16 September the Dutch Channel fleet of 17 ships under admiral Maarten H. Tromp met the Spanish fleet. Oquendo had the windward position and intended to fight at close range where musket fire and boarding might be decisive. The Dutch kept the range open, formed their battle line (line ahead) and concentrated their gunfire on distinct sections of the enemy fleet. The latter was drawn up in a defective formation where many ships could not bring their guns to bear. The battle continued eastward in the Channel for about 60 hours. The Dutch fleet was reinforced by 12 more ships but its total size in displacement was probably less than a third of the Spanish fleet. Two Dutch warships and a Spanish transport were lost but the Spanish ships and crews suffered much damage from gunfire. The disparity in strength between two fleets fighting an *even* battle was so great that the result can be explained only as a vast difference in naval culture. The Spaniards seem to have lacked firepower, seamanship and the tactical imagination to use a much superior force in combat.

Both fleets ran out of ammunition and the Spanish fleet took cover among the sandbanks in the Downs off the English coast at the eastern entrance of the Channel. In the 1630s England had pursued a policy of neutrality which in practice favoured Spain. Spain could transfer money to Flanders through England and English ships shipped soldiers to the war zone (the 'English Road'). In order both to enforce this neutrality and to protect English sovereignty against the three contending powers, Charles I had begun to send out his 'Ship-Money' fleets from 1635, thus causing a grave constitutional crisis in England.[38] In the autumn of 1639 the partially mobilised English fleet had the delicate task of protecting the main Spanish battle fleet in the Downs while it repaired, bought ammunition in London and sent its soldiers and silver across the Channel to Flanders. Meanwhile, the Dutch mobilised everything available in home waters and gradually built up a fleet of about 120 ships which blockaded the Downs. Most of these ships must have been armed merchantmen and small vessels and 16 were fireships.

The Armada of Flanders and the transports had left the Downs and only 38 Spanish warships were serviceable when the Dutch attacked on 21 October. The battle turned into a massacre. Several Spanish ships ran aground in the shallow water while others managed to escape to Flanders or Spain. Fireships and small Dutch warships attacked the Spanish ships which on average were larger and less manoeuvrable in confined waters. A total of 32 warships totalling more than 20,000 tonnes displacement were lost and around 6,000 men died. The English fleet offered only symbolic resistance to the Dutch to uphold the sovereignty which Charles I was so anxious to proclaim. This defeat for Spain contributed to the growing sense of despair which caused a deep political crisis within Habsburg Spain in the 1640s.

J. Alcalá-Zamora has interpreted the battle fleet contest in 1639 as the last attempt of Spain to stem the rising tide of Northern Europe.[39] Economically, technologically and increasingly also politically and militarily, Europe's power centre had shifted from the Mediterranean to the North Sea and even to the Baltic. To send a battle fleet to achieve something which the excellent Army of Flanders had failed to achieve since 1568 seems desperate and reflects the increasing isolation from socio-economic, maritime and military realities which marked the leadership of Olivares. Ironically it was the Dutch, who during the war of 1621–48 had not shown any interest in a battle fleet contest in Europe, who inflicted this defeat on Spain. France, which followed a battle fleet strategy, avoided action when Spain offered it. Qualitatively, Dutch sea power had demonstrated such superiority that the Dutch ruling elite grew over-confident and now believed that their society could improvise battle fleets at very short notice. This was revealed as a dangerous illusion when in 1652–4 they faced a much increased and reinvigorated English battle fleet.

From 1640/1 warfare at sea in Western Europe was governed by new political and strategic conditions. The revolts of Catalonia and Portugal against Spain in 1640 created new opportunities and responsibilities for France and the Dutch. An independent Portuguese navy reappeared and France and the Netherlands sent naval forces to Portugal in order to protect trade and discourage Spain from blockading the rebels. In the Netherlands, the stadholder and the inland provinces thought that the time was ripe for an offensive Dutch battle fleet strategy against Spain in order to support Portugal and possibly even Catalonia. Maritime Holland protested loudly against any policy that might reduce the forces deployed for trade protection, thus revealing the complex interest structure behind the Dutch navy. From 1640 to 1644 the Dutch suffered some of the worst onslaughts of Spanish–Flemish trade warfare. This warfare had by now become something in which much private capital and entrepreneurship was invested, the privateering fleets were large and highly skilled and the Dutch admiralties suffered considerable financial problems in the aftermath of the great mobilisation of 1639. It is probable that Spanish–Flemish trade warfare was self-financing and therefore largely immune to a Dutch battle fleet strategy aiming at inflicting strategic defeats on Spain or blockading its trade with the Indies. Trade warfare had to be persecuted in its bases. In 1644 the French army and the Dutch fleet began to cooperate in a systematic effort to conquer the ports of Flanders and this was to a large extent achieved by 1646. By then, the Spanish–Dutch war was almost at an end. Peace was concluded early in 1648.[40]

From 1640 France and Spain concentrated their naval efforts in the Mediterranean. France hoped to win the war by undermining Spanish positions in Catalonia and Italy and control of the sea lines of communication was essential for this strategy – as it had been during the Italian Wars in 1494–1559. Spain had controlled the western Mediterranean since 1559 but was now challenged by the French battle fleet and a growing French galley fleet. Sailing warships definitely established their supremacy in the Mediterranean in these years, making sea power less dependent on local bases. A series of naval operations of a partly repetitive character dominated this theatre of war until 1648. Both sides showed approximately the same competence in naval warfare.

From 1640 the French supported the Catalan revolt and actually occupied Catalonia. The fleet protected supply lines and attempted to cut off Spanish supplies to Rosas and Tarragona in northern and southern Catalonia, still held by the Spanish army. Spain succeeded in supplying Tarragona through classical galley warfare methods where the galleys ran in the supplies. During 1641 this led to battles of which that of 20 August was a major battle fleet action. It was not decisive and both admirals were dismissed by their dissatisfied governments. In mid-1642 Spain concentrated a large fleet for the relief of Rosas. On 30 June it met the French fleet off Barcelona in a battle that lasted three days. Again neither side was able to inflict a decisive defeat on the other. The French relied much on fireship tactics, but in this battle one of their own largest ships became the victim of a French fireship.

Next year, another major battle was fought off Cartagena on 4 September. It was a French victory, although not a major one, and from 1644 France enjoyed greater freedom of action at sea. The fleet supported attempts to take

Tarragona and the strategically important Finale in Liguria (northern Italy), but in both areas the French army was forced to retreat. In May 1645 Rosas finally fell to the French army and fleet without any interference from the Spanish fleet. France, now under leadership of the Italian-born cardinal Mazarin, concentrated her Mediterranean strategy on conquests in Italy, ultimately aiming at Naples and Sicily. During the spring of 1646 the fleet landed an army in the Presidios, the Spanish-controlled territories on the coast of Tuscany which had been important for the galleys which controlled the sea between the Spanish-controlled Naples and Milan since the sixteenth century. Orbitello was besieged. This was a serious threat to Spain's positions in Italy and the Spanish fleet intervened. A battle took place off Orbitello on 14 June – tactically unusual as it was fought by sailing ships towed by galleys in very light winds. The young French admiral Armand de Maillé-Brézé, Richelieu's nephew and in command of the Mediterranean fleet since 1642, was killed and the French fleet retreated. Orbitello was saved, but in October 1646 the French fleet aided by a Portuguese squadron attacked the Presidios again and took Porto Longone on Elba and Piombino, useful as bases for future attacks against Naples.

Sixteen forty-seven started with renewed French attempts to take Tarragona which again failed. In July a major popular revolt started in Naples. Spain increasingly concentrated its fleet to that area. Surprisingly it was not until November that France had been able to send her fleet to support the revolt. In December the French and Spanish fleets met off Naples. Bad winter weather made operations difficult and the only action which took place seems to have been a skirmish. The French fleet was forced to withdraw in January 1648 and it did not return to Naples until early June. By then, the revolt was crushed. In mid-1648 France herself was shaken by a confused revolt, the Fronde, which for years practically paralysed the navy. Spain took control of the western Mediterranean and began counter-offensives in Catalonia and Italy. Both superpowers of Western Europe were by now seriously affected by political crises which reduced their ability to wage war. The war dragged on until 1659 but the operational naval forces of France and Spain were reduced to very low levels, especially when compared to the great fleets which other European powers sent to sea in these years.

The 1640s was a decade with many political crises in Europe. In 1642 civil war erupted in England. The English navy was controlled by the Parliament. It supported Parliamentary operations on land and as far as possible it tried to hinder import of weapons from abroad to the Royalists. Unlike Spain and France, the civil war in England saw a remarkable increase in the size and efficiency of the navy. By 1650 the English navy, with a total displacement of around 50,000 tonnes, was the largest in the world and it was rapidly expanding. The new English republic was introducing a new naval policy where the permanent navy of the state would be able to undertake both major battle fleet operations and trade protection and could also be used as a major instrument of foreign policy over long distances. In a few years the Dutch Republic, defeated at sea by the English in 1652–4, was forced to follow the same policy. A new phase in naval warfare and state formation had begun where large battle fleets enforced a far more efficient state monopoly of violence at sea than Western Europe had ever experienced. Europe continued its transformation process and conflict at sea remained an important part of it.[41]

11

CONCLUSION

The purpose of this book is to survey various types of warfare at sea as part of the transformation of Europe from 1500 to 1650. This transformation was economic, political and social and it was composed of dynamics as much as of inertia and stagnation. Dynamic performance created new power structures in politics and economy, while inability or unwillingness to change caused decline and loss of power. This is reflected in both maritime trade and the ability of states to use and control violence at sea. Entrepreneurship and the ability to promote creativity and adopt innovation were decisive both for state formation and for the rise of new capitalist power groups. Entrepreneurial ability to use opportunities and to act efficiently under conditions of uncertainty and risk were especially important for Europeans when they created networks of maritime communications around the world. Success and failure in maritime conflicts cannot be explained without an understanding of human ability to innovate and the social, economic and political pre-conditions which created both dynamics and stagnation.

In the early sixteenth century there were several centres of maritime entrepreneurship and technology in Europe. They were fairly equal in their capacity to innovate in maritime technology and organisation. Rulers as well as capital-owners developed ships and guns and used them to gain power and profit through violence, or the threat of it, as well as for protection of trade and territories. The Mediterranean world fell under the domination of two empires, those of the Habsburgs and the Ottomans, which both combined traditional galley technology and tactics with modern powerful guns in a partly old, partly new system of warfare. In Western Europe, guns and improved sailing ship technology created better opportunities for merchants and rulers to co-operate in the development of long-distance shipping. Shipping was increasingly protected and promoted by territorial states which began to assert a monopoly of violence at sea. The Portuguese kings used the same technology and the same idea of bringing politics to sea for a spectacular intrusion into the Indian Ocean. In the Baltic, the two rising Nordic dynasties took this development one step further and used modern naval technology to create an area where violence was controlled by two states which protected foreign shipping. The navies they created were at the same time important for their dynastic interests and for power politics in the Baltic. The maritime cities of the Baltic lost the political leverage which their sea power had given them during the Middle Ages.

From the 1560s to the late sixteenth century the new maritime power structure underwent a profound crisis. The two great empires in the Mediterranean proved unable to control violence at sea and the economy in this region showed increasing signs of stagnation. In Western Europe, English and Dutch sea power, strategically based on each side of the Channel, took control over trade between Northern and Southern Europe. It was the Dutch who used this opportunity to develop their already strong shipping business into a European supremacy in maritime trade. When the Spanish empire attempted to fight back with economic blockade the Dutch used their superior maritime technology and highly developed sense of capitalist entrepreneurship to penetrate the Iberian maritime trade monopolies outside Europe. This challenge was to a large extent successful. It substantially reduced Iberian power in Asia and Europe and it made the Dutch Republic into the first global centre for commerce and shipping. The concentration of maritime trade and naval power to the North Sea/Channel area was part of the economic and political rise of Northern Europe and the corresponding decline of Southern Europe and the Levant – two of the most important aspects of the transformation of Europe. Differences in the ability to develop and use maritime technology and violence at sea are important parts of the explanation for that change. Behind these differences it is possible to discern various socioeconomic power structures where change might be either beneficial or destructive for the power-holders.

Ability to use the sea has mainly been studied in this book by brief analyses of naval operations, battles and maritime trade protected by armed force. One conclusion from the study is that detailed comparative studies of how ships and weapons were used at sea would be rewarding – tactics in battle, logistics, endurance and the ability to sail in adverse weather. European progress in these basic maritime and naval capabilities was evidently very uneven. Various regions and states show marked differences in their capacity to use violence at sea to their own advantage. Better knowledge of this may give us a deeper understanding of the micro-foundations of European transformation and its impact on the rest of the world.

APPENDIX

Major sailing navies and galley navies, 1500–1650

	1500	1520	1545	1570	1600	1630	1650
The Ottoman Empire							
Sailing warships	?	?	–	–	–	–	–
Galleys	15/20	15/25	20/30	50/60	?	20/30	20/30
Venice							
Sailing warships	2/3	?	1/3	3	–	–	–
Galleys	(20)	(25)	(30)	(40)	30/40	25/30	(20)
The Spanish Empire							
Sailing warships	–	–	–	3	40/60	40/60	25/35
Galleys	–	2/3	7/9	18	15/20	12/15	10/14
Portugal							
Sailing warships	?	?	?	?	–	–	20/25
Galleys	?	?	?	?	–	–	–
France							
Sailing warships	8/12	10/15	4/6	2/3	–	27	21
Galleys	(2)	(2)	7	(4/7)	(1)	2	12
England							
Sailing warships	5	14	15	14	27	31	49
Galleys	–	*	*	1	*	–	–
The Dutch Republic							
Sailing warships	–	–	–	–	15/25	40	29
Galleys	–	–	–	–	(1)	–	–
Denmark-Norway							
Sailing warships	?	6/10	7/9	15	(11)	19	22
Galleys	–	–	–	1	1	–	–
Sweden							
Sailing warships	–	(1)	7	21	24	17	28
Galleys	–	–	2	*	1	–	–

Table A.1 The total displacement of warships owned by state navies (thousand tonnes)

Sources: The figures are based on appendices 1 and 2 in J. Glete, *Navies*, pp. 501–704 with some additional information from the literature on which these appendices were based. I have also benefited from additional information about the Danish-Norwegian navy from Niels M. Probst (personal communication) and from J. H. Barfod, *Flådens födsel* and *Christian 3.s flåde*.

Notes

a   Displacement calculations are made by the author. Vessels smaller than 100 tonnes, numerous in some navies during wars, are excluded. Hired and requisitioned vessels are not included, nor are warships owned by private interests, such as privateers and the trading companies. The Dutch West India Company had a navy of probably 15,000 to 20,000 tonnes in 1630. Spanish warships on long-term lease from private owners (*asiento* contracts) are included. Portugal was part of the Spanish empire in 1600 and 1630.

b   All calculated displacements are approximate and data from this period are often uncertain. Figures in parentheses are highly approximated. Two figures divided by a solidus indicate that only a rough indication of the probable size of the navy can be given.

c   The asterisks under English and Swedish galleys indicate that only a few, or one, existed whose total displacement was less than 500 tonnes.

NOTES

1 WARFARE AT SEA IN EUROPEAN HISTORY

1 General works on medieval and Renaissance warfare at sea are C. Cipolla, *Guns and sails in the early phase of European expansion* (London, 1965); F.-F. Olesa Munido, *La organizacion naval de los estados Mediterraneos y en especial de Espana durante los siglos XVI y XVII*, 2 vols (Madrid, 1968); J. F. Guilmartin Jr, *Gunpowder and galleys: Changing technology and Mediterranean warfare at sea in the sixteenth century* (Cambridge, 1974); P. Padfield, *Tide of Empires: Decisive naval campaigns in the rise of the West*: vol. 1, 1481–1654 (London, 1979); R. W. Unger, *The ship in the medieval economy, 600-1600* (London, 1980); G. V. Scammell, *The world encompassed: The first European maritime empires, c. 800–1650* (London, 1981); A. R. Lewis and T. J. Runyan, *European naval and maritime history, 300–1500* (Bloomington, 1985); J. Glete, *Navies and nations: Warships, navies and state building in Europe and America, 1500–1860*, 2 vols (Stockholm, 1993).

2 State building and navies, see J. Glete, *Navies*.

3 A survey in J. D. Tracy (ed.), *The rise of merchant empires: Long-distance trade in the early modern world, 1350–1750* (Cambridge, 1990) and J. D. Tracy (ed.), *The political economy of merchant empires* (Cambridge, 1991). Useful collections of essays: D. A. Irwin (ed.), *Trade in the pre-modern era, 1400–1700*, 2 vols (Cheltenham, 1996); P. Emmer and F. Gastra (eds), *The Organization of interoceanic trade in European expansion* (Aldershot, 1996); and S. Subrahmanyam (ed.), *Merchant networks in the early modern world* (Aldershot, 1996).

4 Naval historiography: J. Glete, *Navies*, pp. 88–93. Several old works are indispensable in spite of being dated. England: M. Oppenheim, *A history of the administration of the Royal Navy and of merchant shipping in relation to the navy* (New York, 1896, 1961). France: C. de La Roncière, *Histoire de la marine francaise*, 6 vols (Paris, 1898–1932). The Netherlands: J. C. de Jonge, *Geschiedenis van het nederlandse zeewezen*, 5 vols (Haarlem, 1858-62, 1st edn 1833-48). Spain: C. Fernandez Duro, *Armada espanola desde la unión de los reinos de Castilla y de Aragón*, 9 vols (Madrid, 1895-1903, 1972-73). Sweden: A. Zettersten, *Svenska flottans historia, 1522–1680*, 2 vols (Stockholm & Norrtälje, 1890-1903), *Svenska flottans historia, 1521–1945*, 3 vols (Malmö, 1942–45). Italy and Venice: C. Manfroni, *Storia della marina italiana dalla caduta di Constantinopoli alla battaglia di Lepanto* (Milano, 1897, 1970); M. Nani Mocenigo, *Storia della marina veneziana de Lepanto alla caduta della Repubblica* (Rome, 1935). More recent standard works: Britain: N. A. M. Rodger, *The safeguard of the sea: A naval history of Britain: vol. 1, 660–1649* (London, 1997). The Netherlands: *Maritieme geschiedenis der Nederlanden*, 4 vols (Bussum, 1976-78); J. R. Bruijn, *The Dutch navy of the seventeenth and eighteenth centuries* (Columbia, 1993); L. Sicking,

Zeemacht en onmacht: Maritieme politiek in de Nederlanden, 1488–1558 (Amsterdam, 1998). Denmark-Norway: J. H. Barfod, Flådens födsel (Copenhagen, 1990); J. H. Barfod, Christian 3.s flåde, 1533–1588 (Copenhagen, 1995); and N. M. Probst, Christian 4.s flåde, 1588–1660 (Copenhagen, 1996).
R. C. Anderson, Naval wars in the Baltic, 1522–1850 (London, 1910, 1969) and R. C. Anderson, Naval wars in the Levant, 1559–1853 (Liverpool, 1952) are indispensable for readers who do not read the languages of the Baltic and the Mediterranean areas as Anderson was careful in comparing what authors from different countries had written about naval operations.

5 Important examples of reinterpretation of post-1650 naval history are D. A. Baugh, British naval administration in the age of Walpole (Princeton, 1965); J. R. Bruijn, De admiraliteit van Amsterdam in rustige jaren, 1713–1751: Regenten en financiën, schepen en zeevarenden (Amsterdam, 1970); G. Teitler, The genesis of the modern officer corps (London, 1977); J. P. Merino Navarro, La armada espanola en el siglo XVIII (Madrid, 1981); B. Lavery, The ship of the line, 2 vols. (London, 1983-84); N. A. M. Rodger, The wooden world: An anatomy of the Georgian navy (London, 1986); C. Buchet, La lutte pour l'espace caraïbe et le facade Atlantique de l'Amerique central et du Sud, 1672–1763, 2 vols (Paris, 1991); M. Vergé-Francheschi, Marine et education sous l'ancien régime (Paris, 1991); R. Harding, Amphibious warfare in the eighteenth century: The British expedition to the West Indies, 1740-1742 (Woodbridge, 1991); J. Pritchard, Anatomy of a naval disaster: The 1746 French naval expedition to North America (Montreal, 1995).

6 Maritime trade and expansion: P. & H. Chaunu, Seville et l'Atlantique, 1504–1650, 11 vols. (Paris, 1955–59); A. Tenenti, Piracy and the decline of Venice, 1580–1615 (Berkeley, 1967); N. Steensgaard, The Asian trade revolution of the seventeenth century (Chicago, 1974); A. Attman, The struggle for Baltic markets: Powers in conflict, 1558–1618 (Gothenburg, 1979); J. C. Boyajian, Portuguese trade in Asia under the Habsburgs, 1580–1640 (Baltimore, 1993); D. D. Hebb, Piracy and the English government, 1616–1642 (Aldershot, 1994). National policy and wars: J. I. Israel, The Dutch Republic and the Hispanic world, 1606–1661 (Oxford, 1982); R. B. Wernham, After the armada: Elizabethan England and the struggle for Western Europe, 1588–1595 (Oxford, 1984); R. B. Wernham, The return of the armadas: The last years of the Elizabethan war against Spain, 1595–1603 (Oxford, 1994). State formation and governance: I. A. A. Thompson, War and government in Habsburg Spain, 1560–1620 (London, 1976); R. Brenner, Merchants and revolution: Commercial change, political conflict, and London overseas traders, 1550-1653 (Cambridge, 1993); M. C. 't Hart, The making of a bourgeois state: War, politics and finance during the Dutch revolt (Manchester, 1994).

7 New interpretation of these historical themes: J. E. Thompson, Mercenaries, pirates, and sovereigns: State-building and extraterritorial violence in early modern Europe (Princeton, 1994); H. Spruyt, The sovereign state and its competitors: An analysis of systems change (Princeton, 1994). State formation, the rise of bureaucracies and the monopolisation of violence to states are themes which were developed in the first half of the twentieth century in classical works by historians and sociologists like Otto Hintze, Max Weber and Norbert Elias.

8 An attempt to answer such questions for this period was made in J. Glete, Navies, pp. 6–15, 102–172.

9 F. Braudel, The Mediterranean and the Mediterranean world in the age of Philip II, 2 vols (London, 1972-73). Other studies in this tradition are P. & H. Chaunu, Seville – a planned volume on political and technological structures was never published; F. Mauro, Le Portugal et l'Atlantique au XVIIe siècle, 1570–1670 (Paris, 1960), G. Benzioni (ed.), Il Mediterraneo nella seconda metà det '500 alla luce di Lepanto (Florence, 1974); A. C. Hess, The forgotten frontier: A history of the sixteenth-century Ibero-African frontier (Chicago, 1978); R. Ragosta (ed.), Le genti del mare Mediterraneo,

NOTES

2 vols. (Naples, 1981); and V. Magalhaes Godinho, *Os descobrimentos e a economia mundial*, 4 vols (2nd edn, Lisbon, 1981-83).

10 J. F. Guilmartin Jr, *Gunpowder*; I. A. A. Thompson, *War and government*; C. Rahn Phillips, *Six galleons for the King of Spain: Imperial defense in the early seventeenth century* (Baltimore, 1986); C. H. Imber, 'The navy of Süleyman the Magnificent', *Archivum Ottomanicum* 6, pp. 211–282, 1980; P. Brummett, *Ottoman seapower and Levantine diplomacy in the Age of Discovery* (Albany, 1994), pp. 89–121; J. Alcala-Zamora y Queipo de Llano, *Espana, Flandes y el Mar del norte, 1618–1639* (Barcelona, 1975). The work of I. Bostan, *Osmanli Bahriye Teskilati: XVII. Yüzilda Tersane-i-Amire* (Ankara, 1992) is summarised in S. Faroqhi et al., *An economic and social history of the Ottoman empire: vol. 2, 1600–1914* (Cambridge, 1994), pp. 461-465.

11 P. Padfield, *Tide of empire* has the connections between trade, plunder and maritime war as its leading theme. Interestingly, Padfield has a background in the mercantile marine, not as a scholarly historian.

12 M. Roberts, *Essays in Swedish history* (London, 1967), pp. 195–225. The article was first published in 1956.

13 G. Parker, *The Military Revolution: Military innovation and the rise of the West, 1500–1800* (Cambridge, 1988).

14 J. Black, *A military revolution? Military change and European society, 1550–1800* (London, 1991).

15 J. R. Hale, *War and society in Renaissance Europe, 1450–1620* (Leicester, 1985); M. S. Anderson, *War and society in Europe of the Old Regime, 1618–1789* (Leicester, 1988).

16 F. Tallett, *War and society in early-modern Europe, 1495–1715* (London, 1992).

17 F. C. Lane, *Profits from power: Readings in protection rent and violence-controlling enterprise* (Albany, 1979). This is a collection of essays from the 1940s on.

18 C. Tilly, 'War making and state making as organized crime', in *Bringing the state back in*, Peter B. Evans et al. (eds.) (Cambridge, 1985), pp. 169–191.

19 C. Tilly, *Coercion, capital, and European states, AD 990–1990* (Oxford, 1990).

20 D. C. North, 'Sources of productivity change in ocean shipping, 1600–1850', *Journal of Political Economy* 76, pp. 953–970, 1968. North emphasises the importance of institutional stability for economic development but he has little to say about war and violence. He acknowledges inspiration from Lane's protection cost theory. D. C. North & R. P. Thomas, *The rise of the Western World: A new economic history* (Cambridge, 1973); D. C. North, *Institutions, institutional change and economic performance* (Cambridge, 1990).

21 W. H. McNeill, *The pursuit of power: Technology, armed force and society since A.D. 1000* (Oxford, 1983), esp. pp. 117–143, 150–151.

22 F. Braudel, *The Mediterranean*; F. Braudel, *Civilization and capitalism, 15th-18th centuries*, 3 vols. (London, 1981-84).

23 I. Wallerstein, *The modern world-system*, vols 1–2 (New York, 1974-80), esp. vol. 2, pp. 36-71.

24 J. I. Israel, *Dutch primacy in world trade* (Oxford, 1989); J. I. Israel, *Empires and entrepots: The Dutch, the Spanish monarchy and the Jews, 1585–1713* ((London, 1990), esp. pp. ix-xiii, 189–212; K. Davids & J. Lucassen (eds.), *A miracle mirrored: The Dutch Republic in European perspective* (Cambridge, 1995), pp. 3, 6, 347. Israel's survey of Dutch history, J. I. Israel, *The Dutch Republic: Its rise, greatness, and fall, 1477–1806* (Oxford, 1995) is less revisionistic than his earlier books in its approach to the role of the Dutch state, and the entrepot theme is not developed.

25 J. Glete, *Navies*. That study was in its theoretical concepts also inspired by authors like W. H. McNeill, G. A. Almond and C. Tilly, although I did not agree with Tilly's interpretation of European state formation as it was stated before 1990. My own interpretation, with emphasis on the growth of navies as the result of political

interest aggregation and the state as seller of protection, is close to the interpretation of state formation as the result of bargaining between rulers and elites about war finance which Tilly presented in C. Tilly, *Coercion*, esp. pp. 11–16. In that study, Tilly has come close to F. C. Lane's ideas about the state as seller of protection.
26 The subsequent development: R. Harding, *Seapower and naval warfare, 1650–1830* (London, 1999).

2 TECHNOLOGY, TACTICS AND STRATEGY

1 A survey of technology, strategy, tactics and naval doctrines: J. Glete, *Navies*, pp. 16–65.
2 Surveys of the debate in M. I. Morton and N. L. Schwartz, *Market structure and innovation* (Cambridge, 1982) and J. Elster, *Explaining technical change: A case study in the philosophy of science* (Cambridge, 1983).
3 Important contributions to these ideas are N. Rosenberg, *Inside the black box: Technology and economics* (Cambridge, 1982) and R. Nelson, *Understanding technical change as an evolutionary process* (Amsterdam, 1987). For network theory in economics and business administration, see G. Thompson (ed.), *Markets, hierarchies and networks: The co-ordination of social life* (London, 1991) and H. Håkansson and I. Snehota (eds), *Developing relationships in business networks* (London, 1997).
4 M. Russell, *Visions of the sea: Hendrick C. Vroom and the origins of Dutch marine painting* (Leiden, 1983); G. S. Keyes, *Mirror of empire: Dutch marine art of the seventeenth century* (Cambridge, 1990). Illustrated catalogues of seventeenth century marine art: M. S. Robinson, *Van de Velde drawings: A catalogue of drawings in the National Maritime Museum made by the Elder and Younger Willem van de Velde*, 2 vols (Cambridge, 1973); M. S. Robinson and R. E. J. Weber, *The Willem van de Velde drawings in the Boymans-Van Beuningen Museum, Rotterdam*, 3 vols (Rotterdam, 1979); M. S. Robinson, *Van de Velde: A catalogue of the paintings of the Elder and Younger Willem van de Velde*, 2 vols (London, 1990).
5 Major excavations of warships from this period are those of *Mary Rose* (sunk 1545) and *Vasa* (sunk 1628). B. Landström, *The Royal warship Vasa* (Stockholm, 1988); H. Soop, *The power and the glory: The sculptures of the warship Wasa* (Stockholm, 2nd rev. edn, 1992), M. Rule, *The Mary Rose: The Excavation and raising of Henry VIII's flagship* (London, 1982). See also M. Guérout *et al.*, *Le navire génois de Villefranche: Un naufrage de 1516 (?)* (Paris, 1989) and C. Martin, *Full fathom five: Wrecks of the Spanish armada* (London, 1975). The leading journal in the field is *The International Journal of Nautical Archaeology (and Underwater Exploration), 1972–*.
6 The development of guns: C. Cipolla, *Guns and sails*; J. F. Guilmartin, *Gunpowder*; V. Schmidtchen, *Bombarden, Befestigungen, Büchsenmeister: Von den ersten Mauerbrechern des Mittelalters zur Belagerungsartillerie der Renaissance* (Düsseldorf, 1977); W. H. McNeill, *The Pursuit*, pp. 79–102; Ph. Contamine, *War in the Middle Ages* (Oxford, 1984), pp. 138–150, 193–207; G. Parker, *The military revolution*; K. DeVries, *Medieval military technology* (Peterborough, 1992); B. Buchanan (ed.), *Gunpowder: The history of an international Technology* (Bath, 1996); J. F. Guilmartin, 'Guns and Gunnery', in *Cogs, caravels and galleons: The sailing ship, 1000–1650*; R. Gardiner and R. W. Unger (eds) (London, 1994), pp. 139–150. K. DeVries, 'The effectiveness of fifteenth-century shipboard artillery', *Mariner's Mirror* 84, pp. 389–399, 1998. Denmark-Norway: M. H. Mortensen, *Dansk Artilleri indtil 1600* (Copenhagen, 1999). England: B. Lavery, *The arming and fitting of English ships of war, 1600–1815* (London, 1987), pp. 80–150; A. B. Caruana, *The History of English sea ordnance, 1523–1875: vol. 1, The Age of evolution, 1523–1715* (Rotherfield, 1994). Sweden: T. Jakobsson, *Sveriges krig 1611–1632: Bilagsband II, Beväpning och beklädnad,* (Stockholm, 1938) and J. Hedberg, *Kungl. Artilleriet:*

Medeltid och äldre Vasatid (Stockholm, 1975).

7 C. de La Roncière, *Histoire*, vol. 3, pp. 9, 65–67; M. H. Mortensen, *Dansk artilleri*, pp. 354, p. 361; B. W. Diffie and G. D. Winius, *Foundations of the Portuguese empire, 1415–1580* (Minneapolis, 1977), pp. 220–221, 224, 238; N. A. M. Rodger, *The Safeguard*, p. 168.

8 J. F. Guilmartin, *Gunpowder*, pp. 277–291.

9 The differences in quality of guns, gun-shot, gun carriages and gun handling technique have been discussed in connection with the Anglo-Spanish confrontation of 1588, see C. Martin, *Full fathom five* (London, 1975) (with an appendix about Spanish gun-shot technology written by Sidney Wingall) and C. Martin and G. Parker, *The Spanish armada* (London, 1988), pp. 195–226. For a Spanish rejoinder, see J. L. Casado Soto, 'Atlantic shipping in sixteenth-century Spain and the 1588 Armada', in *England, Spain and the Gran Armada, 1585–1604*, M. J. Rodriguez-Salgado and S. Adams (eds) (Edinburgh, 1991), pp. 95–132. Gunpowder development: B. S. Hall, 'The corning of gunpowder and the development of firearms in the Renaissance', in *Gunpowder*, Buchanan (ed.), pp. 87–120.

10 N. A. M. Rodger, 'The development of broadside gunnery, 1450–1650', *Mariner's Mirror* 82, pp. 301–324, 1996. Early seventeenth-century Dutch East Indiamen of the larger type often carried two heavy copper guns as bow-chasers and two as stern-chasers with eight to ten small cast-iron guns in the broadsides, see N. Mac Leod, *De Oost-Indische Compagnie als zeemogeenheid in Azië, vol. I, 1602–1632* (Rijswijk, 1927), for example p. 110. Unfortunately, the exact location of guns in ships is seldom mentioned in the sources from this period.

11 Recent general studies with extensive literature lists: R. Unger, *The ship*; R. C. Smith, *Vanguard of empire: Ships of exploration in the age of Columbus* (Oxford, 1993); J. Glete, *Navies*; R. Gardiner and R. W. Unger (eds), *Cogs*; R. Gardiner and J. Morrison (eds), *The age of the galley: Mediterranean oared vessels since pre-classical times* (London, 1995). England: F. Howard, *Sailing ships of war, 1400–1860* (London, 1979); B. Lavery, *The ship of the line*; B. Lavery, *The arming*; I. Friel, *The good ship: Ships, shipbuilding and technology in England, 1200–1520* (London, 1995). Portugal: J. da Gama Pimentel Barata, *Estudos de arqueologia naval*, 2 vols (Lisbon, 1989). Spain: C. Rahn Phillips, *Six galleons*; J. L. Casado Soto, *Los barcos espanoles del siglo XVI y la Gran armada de 1588* (Madrid, 1988); J. L. Rubio Serrano, *Arquitectura de las naos y galeones de las flotas de Indias, 1492–1690*, 2 vols (Málaga, 1991); F. Serrano Mangas, *Función y evolución del galeón en la carrera de Indias* (Madrid, 1992). Denmark-Norway: N. M. Probst, *Christian 4.s flåde*. Sweden: J. Glete, 'Svenska örlogsfartyg 1521–1560: Flottans uppbyggnad under ett tekniskt brytningsskede', *Forum Navale* 30, pp. 5–74, 1976, 31, pp. 23–119, 1977. Venice: F. C. Lane, *Navires et constructeurs á Venise pendant la Renaissance* (Paris, 1965). The Ottoman empire: S. Soucek, 'Certain types of ships in Ottoman-Turkish terminology', *Turcica* 6, pp. 233–249, 1975; C. H. Imber, 'The navy', M. Cizakca, 'Ottomans and the Mediterranean: An analysis of the Ottoman shipbuilding industry as reflected by the Arsenal registers of Istanbul, 1529–1650', in *Le genti*, R. Rosalba (ed.), pp. 773–787. Mediterranean galleys: J. F. Guilmartin, *Gunpowder*; F. F. Olesa Munido, *La organizacion*. Contemporary works on shipbuilding: F. Oliveira, *Livro da fábrica das naus (c. 1565)*, (Lisbon, 1991); T. Cano, *Arte para fabricar y aparejar naos (1611)* (La Laguna, 1964), M. Fernandez, *Livros de tracas carpintaria, 1616* (Lisbon, 1989); W. Salisbury and R. C. Anderson, *A treatise on shipbuilding and a treatise in rigging written about 1620–1625* (London, 1958); J. Furtenbach, *Architectura navalis* (1629), (Hildesheim, 1975); G. Fournier, *Hydrographie* (1643, 1667) (Grenoble, 1973).

12 In the mid-sixteenth century the Swedish navy built some experimental minor warships which attempted to combine galley and sailing ship features with one or a few heavy guns. Type designations such as *bark*, *seidenskepp* and *galleon* were in use,

J. Glete, 'Svenska örlogsfartyg 1521–1560'.

13 J. Glete, *Navies*, pp. 161–167.

14 This traditional view was effectively demolished by J. F. Guilmartin, *Gunpowder*. The early use of guns on galleys: J. F. Guilmartin, 'The early provision of artillery armament on Mediterranean war galleys', *Mariner's Mirror* 59, pp. 257–280, 1973.

15 See Appendix and J. Glete, *Navies*, pp. 102–172, esp. pp. 139–140 and 501–521.

16 J. Hook, 'Fortifications and the end of the Sienese state', *History* 62, pp. 372–387, 1987.

17 R. Reinders and K. Paul, *Carvel construction technique: Skeleton-first, shell-first* (Oxford, 1991); E. Rieth, 'Principe de construction "charpente première" et procédés de construction "bordé premier" au XVII siècle', *Neptunia* 153, pp. 21–31, 1984.

18 G. Parker, 'The *Dreadnought* revolution of Tudor England', *Mariner's Mirror* 82, pp. 269–300, 1996 represents a pioneering attempt in this direction.

19 The importance of gun-armed western merchantmen in the late sixteenth-century Mediterranean was noticed by F. Braudel, *The Mediterranean*, pp. 295–312, 606–642 and the theme was developed by A. Tenenti, *Piracy*. V. Barbour, 'Dutch and English merchant shipping in the seventeenth century', *Economic History Review* 2, pp. 261–290, 1929–30 is a classical text on the economic importance of armed and unarmed merchantmen.

20 It is possible that these regulations became an obstacle to the development of efficient cargo carriers in competition with Northern and Western Europe, see for example an undated memorandum to Philip II from the last years of his reign printed in C. Fernandez Duro, *Armada espanola*, vol. 2, pp. 443–448. On the other hand, Spanish shipbuilders showed great ingenuity in circumventing regulations, producing warships which sacrificed fighting capabilities in order to carry more cargo – see F. Serrano Mangas, *Los galeones de la carrera de Indias, 1650–1700* (Seville, 1985).

21 C. Cipolla, *Guns and sails*, pp. 80–81.

22 J. Glete, *Navies*, p. 705.

23 G. Parker and C. Martin, *The Spanish armada*, pp. 195–226. This question is not finally answered but Parker and Martin's interpretation is a methodologically interesting case of combination of evidence from manuscript sources and nautical archaeology.

24 F. F. Olesa Munido, *La organizacion*; J. F. Guilmartin, *Gunpowder*.

25 Important texts about sixteenth and early seventeenth-century naval tactics: L. G. Carr Laughton, 'Gunnery, frigates and the line of battle', *Mariner's Mirror* 14, pp. 339–363, 1928, a seminal paper which challenged established thinking; P. Padfield, *Guns at sea* (London, 1973), esp. pp. 57–69; B. Lavery, 'The revolution in naval tactics, 1588–1653', in *Les marines de guerre europénnes, XVIIe-XVIIIe siècles*, M. Acerra et al. (eds) (Paris, 1985), pp. 167–174 and N. A. M. Rodger, 'The development of broadside gunnery', which includes a detailed bibliography. Publications of fighting instructions: J. S. Corbett, *Fighting instructions, 1530–1816* (London, 1905, 1971); J. K. Oudendijk, *Een Bourgondisch ridder over ten oorlog ter zee: Philips van Kleef als leermeester van Karel V* (Amsterdam, 1941) and R. E. J. Weber, *De seinboken voor nederlandse oorlogsvloten en konvoien tot 1690* (Amsterdam, 1982). The enormous literature about the Armada of 1588 has much to say about tactics, but much of it is written under the misconception that this battle was the first major contest at sea with guns in Europe.

26 To set ships afire and leave them to drift into an enemy fleet was an old tactic but, apparently in the 1630s, the French navy developed a new type of fireship filled with combustible material which could be sailed close to an enemy by an elite crew and rapidly set afire. The crew was supposed to escape in a boat.

27 J. S. Corbett, *Fighting instructions*, pp. 18–24; P. Pierson, *Commander of the Armada: The seventh duke of Medina Sidonia* (New Haven, 1989), pp. 133–139,

235–243.

28 N. M. Probst, 'Nordisk sötaktik i 1500- og 1600-tallet – og slaget i Köge Bugt den 1. Juli 1677', *Marinehistorisk Tidsskrift* 25, pp. 4–6, 1992 and section 7.2.

29 J. S. Corbett, *Fighting instructions*, pp. 27–77; B. Lavery, 'The revolution in naval tactics', N. A. M. Rodger, 'The development', p. 309.

30 M. G. de Boer, *Tromp en de armada van 1639* (Amsterdam, 1941), pp. 71–72.

31 N. A. M. Rodger, 'The development', p. 315.

32 Analysis of this development: W. S. Maltby, 'Politics, professionalism, and the evolution of sailing-ship tactics, 1650–1714', in *Tools of war: Instruments, ideas and institutions of warfare, 1445–1871*, J. A. Lynn (ed.), (Urbana, Ill., 1990), pp. 53–73 and M. A. J. Palmer, 'The "Military Revolution" afloat: The Era of the Anglo-Dutch wars and the transition to modern warfare at sea', *War in History* 4, pp. 123–149, 1997.

3 SEAMEN, SOLDIERS AND CHANGING MARITIME SOCIETIES

1 This introductory section is based on several works about the maritime world from 1500 to 1650; see J. Glete, *Navies*, pp. 105–123 and the literature mentioned there. Among later studies J. R, Bruijn, *The Dutch navy*; Ph. Masson and M. Vergé-Franceschi, *La France et la mer au siècle des grandes découvertes* (Paris, 1993); D. D. Hebb, *Piracy*; N. A. M. Rodger, *The safeguard* and P. E. Pérez-Malla'na, *Spain's men of the sea: Daily life on the Indies fleets in the sixteenth century* (Baltimore, 1998) are especially important. A survey of recent research on European seamen: P. C. van Royen, J. R. Bruijn and J. Lucassen (eds), *'Those emblems of hell'?: European sailors and the maritime labour market, 1570–1870* (St. John's, Newfoundland, 1997).

2 Among important books about early modern entrepreneurship, private violence at sea and the use of private contractors in warfare at sea might be mentioned N. Mac Leod, *De Oost-Indische*; C. R. Boxer, *The Dutch in Brazil, 1624–1654* (Oxford, 1957); P. W. Klein, *De Trippen in de 17e eeuw: Een studie over het ondernemergedrag op de hollandse stapelmarkt* (Assen, 1965); A. Tenenti, *Piracy*; C. C. Goslinga, *The Dutch in the Caribbean and on the Wild Coast, 1580–1680* (Assen, 1971); N. Steensgaard, *The Asian trade revolution*; I. A. A. Thompson, *War and government*; K. R. Andrews, *The Spanish Caribbean: Trade and plunder, 1530–1630* (New Haven, 1978); L. Blussé and F. Gaastra (eds), *Companies and trade: Essays on overseas trading companies during the Ancien Régime* (The Hague, 1981); K. R. Andrews, *Trade, plunder and settlement: Maritime enterprise and the genesis of the British empire, 1480–1630* (Cambridge, 1984); C. Rahn Phillips, *Six galleons*, and A. P. van Vliet, *Vissers en kapers: De zeevisserij vanuit het Maasmondgebied en de Duinkerker kapers (c. 1570–1648)* (The Hague, 1994). Early modern interest aggregation behind navies and the role of mercantile groups in that process: J. Glete, *Navies*, pp. 123–172. Early modern military entrepreneurship: F. Redlich, *The German military enterpriser and his work force: A study of European economic and social history*, 2 vols (Wiesbaden, 1964–65).

3 General: G. Teitler, *The genesis*. The nobility and the state: R. G. Asch and A. M. Birke, *Princes, patronage, and the nobility: The court at the beginning of the modern age, c. 1450–1650* (Oxford, 1991); H. M. Scott (ed.), *The European nobilities in the seventeenth and eighteenth centuries*, 2 vols (London, 1995).

4 This idea, that social status was required to command men at sea (and on land) is often mentioned but in my opinion too little emphasised. The development of the officer corps might be seen as an effort by the state to create a new order of status (an alternative to family connections, nobility and land-ownership) which suited the interests of the state and in which men with abilities and loyalties which were important to the state could be given social authority.

5 Britain: S. F. Gradish, *The manning of the British navy during the Seven Years' War* (London, 1980); N. A. M. Rodger, *The wooden world*; B. Capp, *Cromwell's navy: The*

fleet and the English revolution, 1648–1660 (Oxford, 1989); J. D. Davies, *Gentlemen and tarpaulins: The officers and men of the Restoration navy* (Oxford, 1992). France: E. L. Asher, *The resistance to the maritime classes: The survival of feudalism in the France of Colbert* (Berkeley, 1960); P. W. Bamford, *Fighting ships and prisons: The Mediterranean Galleys of France in the Age of Louis XIV* (Minneapolis, 1973); J. Aman, *Les officiers bleus dans la marine française au XVIIIeme siècle* (Paris-Genève, 1976); A. Zysberg, *Les galerien: Vies et destins de 60,000 forcats sur les galères de France, 1680–1748* (Paris, 1987); M. Vergé-Franceschi, *Les officiers généraux de la marine royale, 1715–1774*, 15 vols (Paris, 1990). The Netherlands: P. C. van Royen, *Zeevarenden op de koopvardivloot omstreeks 1700* (Amsterdam, 1987).

6 J. S. Corbett, *Drake and the Tudor navy*, 2 vols (London, 1898, Aldershot, 1988); J. A. Williamson, *Hawkins of Plymouth: A new history of Sir John Hawkins and of other members of his family prominent in Tudor England* (2nd edn, London, 1969); J. K. Oudendijk, *Maerten Harpertszoon Tromp* (The Hague, 1952); A. Tenenti, *Cristoforo Da Canal: La marine Vénitienne avant Lepante* (Paris, 1962); E. Bradford, *The Sultan's admiral: The life of Barbarossa* (London, 1969); P. Pierson, *Commander*. For the Swedish and Danish-Norwegian navies there are valuable although dated lists of sea officers with biographical information: H. D. Lind, *Kong Kristian den fjerde og hans maend paa Bremerholm* (Copenhagen, 1889, 1974); H. Börjeson and G. Hafström, *Skeppshövidsmän vid örlogsflottan under 1500-talet: Biografiska anteckningar* (Uppsala, 1949). U. M. Ubaldini, *La marina del sovrano militare ordine di San Giovanni di Gerusalemme di Rodi e di Malti* (Rome, 1971) has lists of commanders of warships belonging to the Order of St John (Malta).

7 General and comparative works: G. Teitler, *The genesis; Course et piraterie*, 2 vols (Mimeo. Paris, 1975); P. Adam, *Seamen in society* (Mimeo, 1980); R. Ragosta (ed.), *Le genti del mare Mediterraneo*, 2 vols (Naples, 1981), pp. 725–1048.

8 A well-known example is the complicated command structure in the Spanish Armada of 1588. Earlier it was thought that the division of the Armada into ten squadrons, each with a *General* and an *Almirante* (1st and 2nd in command) which is normally used when its ships are listed, represented a battle order but it is now known that it was only an administrative division and that some of the flag officers fought in ships other than their administrative flagship. The leading army officers (the *Maestre de Campo*) were dispersed on some of the more important combat units of the Armada, apparently according to a principle that all important ships should have either a senior sea officer *or* a senior army officer on board. See P. Pierson, *Commander*, pp. 235–243.

9 This section on the changes of command structures in the navies is based on the literature concerning individual navies mentioned in the subsequent notes of this chapter. See also G. Teitler, *The Genesis*.

10 The Christian Mediterranean galley fleets were commanded by men who may be described as professional (skilled specialists trained according to a formalised tactic and normally loyal to a state), but they were entrepreneurs or aristocrats (nobles or member of city oligarchies), not members in formally established officer corps. F.-F. Olesa Munido, *La organizacion naval*; J. F. Guilmartin, *Gunpowder and galleys*; G. Hanlon, *The twilight of a military tradition: Italian aristocrats and European conflicts, 1560–1800* (London, 1998), pp. 9–46 and the literature listed in J. Glete, *Navies*, pp. 139–146, 501–521.

11 J. H. Barfod, *Christian 3.s flåde*; N. M. Probst, *Christian 4.s flåde*.

12 A. Zettersten, *Svenska flottans historia*. M.A. Ingvar Sjöblom, Stockholm university, is preparing a thesis on the development of the Swedish sea officer corps and I have used his preliminary results.

13 B. Capp, *Cromwell's navy*; J. D. Davies, *Gentlemen*; N. A. M. Rodger, *The safeguard*, pp. 131–142, 297–310, 395–426.

14 J. R. Bruijn, *The Dutch navy*, pp. 40–53.
15 See note 10 above. Venice: F. C. Lane, *Venice: A maritime republic* (Baltimore, 1973), pp. 342–344, 365–367, 414–415. The Order of St John as an international cadet school: P. W. Bamford, 'The Knights of Malta and the King of France, 1665–1700', *French Historical Studies* 3, pp. 429–453, 1964.
16 C. Rahn Phillips, *Six Galleons*, pp. 119–151; D. Goodman, *Spanish naval power, 1589–1665: Reconstruction and defeat* (Cambridge, 1997), pp. 221–261.
17 C. R. Boxer, *The Portuguese seaborne empire, 1415–1825* (Harmondsworth, 1973) pp. 213–221; A. J. R. Russell-Wood, 'Seamen ashore and afloat: The social environment of the *Carreira da India*, 1550–1750', *Mariner's Mirror* 69, pp. 35–52, 1983.
18 M. Mollat du Jourdin, *La vie quotidienne des gens de mer en Atlantique, IXème-XVIème siècles* (Paris, 1983); M. Mollat, 'The French maritime community: A slow progress up the social scale from the Middle Ages to the sixteenth century', *Mariner's Mirror* 69, pp. 115–128, 1983.
19 C. de La Roncière, *Histoire*, vol. 4, pp. 599–601; G. Lacour-Gayet, *La marine militaire de la France sous les règnes de Louis XIII et Louis XIV* (Paris, 1911), pp. 32–44, 80–88; M. Vergé-Franceschi, *Marine*, pp. 5–102.
20 C. H. Imber, *The navy*, pp. 251–260.
21 The higher officers of the Armada: P. Pierson, *Commander*, pp. 76–127.
22 C. H. Imber, *The navy*, pp. 226–227, 247–260.
23 J. F. Guilmartin, *Gunpowder*, pp. 131–135, 174, 268–269.
24 J. H. Barfod, *Christian 3.s flåde*; N. M. Probst, *Christian 4.s flåde*, pp. 24–30; A. Zettersten, *Svenska flottans historia*; N. E. Villstrand, 'Manskap och sjöfolk inom den svenska örlogsflottan, 1617–1644', *Historisk Tidskrift för Finland* 71, pp. 24–72, 1986.
25 N. A. M. Rodger, *The safeguard*, pp. 153–163, 311–326, 395–426; G. V. Scammell, 'The sinews of war: Manning and provisioning English fighting ships, c. 1550–1650', *Mariner's Mirror* 73, pp. 351–367, 1987.
26 D. Goodman, *Spanish*, pp. 181–220; C. Rahn Phillips, *Six galleons*, pp. 119–151; R. A. Stradling, *The Armada of Flanders: Spanish maritime policy and European war, 1568–1665* (Cambridge, 1992), pp. 153–164; P. E. Pérez-Mallaína, *Spain's Men*; J. Varela Marcos, 'El seminario de marinos: Un intento de formación de los marineros para la armadas y flotas de Indias', *Revista de historia de America*, no. 87, pp. 9–36, 1979. Portugal, see note 17.
27 J. R, Bruijn, *The Dutch navy*, pp. 54–63.
28 A. Tenenti, *Cristoforo Da Canal*, pp. 61–115; A. Tenenti, *Piracy*, pp. 89–109; F.-F. Olesa Munido, *La organizacion naval*, pp. 749–788; F. C. Lane, *Venice*, esp. pp. 365–369, 414; J. F. Guilmartin Jr, *Gunpowder*, pp. 113–119, 222–228, 267–270; M. Aymard, 'Chiourmes et galères dans la seconde moitie du XVIe siècle', in *Il Mediterraneo nella secunda metà del '500 alla luce di Lepanto*, G. Benzione (ed.)(Florence, 1974), pp. 71–94; R. Ragosta (ed.), *Le genti*.
29 J. F. Guilmartin, Jr, 'The tactics of the battle of Lepanto clarified: The impact of social, economic, and political factors on sixteenth-century galley warfare', in *New aspects of naval history*, Craig L. Symonds (ed.)(Annapolis, 1981), pp. 41–65; C. H. Imber, *The navy*, pp. 265–269..
30 In the sixteenth and eighteenth centuries Baltic galley forces, soldiers were used as oarsmen.

4 STATES, ORGANISATIONS AND MARITIME WARS

1 For recent research on early modern European states, see R. Bonney, *The European dynastic states, 1494–1660* (Oxford, 1991); R. Bonney (ed.), *Economic systems and state finance* (Oxford, 1995); W. Reinhard (ed.), *Power elites and state building* (Oxford, 1996); P. Blickle, *Resistance, representation, and community* (Oxford, 1997).

2 Surveys of early modern state formation studies are found in C. Tilly, *Coercion*, pp. 1–37, W. Reinhard, *Power elites*, pp. 1–18 and T. Ertman, *Birth of the Leviathan: Building states and regimes in medieval and early modern Europe* (Cambridge, 1997), pp. 1–19. On war as a question in domestic and international politics: J. Black (ed.), *The origins of war in early modern Europe* (Edinburgh, 1987).

3 Earlier works on early modern state formation: O. Hintze, *The historical essays of Otto Hintze* (ed. F. Gilbert) (Oxford, 1975); G. Oestreich, *Neostoicism and the early modern state* (Cambridge, 1982); P. Anderson, *Lineages of the absolutist state* (London, 1974); and C. Tilly (ed.), *The formation of states in Western Europe* (Princeton, 1975).

4 C. Tilly, *Coercion*. A later attempt to formulate a theory of European state building is that of Thomas Ertman. It is of little use in a study about maritime history as it excludes all non-territorial states and all federal republics: T. Ertman, *Birth*, pp. 5–6.

5 C. Tilly, *Coercion*, pp. 11, 53–54, 59–60, 76.

6 I intend to compare the Dutch army and navy with a few other early military states of Europe in a forthcoming study.

7 There is nothing in capital and capitalism that make them inherently hostile to big structures and complex organisations, provided that capital owners remain in control. Renaissance Italian states and maritime empires were organisationally advanced in their day and so were the East India companies. In the twentieth century the number of privately controlled complex organisations has increased dramatically. Tilly's assumption that the complex organisation 'the early modern European state' was designed solely by territorial coercion-wielders who in some cases co-operated productively with capital is not an established historical fact. For a radically different sociological perspective, in which the development of the Dutch army is regarded as an important part of the development of modern organisation, see J. A. A. Van Doorn, *Sociologie van de organisatie: Beschouwingen over organiseren in het bijzonder gebaseerd op een onderzoek van het militaire systeem* (Leiden, 1956). Van Doorn gives the Dutch army reforms around 1600 a central place in the development of modern organisation.

8 I attempted to bring it into that discussion with J. Glete, *Navies*.

9 One major attempt at reinterpretation is J. Brewer, *The sinews of power* (London, 1989). One attempt to restate the old ideas of a causal interconnection between low domestic resource extraction for war and strong representative institutions is B. M. Downing, *The military revolution and political change: Origins of democracy and autocracy in early modern Europe* (Princeton, 1992). The conclusions presented in that study are untenable. They have been presented without any critical study of the level of resource extraction per capita in the six cases on which it is based.

10 There is little about this in recent works like W. Reinhard, *Power elites* and J.-Ph. Genet and G. Lottes, *L'état moderne et les élites, XIIIe-XVIIIe siècles: Apports et limites de la methode prosopographique* (Paris, 1996).

11 The importance of elite group participation in administration during the early phase of state formation will be discussed in a forthcoming study.

12 General: G. Scammell, *The world encompassed*; W. Brulez, 'Shipping profits in the early modern period', *Acta Historiae Neerlandicae* 14, pp. 65–84, 1981 and R. S. Menard, 'Transport costs and long-range trade, 1300–1800: Was there a European "transport revolution" in the early modern era?', in *The political economy*, J. D. Tracy (ed.), pp. 228–275. Venice: F. C. Lane, *Venice*. Genoa: J. Heers, *Gênes au XVe siécle: Activité économique et problèmes sociaux* (Paris, 1961); T. A. Kirk, *Genoa and the sea: Ships and power in the early modern Mediterranean, 1559–1680* (PhD thesis, European University Institute, Florence, 1996). I am grateful to have been sent a copy of this dissertation from Dr. Kirk before its publication. Spain: W. D. Phillips, Jr, 'Spain's northern shipping industry in the sixteenth century', *Journal of European Economic History* 17, pp. 267–301, 1988. Normandy: M. Mollat, *Le commerce maritime normand*

a la fin du moyen age (Paris, 1952). Brittany: H. Touched, *Le commerce maritime breton à la fin du moyen âge* (Paris, 1967). The Netherlands: J. Israel, *Dutch primacy*. The Hanse: P. Dollinger, *The German Hansa* (London, 1970).

13 England: ship-list in N. A. M. Rodger, *The safeguard*, pp. 476–478; France, C. de La Roncière, *Histoire*, vol. 3, pp. 3, 7, 45, 48, 66.

14 J. Glete, *Navies*, pp. 146–152.

15 J. Glete, *Navies*, pp. 123–139. Scotland also had a royal navy in the early sixteenth century but the Scottish naval efforts were too sporadic to create a permanent navy, N. A. M. Rodger, *The safeguard*, pp. 166–172.

16 In the early eighteenth century tsar Peter I founded St Petersburg as the main naval base and the leading port of Russia. He also found it useful or necessary to move the capital from inland Moscow to this new maritime centre.

17 J. Paviot, *La politique navale des ducs de Bourgogne, 1384–1482* (Lille, 1995); L. Sicking, *Zeemacht.*

18 J. Glete, *Navies*, pp. 146–152.

19 The most entrepreneurial-oriented study of this period is P. W. Klein, *De Trippen*. The impact in Asia of changing European institutions and new combinations of violence and entrepreneurship: N. Steensgaard, *The Asian trade revolution*. The Dutch: J. I. Israel, *Dutch primacy*. The English: K. R. Andrews, *Trade, plunder and settlement*. English entrepreneurs in privateering, trade and naval administration: J. A. Williamson, *Hawkins of Plymouth* (London, 1969); R. T. Spence, *The privateering earl: George Clifford, 3rd earl of Cumberland, 1558–1605* (Stroud, 1995). The role of merchants and investors interested in English maritime expansion in the opposition against Charles I and their central role in the post-Civil War expansion of the English navy: R. Brenner, *Merchants and Revolution*.

20 Weberian and neoweberian organisation theory: C. Perrow, *Complex organizations: A critical essay* (3rd edn, New York, 1986).

21 The separation was of course not complete and no state has ever been completely uninfluenced by the power structure in the surrounding local societies. But the important thing is that the development of the state provided an alternative to the traditional local power structure, an alternative with which traditional powerholders must make compromises .

22 H. Simon, *Administrative behavior* (3rd edn, New York 1976, 1st edn 1947); A. D. Chandler, *Strategy and structure* (Cambridge, Mass., 1962); O. E. Williamson, *Markets and hierarchies: Analysis and antitrust implications* (New York, 1975); O. E. Williamson, *The economic institutions of capitalism: Firms, markets, relational contracting* (New York, 1985).

23 C. Perrow, *Complex organizations* (1986), pp. 236–238. 'Asset specificity': a high degree of specialisation of skills and hardware which makes them highly attractive under certain conditions but also of little use under different conditions. Specialised warships or trained formations of soldiers are typical examples.

24 Path-dependence: R. R. Nelson and S. G. Winter, *An evolutionary theory of economic change* (Boston, 1982).

25 Compare Chapter 2, pp. 17–20.

26 F. C. Lane, *Profit*; N. Steensgaard, *The Asian trade revolution*, esp. pp. 60–153, N. Steensgaard, 'Violence and the rise of capitalism: Frederic C. Lane's theory of protection and tribute', *Review* 2, pp. 247–273, 1981.

27 The entrepôt theory was originally developed by T. P. van der Kooy, *Hollands stapelmarkt en haar verval* (Amsterdam, 1931) and later used by P. W. Klein, *De Trippen*, esp. pp. 1–17 and J. I. Israel, *Dutch primacy*. F. Braudel, *Civilization and capitalism* and I. Wallerstein, *The modern world-system* have also put great emphasis on entrepôts and shifting hegemonies in world trade.

28 These conclusions are mainly based on J. I. Israel, *The Dutch Republic and the Hispanic*

world and J. I. Israel, *Empires*. See also K. Davids and J. Lucassen, *A miracle mirrored*, J. de Vries and A. van der Woude, *The first modern economy: Success, failure and perseverance of the Dutch economy, 1500–1815* (Cambridge, 1997), esp. pp. 667–668, 691–692, 714–715 and J. Alcalá-Zamora, *Espana*.

5 THE PORTUGUESE IN MARITIME ASIA, 1498–1600

1 J. Needham, *Science and civilisation in China*, vol. 4, part III (Cambridge, 1971), pp. 479–535; L. Levathes, *When China ruled the seas: The treasure fleet of the Dragon Throne, 1405–1433* (Oxford, 1994). For the political context, see *The Cambridge history of China*, vol. 8 (Cambridge, 1998), pp. 301–333.

The length and beam of the fifteenth century Imperial Chinese ships have reached fantastic proportions in the literature. The reported dimensions do not correspond with the (realistic) cargo capacity and displacement given by the same authors. They are rather the dimensions of ships which are 10 to 15 times larger and thus incredible. For a critical review, see R. Barker, 'The size of the "treasure ships" and other Chinese vessels', *Mariner's Mirror* 75, pp. 273–275, 1989 and A. Wegener Sleeswyk, 'The *liao* and the displacements of ships in the Ming navy', *Mariner's Mirror* 82, pp. 3–13, 1996. See also the discussion of measurement problems in C. Wake, 'The great ocean-going ships of Southern China in the age of Chinese maritime voyaging to India, twelfth to fifteenth centuries', *International Journal of Maritime History* 9, pp. 51–81, 1997.

2 Asian trade: K. N. Chaudhuri, *Trade and civilisation in the Indian Ocean: An economic history from the rise of Islam to 1750* (Cambridge, 1985). Portuguese activities: C. R. Boxer, *The Portuguese seaborne empire*; B. W. Diffie and G. D. Winius, *Foundations*; M. N. Pearson, *The Portuguese in India* (Cambridge, 1987); S. Subrahmanyam, *The Portuguese empire in Asia, 1500–1700: A political and economic history* (London, 1993). Portuguese trade: M. A. P. Meilink-Roelofsz, *Asian trade and European influence in the Indonesian archipelago between 1500 and about 1630* (The Hague, 1962); V. Magalhaes Godinho, *Os descobrimentos*; J. C. Boyajian, *Portuguese trade*. The early decades: S. Subrahmanyam, *The career and legend of Vasco da Gama* (Cambridge, 1997). Naval actions: P. Padfield, *Tide of empires*, vol. 1, pp. 19–73; S. Monteiro, *Batalhas e combates da marinha Portuguesa, 1139–1579*, 3 vols (Lisbon, 1989–92). The Muslim empires, the Indian Ocean and the Portuguese: H. Inalcik, *An economic and social history of the Ottoman empire*, vol. 1, *1300–1600* (Cambridge, 1994), pp. 315–363 and N. M. Farooqi, 'Moguls, Ottomans, and pilgrims: Protecting the routes to Mecca in the Sixteenth and Seventeenth Centuries', *International History Review* 10, pp. 198–220, 1988.

3 Surveys: J. E. Wills, 'Maritime Asia, 1500–1800: The interactive emergence of European domination', *American Historical Review* 98, pp. 83–105, 1993 and A. R. Lewis, 'Maritime skills in the Indian Ocean, 1368–1500', *Journal of the Economic and Social History of the Orient* 16, pp. 238–264, 1973.

4 The Muslim response: A. C. Hess, 'The evolution of the Ottoman seaborne empire in the Age of the oceanic discoveries, 1453–1525', *American Historical Review* 75, pp. 1892–1919, 1970 and P. Brummett, *Ottoman seapower and Levantine diplomacy in the Age of discovery* (Albany, 1994), pp. 51–122.

5 Protection selling and convoys in western India: M. N. Pearson, *Merchants and rulers in Gujarat: The response to the Portuguese in the sixteenth century* (Berkeley, 1976), esp. pp. 30–56.

6 Portuguese warship development: J. da Gama Pimentel Barata, *Estudos*.

7 Estimate of manpower from C. R. Boxer, *The Portuguese seaborne empire*, p. 53.

8 J. F. Guilmartin Jr, *Gunpowder*, pp. 7–15.

9 A. C. Hess, 'The evolution'; P. Brummett, *Ottoman seapower*; H. Inalcik, *Economic and social history*, pp. 319–340.

10 C. H. Imber, 'The navy'.
11 C. R. Boxer, *The Portuguese seaborne empire*, p. 58; S. Subrahmanyam, *The Portuguese empire*, pp. 134–135.
12 C. R. Boxer, 'A note on Portuguese reactions to the revival of the Red Sea spice trade and the rise of Atjeh, 1540–1600', in C. R. Boxer, *Portuguese conquest and commerce in Southern Asia, 1500–1750* (Aldershot, 1985, first published 1969) and H. Inalcik, *Economic and social history*, pp. 327–331. The role of the Ottomans in supplying artillery technology to Aceh and to other rulers in the Indian Ocean who fought the Portuguese: H. Inalcik, 'The socio-political effects of the diffusion of firearms in the Middle East', in *War, technology and society in the Middle East*, V. J. Parry and M. E. Yapp (eds), (Oxford, 1975).
13 C. R. Boxer, *The Great Ship from Amacon: Annals of Macao and the Old Japan trade, 1555–1640* (Lisbon, 1959).
14 See Chapters 9 and 10.
15 F. C. Lane, *Profits*, pp, 12–49 (first published 1941–50). Lane's texts are only brief interpretations based on his research on the Venetian spice trade and its interaction with Portuguese Indian Ocean policy.
16 V. Magalhaes Godinho, *Os descobrimentos*, esp. vol. 1, pp. 51–62.
17 N. Steensgaard, *The Asian trade revolution*.
18 M. N. Pearson, *Merchants and rulers*; M. N. Pearson, *The Portuguese in India*; M. N. Pearson, 'Merchants and states', in *The political economy*, J. D. Tracy (ed.), pp. 41–116.
19 S. Subrahmanyam, *The political economy of commerce: Southern India, 1500–1650* (Cambridge, 1990); S. Subrahmanyam, *Improvising empire: Portuguese trade and settlement in the Bay of Bengal, 1500–1700* (Oxford, 1990); S. Subrahmanyam and L. F. Thomas, 'Evolution of empire: The Portuguese in the Indian Ocean during the sixteenth century', in *The political economy*, J. D. Tracy (ed.); S. Subrahmanyam, *The Portuguese empire* and the 'Roundtable' about this book in *International Journal of Maritime History* 5, pp. 211–253, 1993.
20 J. C. Boyajian, *Portuguese trade*.
21 C. Cipolla, *Guns and sails*, pp. 101–103, 132–148; G. Parker, *Military revolution*, pp. 104–106. The same argument is found in C. R. Boxer, *The Portuguese seaborne empire*, pp. 49–50; P. Padfield, *Tide of Empires*, pp. 42–53, 71, B. W. Diffie and G. D. Winius, *Foundations*, pp. 214–219; W. H. McNeill, *The pursuit of power*, p. 95 and M. N. Pearson, *The Portuguese in India*, pp. 57–60, 133. H. Inalcik, 'The socio-political effects' also underlines the importance of guns in the Indian Ocean.
22 P. J. Marshall, 'Western arms in maritime Asia in the early phases of expansion' and G. V. Scammell, 'Indigenous assistance in the establishment of Portuguese power in Asia in the sixteenth century', both in *Modern Asia studies* 14, pp. 11–28, 1980.
23 General: The *Cambridge history of China*, vols 7–8 (Cambridge, 1988–98), esp. vol. 8, pp. 333–375 (by J. E. Wills Jr); W. H. McNeill, *The Pursuit of Power*, pp. 42–62. Chinese maritime technology: J. Needham, *Science*, vol. 4, part III, pp. 379–699. Chinese gunpowder technology: J. Needham, *Science*, vol. 5, part VII (Cambridge, 1986).
24 A. L. Sadler, 'The naval campaign in the Korean war of Hideyoshi (1592–8)', *Transactions of the Asiatic society of Japan*, 2nd series 14, pp. 177–208, 1937 (a fundamental article, much used by later authors. I have been unable to read it). A. J. Marder, 'From Jimmu Tenno to Perry: Sea power in early Japanese history', *American Historical Review* 51, pp. 1–34, 1945; D. M. Brown, 'The impact of firearms on Japanese warfare, 1543–98', *Far Eastern Quarterly* 7, pp. 236–253, 1948; Park Yune-hee, *Admiral Yi Sun-shin and his turtleboat armada: A comprehensive account of the resistance of Korea to the 16th century Japanese invasion* (Seoul, 1973); G. Parker, *The military revolution*, pp. 108–110, 140–145.

25 Park, *Admiral Yi Sun-shin*, pp. 74–76 gives data, probably derived from preserved Korean guns.
26 The turtle-ships were reportedly built to a standardised design but the reported dimensions differ and they may actually have been built in more than one size. A reported length of 33 metres and a beam of 8 metres seems to suit a reported broad-side armament of 12 guns on each side, J. Needham, *Science*, vol. 4, part III, pp. 682–685. Another source gives a length of around 45 metres, a beam of around 7.5 metres, around 40 guns, 2 masts and 20 to 30 (pairs of?) oars, possibly with six men to each oar, D. M. Brown, 'The Impact', pp. 250. Smaller dimensions are reported for turtle-ships in the late eighteenth century, Park, *Admiral Yi Sun-shin*, pp. 70–74. As oared ships they had large crews and can have been suitable only for short-distance operations but that was all what was required of them in the Korean-Japanese wars.

The turtle-ships are often described as armoured with wrought iron but this is doubtful. Such armour must have been very thin and wood ought in any case to have given adequate cover against Japanese naval weapons, including muskets. In additions to guns, the Koreans also used fire-arrows, incendiary bombs and possibly toxic smoke.
27 A. J. Marder, *From Jimmu Tenno*, p. 22; D. M. Brown, 'The impact', pp. 250, 252.

6 THE MEDITERRANEAN: THE FAILURE OF EMPIRES

1 The war of 1499–1502: F. C. Lane, 'Naval actions and fleet organization, 1499–1502', in *Renaissance Venice*, J. R. Hale (ed.), (Totowa, N. J., 1973); pp. 146–173, S. Pepper, 'Fortress and fleet: The defence of Venice's mainland Greek colonies in the late fifteenth century', in *War, society and culture in Renaissance Venice: Essays in honour of John Hale*, D. S. Chambers et al. (eds), (London, 1993).
2 The displacement estimates are those of the author. They are highly approximate.
3 Old standard works on the Mediterranean navies with references to the sources are C. Fernandez Duro, *Armada espanola*, C. Manfroni, *Storia* and C. de La Roncière, *Histoire*. In the absence of recent studies, the information about naval operations in this chapter has mainly been derived from them. A. C. Hess, *The forgotten frontier* has a fresh approach to the sources but covers only a selection of the major operations. J. F. Guilmartin, *Gunpowder* is a major step forward in interpretation of galley war-fare. It has been influential in this chapter although Guilmartin's conclusions must sometimes be seen as hypotheses. Trade, warfare and political events: the most influential synthesis is F. Braudel, *The Mediterranean*. Navies as organisations for protection selling and violence control: J. Glete, *Navies*.
4 J. Heers, *Gênes*; R. Romano, 'La marine marchande vénitienne au XVIe siècle', in *Les sources de l'histoire maritime en Europe, du moyen age au XVIIIe siècle*, M. Mollat (ed.), (Paris, 1962); M. E. Mallett, *The Florentine galleys in the fifteenth century* (Oxford, 1967), *Guerra e commercio nell'evoluzione della marina genovese tra XV e XVII secolo*, 2 vols (Genoa, 1970–73); F. C. Lane, *Venice*; J.-C. Hocquet, *Le sel et la fortune de Venise*; vol. 2: *Voiliers et commerce en Méditerranée, 1200–1650* (Lille, 1982); E. Ashtor, *Levant trade in the later Middle Ages* (Princeton, 1983); S. Epstein, *Genoa and the Genoese, 958–1528* (Chapel Hill, 1996); T. A. Kirk, *Genoa*.
5 Ottoman imperial expansion: *The Cambridge history of Islam*, vol. 1 (Cambridge, 1970), pp. 293–353 (by H. Inalcik): H. Inalcik, *The Ottoman empire: The classical age, 1300–1600* (London, 1973). Ottoman sea power: A. C. Hess, 'The evolution', A. C. Hess, 'The battle of Lepanto and its place in Mediterranean history', *Past and Present* 57, pp. 53–73, 1972; A. C. Hess, 'The Ottoman conquest of Egypt (1517) and the beginning of the sixteenth-century world war', *International Journal of Middle East Studies* 4, pp. 55–76, 1973; A. C. Hess, *The forgotten frontier*, J. H. Pryor, *Geography, technology, and war: Studies in the maritime history of the Mediterranean, 649–1571*

(Cambridge, 1988), pp. 165–196; P. Brummett, *Ottoman seapower*. Ottoman land warfare: R. Murphey, *Ottoman warfare, 1500–1700* (London, 1999).

6 J.-L. Bacque-Grammont, 'Soutien logistique et présence navale ottomane en Méditerranée en 1517', *Revue de l'occident musulmane et de la Méditerranée* 39, pp. 7–34, 1985.

7 The Ottoman navy on the Danube: C. H. Imber, 'The navy', pp. 275–277.

8 P. Brummett, *Ottoman seapower*. Ottoman sea power and the economy: H. Inalcik. *An economic and social history*, esp. pp. 44–54.

9 J. N. Hillgarth, *The Spanish kingdoms, 1250–1516*, vol. 2, *1410–1516* (Oxford, 1978), esp. pp. 534–584; A. C. Hess, *The forgotten frontier*.

10 The Italian wars at sea: C. de La Roncière, *Histoire*, vol. 3, has the most detailed general account, but the subject requires a modern study. The political background: R. Bonney, *The European dynastic states*, pp. 79–130 and M. S. Anderson, *The origins of the modern European state system, 1494–1618* (London, 1998), pp. 69–138.

11 A. C. Hess, *The forgotten frontier*, pp. 26–70; S. Soucek, 'The rise of the Barbarossa in North Africa', *Archivum Ottomanicum* 3, pp. 238–250, 1971. A popular biography: E. Bradford, *The Sultan's admiral*.

12 General: J. B. Wolf, *The Barbary coast: Algeria under the Turks* (New York, 1979).

13 Doria, Genoa and Spain: T. A. Kirk, *Genoa*.

14 The Order of St John and its navy have been popular subjects. Recent general accounts: U. B. Ubaldini, *La Marina*; R. L. Dauber, *Die Marine des Johanniter-Malteser-Ritter-Ordens: 500 Jahre Seekrieg zur Verteidigung Europas* (Graz, 1989); J.-D. Brandes, *Korsaren Christi: Johanniter und Malteser. Die Herren des Mittelmeers* (Sigmaringen, 1997), J. M. Wismayer, *The fleet of the Order of St. John, 1530–1798* (Valletta, 1997);

15 The literature is often uncertain about whether an invasion was intended or not. H. Inalcik in *Cambridge history of Islam*, p. 327 unambiguously states that this was the Sultan's intention.

16 The analysis of Prevesa in J. F. Guilmartin, *Gunpowder*, pp. 42–56 make sense and has been used here, but there are errors (or misprints) in its chronology. On p. 52 Guilmartin says that Doria's fleet had been off Prevesa for about three weeks when it retired, but different information is given on pp. 45 and 48. All accounts in the literature available to me are silent on this crucial point. Traditionally, Prevesa has often been interpreted as a 'political' battle, determined by secret negotiations, treason and jealousy between the Genoese Doria and the Venetians.

17 C. H. Imber, 'The cost of naval warfare: The accounts of Hayreddin Barbarossa's Herceg Novi campaign in 1539', *Archivum Ottomanicum* 4, pp. 203–216, 1972.

18 J. Laroche, 'L'expédition en Provence de l'armée de mer du sultan Suleyman sous le commandement de l'amiral Hayreddin Pacha, dit Barberousse (1543–1544)', *Turcica* 1, pp. 161–165, 1969.

19 F. Braudel, *The Mediterranean*, pp. 904–1185 provides a general account of politics and war from the late 1540s to 1580.

20 G. Veinstein, 'Les préparatifs de la campagne navale Franco-Turque de 1552 à travers les ordres du divan Ottoman', *Revue de l'occident musulman et de la Méditerannée* 39, pp. 35–67, 1985.

21 From 1559, R. C. Anderson, *Naval wars in the Levant* provides a year by year account of naval operations.

22 At this time, the 93 year old Andrea Doria was still commander of the Spanish Mediterranean fleet, but too old for seagoing command – he died in 1560. His young relative, Gian Andrea Doria, acted as commander in his place.

23 An analysis of Djerba: J. F. Guilmartin, *Gunpowder*, pp. 123–134. Guilmartin has not used C. Monchicourt, *L'expédition espagnole contre l'île de Djerba* (Paris, 1913) which according to F. Braudel, *The Mediterranean*, p. 973, note 21, is the major work on the subject.

24 This interpretation in J. F. Guilmartin, *Gunpowder*, pp. 131–134.

25 E. Bradford, *The great siege* (London, 1961). An analysis which makes the Spanish strategy look more sophisticated than in earlier literature is J. F. Guilmartin, *Gunpowder*, pp. 176–193. This text follows Guilmartin's analysis.

26 This explanation in J. F. Guilmartin, *Gunpowder*, p. 236. There are other explanations in the literature, but Guilmartin has emphasised the limits of galley warfare as important. A Spanish work on this war is R. Cerezo Martinez, *Anos cruciales en la historia del Mediterraneo, 1570–1574* (Madrid, 1971).

27 This analysis follows J. F. Guilmartin, *Gunpowder*, pp. 221–252 and J. F. Guilmartin, 'The tactics of the battle of Lepanto'. See also G. Benzione (ed.), *Il Mediterraneo*.

28 Three specialists give these figures: R. C. Anderson, *Naval wars in the Levant*, p. 45: 30,000 Turks and 9,000 Christians lost. F. Braudel, *The Mediterranean*, p. 1102: the Turks lost over 30,000 dead and wounded, 3,000 prisoners and 15,000 of their galley slaves were freed, the Christians had 8,000 killed and 21,000 wounded. J. F. Guilmartin, *Gunpowder*, p. 251: 30,000 Turks killed, 3,468 taken prisoner and some 15,000 Christian galley slaves freed.

29 J. F. Guilmartin, *Gunpowder*, esp. pp. 253–273.

30 A general history of the Mediterranean after 1580 during the 'decline of empires' is lacking and the maritime aspect of Spanish-Italian history in this period is also neglected. Individual states: T. A. Kirk, *Genoa*; F. C. Lane, *Venice*, pp. 384–417; *The Cambridge history of Islam*, vol. 1, pp. 336–353 (by H. Inalcik); S. Faroqhi *et al.*, *An economic and social history of the Ottoman empire*, vol. 2, *1600–1914*, pp. 411–636 (by S. Faroqhi). Naval operations: R. C. Anderson, *Naval wars in the Levant*, pp. 55–147; C. Fernandez Duro, *Armada espanola*, vols 2–4; M. Nani Mocenigo, *Storia*; C. Manfroni, 'La marina da guerra del Granducato Mediceo' (in 7 parts), *Rivista Maritima* 28–29, 1895–96; G. Guarnieri, *I cavalieri di Santo Stefano nella storia della marina italiana, 1562–1859* (3rd edn, Pisa, 1960). Trade: A. C. Wood, *A history of the Levant Company* (Oxford, 1935, 1964); F. Braudel and R. Romano, *Navires et marchandises à l'entrée du port de Livourne, 1547–1611* (Paris, 1951); *Aspetti e cause della decadenza economica veneziana nel secolo XVII* (Venice and Rome, 1961); M. Aymard, *Venise, Raguse et le commerce de blé pendant la seconde moitié du XVIe siècle* (Paris, 1966); B. Pullan (ed.), *Crisis and change in the Venetian economy in the fifteenth and sixteenth centuries* (London, 1968); J. I. Israel, 'The phases of the Dutch *Straatvaart*, 1590–1713: A chapter in the economic history of the Mediterranean', *Tijdschrift voor Geschiedenis* 99, pp. 133–162, 1986; D. Goffman, *Izmir and the Levantine world, 1550–1650* (Seattle, 1990).

31 Privateering and piracy: A. Tenenti, *Naufrages, corsaires et assurances maritimes à Venise, 1592–1609* (Paris, 1959); A. Tenenti, *Piracy*; P. Earl, *Corsairs of Malta and Barbary* (London, 1970); M. Fontenoy and A. Tenenti, 'Course et piraterie Méditerrannéennes de la fin du moyen-age au debut de XIXe siècle', in *Course et piraterie*, pp. 78–136; J. B. Wolf, *The Barbary Coast*; C. Manca, 'Uomini per la corsa: Rapporti di classe e condizioni sociali nelle città marittime Barbaresche dopo Lepanto', in *Le genti*, R. Ragosta (ed.), pp. 725–772; M. Fontenoy, 'Corsaires de la foi ou rentiers du sol? Les chevaliers de Malte dans le "corso" Méditerranéen au XVIIe siècle', *Revue d'histoire moderne et contemporaine* 35, pp. 361–384, 1988; S. Bono, *Corsari nel Mediterraneo: Cristiani e musulmani fra guerra, sciavitù e commercio* (Milan, 1993); D. D. Hebb, *Piracy*; G. Hanlon, *The twilight*, pp. 26–46.

32 J. I. Israel, 'The Phases' argues that Braudel has underestimated the efficiency of the Spanish embargoes on Dutch and English shipping. But even Israel shows that the ships of Spain's enemies passed in and out of the Mediterranean up to 1598.

33 C. W. Bracewell, *The Uskoks of Senj: Piracy, banditry, and holy war in the sixteenth-century Adriatic* (Ithaca, 1992).

34 For an enthusiastic account, see C. Fernandez Duro, *El Gran Duque de Osuna y su marina: Jornadas contra Turcos y Veneciana* (Madrid, 1885). R. C. Anderson, *Naval wars*

in the Levant, pp. 77–105 gives a more balanced account. Political background: L. Barbe, *Don Pedro Téllez Girón, duc d'Osuna, Vice-roi de Sicile, 1610–1616: Contribution à l'étude du règne de Philippe III* (Grenoble, 1992).

35 I. A. A. Thompson, *War and government*, p. 199.

36 R. E. J. Weber, *De beveiling van de zee tegen europeesche en barbarische zeerovers, 1609–1621* (Amsterdam, 1936); D. D. Hebb, *Piracy*.

37 *Cambridge history of Islam*, vol. 1, p. 351.

38 The Ottoman empire as a contender for world power status is underlined by Halil Inalcik, Andrew C. Hess and Palmira Brummett.

7 MARITIME STATE FORMATION AND EMPIRE BUILDING IN THE BALTIC

1 This 'protection selling' interpretation (based on F. C. Lane's theory) of German–Dutch–Nordic relations from the fifteenth to the seventeenth century was first presented in J. Glete, *Navies*, pp. 110–114, 133–139, with more extensive references to the literature than in this chapter. For more information about the Baltic navies, see that study. See also G. Rystad et al., *In quest of trade and security: The Baltic in power politics, 1500–1990: vol. 1, 1500–1890* (Lund, 1994), esp. the contributions by J. Glete, A. Tjaden, K. J. V. Jespersen and K.-R. Böhme. Recent general surveys of Baltic history in English: D. Kirby, *Northern Europe in the early modern period: The Baltic world, 1492–1772* (London, 1990) and S. Oakley, *War and peace in the Baltic, 1560–1790* (London, 1992).

2 Medieval Baltic, Scandinavia and the Hanse: P. Dollinger, *The German Hansa*; K. Kumlien, *Sverige och hanseaterna: Studier i svensk politik och utrikeshandel* (Stockholm, 1953); E. Albrectsen, *Danmark-Norge 1380–1814: vol. 1, Faelleskabet bliver til, 1380–1536* (Oslo, 1997); K. Fritze and G. Krause, *Seekriege der Hanse: Das erste Kapitel deutscher Seekriegsgeschichte* (Berlin, 1997). The Hanse and the Dutch: D. Seifert, *Kompagnons und Konkurrenten: Holland und die Hanse im späten Mittelalter* (Köln, 1997). The Hanse and England: J. D. Fudge, *Cargoes, embargoes, and emissaries: The commercial and political interaction of England and the German Hanse, 1450–1510* (Toronto, 1995). Eastern Baltic: E. Christiansen, *The Northern Crusades: The Baltic and the Catholic frontier, 1100–1525* (London, 1980).

3 The Sound Toll: M. Venge, *Dansk toldhistorie: vol. I, Fra åretold till toldetat: Middelalderen indtil 1660* (Copenhagen, 1987). Danish state finance in the sixteenth century: S. Balle, *Statsfinanserne på Christian 3.s tid* (Aarhus, 1992), which also has information about the Danish navy.

4 A. Attman, *The struggle*; S. Troebst, *Handelskontrolle, 'Derivation', Eindämmerung: Schwedische Moskaupolitik, 1617–1661* (Wiesbaden, 1997). There is a long scholarly debate about the ultimate motives for Swedish imperial expansion. Here it is enough to say that control of trade was one motive.

5 A. E. Christensen, *Dutch trade to the Baltic about 1600: Studies in the Sound toll register and Dutch shipping records* (Copenhagen, 1941); P. W. Klein, *De Trippen*; A. Attman, *The Russian and Polish markets in international trade, 1500–1650* (Gothenburg, 1973); Å. Sandström, *Mellan Torneå och Amsterdam: En undersökning av Stockholms roll som förmedlare av varor i regional- och utrikeshandel* (Stockholm, 1990); J. Israel, *Dutch primacy*; P. Jeannin, *Marchands du Nord: Espaces et trafics à l'époque moderne* (Paris, 1996).

6 This section and the rest of the chapter is based on several old and new books and articles on Baltic and Nordic history. General: E. Albrectsen, *Danmark-Norge, 1380–1536*; Ö. Rian, *Danmark-Norge, 1380–1814: vol. II, Den aristokratiske fyrstestaten, 1536–1648* (Oslo, 1997); M. Roberts, *The early Vasas: A history of Sweden, 1523–1611* (Cambridge, 1968). Naval operations: Denmark-Norway: J. H. Barfod, *Flådens födsel*; J. H. Barfod, *Christian 3.s flåde*. Lübeck: K. Fritze and G. Krause,

Seekriege, pp. 142–187 (unreliable about battles). Sweden: B. C: son Barkman, *Kungl. Svea Livgardes historia, vol. I, 1523–1560* (Stockholm, 1937) gives the best account of Swedish army and navy operations 1521–1560. Dutch and Habsburg participation in Baltic warfare: L. Sicking, *Zeemacht en onmacht*, pp. 109–122. This chapter is partly based on the author's own research on Baltic naval history, partly published in J. Glete, 'Svenska örlogsfartyg, 1521–1560'. R. C. Anderson, *Naval wars in the Baltic* pp. 1–70 is reliable but dated.

7 This admiral is a legend in Nordic history: L. J. Larsson, *Sören Norby och Öster-sjöpolitiken, 1523–1525* (Lund, 1986); B. Graffton, *Sören Norby: Sjökrigare i Östersjön på 1500–talet* (Visby, 1995).

8 Swedish trade and foreign policy: S. Lundkvist, *Gustav Vasa och Europa: Svensk handels- och utrikespolitik, 1534–1557* (Uppsala, 1960).

9 G. Landberg, *De nordiska rikena under Brömsebroförbundet* (Uppsala, 1925), maritime and naval aspects, pp. 72–89.

10 The latest detailed study of this war is F. P. Jensen, *Danmarks konflikt med Sverige, 1563–1570* (Copenhagen, 1982). Naval operations: H. D. Lind, *Fra kong Frederik den andens tid: Bidrag til den dansk-norske sömagts historie, 1559–1588* (Copenhagen, 1902), pp. 1–162; E. Briand de Crèvecoeur, *Herluf Trolle: Kongens Admiral och Herlufsholms Skoles stifter* (Copenhagen, 1959), pp. 69–138; *Svenska flottans historia, vol. I, 1521–1679*, esp. pp. 155–157, 168–172, 508–515 (text by C. Ekman and G. Unger); C. Ekman, 'Några data om Erik XIV: s sjökrigskonst', *Tidskrift i Sjöväsendet* 109, pp. 50–83, 1946; H. Kloth, 'Lübecks Seekriegswesen in der Zeit des nordischen Siebenjährige Krieges, 1563–1570: Ein Beitrag zur deutschen Seekriegsgeschichte im 16. Jahrhundert', *Zeitschrift des Vereins für Lübeckische Geschichte und Altertumskunde* 21, pp. 1–51, 185–256, 1923, 22, pp. 121–152, 325–379, 1925. The present text is also based on the author's unpublished research, mainly in the Swedish naval archives at Riksarkivet, Stockholm and Krigsarkivet, Stockholm. Swedish naval accounts are well preserved, while there are more narrative texts preserved on the allied side.

11 M. H. Mortensen, *Dansk artilleri*, pp. 207–215.

12 The orders of battle of the fleets in the war of 1563–70 are often uncertain. The estimates of the number of ships are those of the author. Only ships which according to the author's estimate were of around 300 tonnes displacement or larger are included in order to facilitate comparisons of the sizes of the fleets. Smaller ships were seldom of much importance in major actions.

13 Slow loading procedure has been suggested as an explanation of the Armada's failure to inflict much damage on the English fleet in 1588, C. Martin and G. Parker, *The Spanish Armada*, pp. 195–226.

14 Nordic history in general: M. Roberts, *The early Vasas*; Ö. Rian, *Danmark-Norge, 1536–1648*.

15 A. Attman, *The struggle*.

16 The post-1570 naval competition between the Nordic states will be treated in a future study of the Swedish navy.

17 Danish naval operations up to 1588: H. D. Lind, *Fra kong Frederik*, pp. 163–236; J. H. Barfod, *Christan 3.s flåde*, pp. 223–274. From 1588 on: N. M. Probst, *Christan 4.s flåde*.

18 S. U. Palme, *Sverige och Danmark, 1596–1611* (Uppsala, 1942), the maritime conflict, pp. 558–567.

19 *Sveriges Krig, 1611–1632: Bilagsband I, Sveriges Sjökrig, 1611–1632* (Stockholm, 1937), pp. 63–122. N. M. Probst, *Christian 4.s flåde*, pp. 107–122. For the Danish navy in the years 1611–50 I rely on N. M. Probst's calculation of displacements.

20 M. Roberts, *Gustavus Adolphus: A history of Sweden, 1611–1632*, 2 vols (London, 1953–58). Swedish naval operations 1613–32: *Sveriges sjökrig, 1611–1632*, pp. 122–232.

21 The indirect effects on Denmark of Swedish expansion in the eastern Baltic: L. K. Tandrup, *Mod triumf eller tragedie: En politisk-diplomatisk studie over forløbet af den dansk-svenske magtkamp fra Kalmarkrigen til Kejserkrigen*, 2 vols (Aarhus, 1979). A survey in English: P. D. Lockhart, *Denmark in the Thirty Years' War, 1618–1648: King Christian IV and the decline of the Oldenburg state* (Selinsgrove, 1996).

22 E. Koczorowski, *Bitwa pod Oliwa* (Gdansk, 1976).

23 J. I. Israel, 'The politics of international trade rivalry during the Thirty Years War: Gabriel de Roy and Olivares' mercantilist projects, 1621–1645', *International History Review* 8, pp. 517–549, 1986.

24 The war at sea 1643–45: Försvarsstaben, *Slaget vid Femern 1644* (Gothenburg, 1944), O. Bergersen, *Fra Henrik Bielke til Iver Huitfeldt: Utsyn over den dansk-norske fellesflådes historie i perioden 1630 til 1710*, vol. 1 (Trondheim, 1953), pp. 29–293; N. M. Probst, *Christian 4.s flåde*. pp. 227–256. Dutch and English armed merchantmen: see pp. 108–111 and Chapter 10.

25 Dimensions and armament for the hired Dutch ships from Louis De Geer's papers, Leufstasamlingen, vol. 47, Riksarkivet, Stockholm. The displacement calculations are those of the author. The sources for the battles are discussed by J. M. Fahlström, 'Kring den politiska och militära bakgrunden till slagen i Listerdyb den 16 och 25 maj 1644', *Skrifter utgivna av Sjöhistoriska samfundet* 6, pp. 79–109, 1945. The demise of armed merchantmen in battle fleets after 1650: J. Glete, *Navies*, pp. 180–184, 196–206.

26 Only ships of 300 tonnes and more are counted.

27 Only ships of 300 tonnes and more are counted.

28 G. W. Kernkamp, *De sleutels van de Sont: Het aandeel van de Republiek in den Deensch-Zweedschen oorlog van 1644–1645* (The Hague, 1890).

8 WAR IN WESTERN EUROPE UNTIL 1560

1 Economy, trade and shipping: for surveys with extensive bibliographies, see B. Yun, 'Economic cycles and structural changes' and J. H. Munro, 'Patterns of trade, money, and credit', both in T. A. Brady *et al.*, *Handbook of European history, 1400–1600: Late Middle Ages, Renaissance and Reformation*, vol. 1 (Leiden, 1994), pp. 113–196. The Netherlands: J. de Vries and A. van der Woude, *The first modern economy*; R. W. Unger, 'Shipping in the Northern Netherlands, 1490–1580', in R. W. Unger, *Ships and shipping in the North Sea and Atlantic, 1400–1800* (Aldershot, 1997), pp. 1–18 (with an extensive bibliography). Spain: W. D. Phillips, Jr, 'Spain's northern shipping industry in the sixteenth century', *Journal of European Economic History* 17, pp. 267–301, 1988; C. Rahn Phillips and W. D. Phillips, Jr, *Spain's golden fleece: Wool production and the wool trade from the Middle Ages to the nineteenth century* (Baltimore, 1997), pp. 210–248. France: M. Mollat, *Le commerce maritime normand*; H. Touchard, *Le commerce maritime breton*; J. Bernard, *Navires et gens de mer à Bordeaux*. England: D. Burwash, *English merchant shipping, 1460–1540*; G.V. Scammell, 'English merchant shipping at the end of the Middle Ages: Some east coast evidence', *Economic History Review* 2: 13, pp. 327–341, 1961; G. V. Scammell, 'Shipowning in England, c. 1450–1550', *Transactions of the Royal Historical Society* 5: 12, pp. 105–122, 1962; G. V. Scammell, 'Shipowning in the Economy and Politics of Early Modern England', *Historical Journal* 15, pp. 385–407, 1972.

2 T. A. Brady *et al.*, *Handbook*, vols 1–2; R. Bonney, *The European dynastic states*; D. Potter, *A history of France, 1460–1560: The emergence of a nation state* (London, 1995); J. N. Hillgarth, *The Spanish kingdoms*, vol. 2; J. Lynch, *Spain, 1516–1598: From nation-state to world empire* (Oxford, 1991); J. D. Tracy, *Holland under Habsburg rule, 1506–1566: The formation of a body politic* (Berkeley, 1990).

3 See Chapters 6 and 7.

4 J. Glete, *Navies*, pp. 9–17, 117–120, 122–132, 146–172. A recent study of sea power and state formation in the Netherlands in this period is L. Sicking, *Zeemacht*.
5 M. Mollat, 'Guerre de course et piraterie à la fin du moyen age: Aspects économiques et sociaux. Positions de problemes', *Hansische Geschichtsblätter* 90, pp. 1–14, 1972; M. Mollat, 'De la piraterie sauvage à la course réglementée (XIVe-XVe siècle)', in M. Mollat, *Études d'histoire maritime (1938–1975)* (Turin, 1977), pp. 591–609; A. Pérotin-Dumon, 'The pirate and the emperor: Power and the law on the seas, 1450–1850', in *The political economy*, J. D. Tracy (ed.), pp. 196–227.
6 The admirals of Normandy and Picardy were also Admirals of France. There is very little research on the administration of the sixteenth-century French navy and it is possible that it was more complex than outlined here. The galley fleet seems to have been more centralised than the sailing fleet. The traces of the naval administration are scattered in regional archives and private collections (see the extensive references in C. de La Roncière, *Histoire*) and there are few traces of a central naval administration before the 1620s.
7 France: C. de La Roncière, *Histoire*, vols 2–3; Ph. Contamine (ed.), *Histoire militaire de la France: Des origines à 1715* (Paris, 1992), pp. 279–301; P. Masson and M. Vergé-Franceschi, *La France et la mer*. Brittany: J. Kerhervé, *L'état breton aux 14e et 15e siècles: Les ducs, l'argent et les hommes*, 2 vols (Paris, 1987). The Netherlands: J. D. Tracy, 'The Habsburg Netherlands and the struggle for control of the North Sea, c. 1520–1560', *Sixteenth Century Journal* 24, pp. 249–272, 1993; L. Sicking, *Zeemacht*. England: D. Loades, *The Tudor navy*, pp. 11–177; N. A. M. Rodger, *The safeguard*, pp. 143–237.
8 W. D. Phillips, Jr, 'Spain's Northern Shipping'; C. Rahn Phillips and W. D. Phillips, Jr, *Spain's golden fleece*, pp. 219–230; the American convoys: P. and H. Chaunu, *Seville*.
9 R. B. Wernham, *Before*, pp. 11–26.
10 International conflicts: R. Bonney, *The European dynastic states*, pp. 79–130; R. B. Wernham, *Before*, pp. 11–243.
11 L. Sicking, *Zeemacht*.
12 For example by D. Loades, *The Tudor navy*, p. 49. In spite of that he gives evidence to the contrary on pp. 43, 49 and 60.
13 Major French warships and their armament: C. de La Roncière, *Histoire*, vol. 3, pp. 1–116 and 168, esp. pp. 32, 42, 79–80, 97; A. Anthiaume, *Le navire: Sa construction en France et principalement chez les Normands* (Paris, 1922, Marseille, 1980), pp. 211–219.
14 N. A. M. Rodger, *The safeguard*, pp. 167–169; N. MacDougall, "The greatest scheip that ewer saillit in Ingland or France": James IV's "Great Michael", in *Scotland and war, AD 79–1918*, N. MacDougall (ed.), (Edinburgh, 1991), pp. 36–60. I wish to thank Dr N. A. M. Rodger for sending me a copy of this article.
15 N. A. M. Rodger, *The safeguard*, pp. 162–163; L. G. Carr Laughton, 'Early Tudor ship-guns' (ed. by M. Lewis), *Mariner's Mirror* 46, pp. 242–285, 1960.
16 The war of 1512–14: C. de La Roncière, *Histoire*, vol. 3, pp. 89–116; D. Loades, *The Tudor navy*, pp. 55–68; N. A. M. Rodger, *The safeguard*, pp. 169–172.
17 An account of the battle in A. McKee, *Mary Rose* (London, 1973), pp. 31–38. La Cordelière main armament was 16 stoneguns firing stones of 100 to 120 pounds, C. de La Roncière, *Histoire*, vol. 3, p. 97. Stoneguns were considerably lighter in proportion to the weight of the shot than guns firing iron shot, see J. F. Guilmartin, *Gunpowder*, pp. 166–167.
18 The war of the 1520s: C. de La Roncière, *Histoire*, vol. 3, pp. 164–185; D. Loades, *The Tudor navy*, pp. 103–111; N. A. M. Rodger, *The safeguard*, pp. 174–177; L. Sicking, *Zeemacht*, pp. 163–164.
19 The war of 1542–46: C. de La Roncière, *Histoire*, vol. 3, pp. 395–431; C. Fernández Duro, *Armada espanola*, vol. 1, pp. 366–373; D. Loades, *The Tudor navy*, pp. 123–138; N. A. M. Rodger, *The safeguard*, pp. 179–184; L. Sicking, *Zeemacht*, pp. 165–167.

20 An account of naval operations in 1545 from an English perspective: A. McKee, *Mary Rose*, pp. 47–90.
21 The successful Dutch invasion in 1688 should not be forgotten but the circumstances were exceptional and not comparable.
22 See pp. 100–101
23 C. de La Roncière, *Histoire*, vol. 3, pp. 432–443; D. Loades, *The Tudor navy*, pp. 139–147; N. A. M. Rodger, *The safeguard*, pp. 184–187; E. Bonner, 'The recovery of St Andrews Castle in 1547: French naval policy and diplomacy in the British isles', *English Historical Review* 111, pp. 578–598, 1996.
24 C. de La Roncière, *Histoire*, vol. 3, pp. 453–462.
25 The wars of 1549–56: C. de La Roncière, *Histoire*, vol. 3, pp. 443–452, 480–504; C. Fernández Duro, *Armada espanola*, vol. 1, pp. 309–322; J. Craeybeckx, 'De Organisatie en de konvooiering van de koopvaardijvloot op het einde van de regering van Karel V', *Bijdragen van de Geschiedenis der Nederlanden* 3, pp. 179–208, 1949; D. Loades, *The Tudor navy*, pp. 147–149; N. A. M. Rodger, *The safeguard*, pp. 186–189.
26 The war 1557–59: C. de La Roncière, *Histoire*, vol. 3, pp. 552–569; T. Glasgow, 'The navy in Philip and Mary's War, 1557–1558', *Mariner's Mirror* 53, pp. 321–342, 1967; T. Glasgow, 'Maturing of naval administration, 1556–1564', *Mariner's Mirror* 56, pp. 3–26, 1970; D. Loades, *The Tudor navy*, pp. 190–196; N. A. M. Rodger, *The safeguard*, pp. 190–196;, L. Sicking, *Zeemacht*, pp. 140–145, 170–172.

9 ATLANTIC WARFARE UNTIL 1603

1 The emerging Atlantic economy: J. H. Parry, *The discovery of the sea* (London, 1974; P. and H. Chaunu, *Seville*; V. Magalhaes Godinho, *Os descubrimentos*; F. Mauro, *Le Portugal et l'Atlantique*; K. R. Andrews, *Trade, plunder*; J. I. Israel, *Dutch primacy*, pp. 1–81; C. Gomez-Centurion Jimenez, *Felipe II, la empresa de Inglaterra y el comercio septentrional, 1566–1609* (Madrid, 1988).
2 French overseas ambitions in the sixteenth century: C. de La Roncière, *Histoire*, vols 3–4, remains the standard work. See also Ph. Masson and M. Vergé-Franceschi, *La France et la mer*.
3 R. Bonney, *The European dynastic states*, pp. 131–187; M. P. Holt, *The French Wars of Religion, 1562–1629* (Cambridge, 1995); G. Parker, *The Dutch revolt* (London, 1977); J. I. Israel, *Dutch primacy*, pp. 12–79; R. B. Wernham, *Before*, pp. 244–408; R. B. Wernham, *After*; R. B. Wernham, *The return*; J. Lynch, *Spain, 1516–1598*.
4 P. and H. Chaunu, *Seville*; R. Pike, *Aristocrats and traders: Sevillian society in the sixteenth century* (Ithaca, 1972); P. E. Hoffman, *The Spanish crown and the defense of the Caribbean, 1535–1585: Precedent, patrimonialism and royal parsimony* (Baton Rouge, 1980); K. R. Andrews, *The Spanish Caribbean*; B. Torres, *La marina en el gobierno y administración de Indias* (Madrid, 1992); P. E. Pérez-Mallaína, *Spain's Men*.
5 O. H. K. Spate, *The Spanish lake* (Minneapolis, 1979).
6 C. Buchet, *La lutte*.
7 Conflicts with Portugal: C. de La Roncière, *Histoire*, vol. 3, pp. 243–306, vol. 4, pp. 10–14; P. E. Hoffman, *The Spanish Crown*, pp. 27–37; K. R. Andrews, *Trade, plunder*, pp. 101–115. A minor encounter at sea during these conflicts is analysed in J. F. Guilmartin, *Gunpowder*, pp. 85–94.
8 Detailed information about yearly convoys and their escorts in the statistical volumes of P. and H. Chaunu, *Seville*. See also Map 4 of this volume.
9 General works on conflicts at sea in this period are C. Fernandez Duro, *Armada espanola*, vol. 2, now partly replaced by R. Cerezo Martinez, *Las armadas de Felipe II* (Madrid, 1988) and M. de Pazzis Pi Corrales, *Felipe II y la lucha por el dominio del mar* (Madrid, 1989); C. de La Roncière, *Histoire*, vol. 4; D. B. Quinn and A. N. Ryan,

England's sea empire, 1550–1642 (London, 1983), pp 19–91; D. Loades, *The Tudor navy*, pp. 178–243; N. A. M. Rodger, *The Safeguard*, pp. 190–203, 238–253; R. E. J. Weber, 'Met smakzeilen en spiegelschepen tegen den Spanjaard', in J. Romein *et al.*, *De Tachtigjarige oorlog* (Amsterdam, 1941), pp. 132–158; *Maritieme geschiedenis*, vol. 1, pp. 326–335 (by J. C. A. de Meij); M. Acerra and G. Martinière (eds), *Coligny, les protestants et la mer* (Paris, 1997), esp. pp. 35–44, 91–108, 119–144, 155–176.

10 T. Glasgow, 'The navy in the first Elizabethan undeclared war, 1559–1560', *Mariner's Mirror* 54, pp. 23–37, 1968.

11 T. Glasgow, 'The navy in the Le Havre expedition, 1562–1564', *Mariner's Mirror* 54, pp. 281–296, 1968.

12 M. Augeron, 'Coligny et les Espagnols à travers la course (c. 1560–1572): Une politique maritime au service de la Cause protestante', in *Coligny*, M. Acerra and G. Martinière (eds), pp. 155–176. Spanish convoy protection: see the yearly convoy lists in P. and H. Chaunu, *Seville*.

The international connections between Protestants and French trans-oceanic trade were still important in the seventeenth and eighteenth centuries: J. F. Bosher, *Business and religion in the age of New France, 1600–1760* (Toronto, 1994).

13 G. Parker, *The Army of Flanders and the Spanish Road, 1567–1659* (Cambridge, 1972).

14 J. C. A. de Meij, *De watergeuzen en de Nederlanden, 1568–1572* (Amsterdam, 1972).

15 B. Dietz, 'The Huguenot and English corsairs during the Third Civil War in France, 1568 to 1570', *Proceedings of the Huguenot Society* 19, pp. 278–294, 1952–58, based on B. Dietz dissertation on Protestant privateering 1568–72.

16 The early history of one of the Dutch admiralties: H. G. van Grool, *Het Beheer van het Zeeuwsche zeewezen, 1577–1587* (Flushing, 1936).

17 V. Enthoven, *Zeeland en de opkomst van de Republiek: Handel en strijd in de Scheldedelta, c. 1550–1621* (Leiden, 1996).

18 M. Pi Corrales, *Espana y las potencias nórdicas: 'La otra invencible' 1574* (Madrid, 1983).

19 I intend to discuss this episode in another study.

20 Drake's voyage was also a major success in exploration as well as the second circumnavigation of the globe; O. H. K. Spate, *The Spanish lake*, pp. 229–264; K. R. Andrews, *Trade, plunder*, pp. 135–166.

21 The main Spanish work on the events in 1582–83 remains C. Fernandez Duro, *La conquista de las Azores en 1583* (Madrid, 1886). The French story: C. de La Roncière, *Histoire*, vol. 4, pp. 167–205.

22 It is usually called the battle of Terceira after another island in the Azores.

23 C. de La Roncière, *Histoire*, vol. 4, p. 189 states that four ships and about 1,500 men were lost while the Spanish literature gives the losses as ten or more ships and about the same number of men. The French flagship was among the ships lost.

24 Classical studies of this war: J. S. Corbett, *Drake and the Tudor navy*, 2 vols (London, 1898, new edn. with an introduction by R. B. Wernham, London, 1988); J. S. Corbett, *The successors of Drake* (London, 1900) and C. Fernandez Duro, *Armada espanola*, vols 2–3. More recent works: R. B. Wernham, *Before*; R. B. Wernham, *After*; R. B. Wernham, *The return*; K. R. Andrews, *Elizabethan privateering: English privateering during the Spanish War, 1585–1603* (Cambridge, 1964); D. Loades, *The Tudor navy*, pp. 233–281; N. A. M. Rodger, *The Safeguard*, pp. 238–296; R. Cerezo Martinez, *Las Armadas*, pp. 305–418; M. (de Pazzis) Pi Corrales, *Felipe II*, pp. 263–335; R. E. J. Weber, 'Met smakzeilen'. Spanish convoys: H. and P. Chaunu, *Seville*.

25 Examples of interpretations of Philip's intentions with the Armada and its possible effects had it been successful: G. Parker, 'If the Armada had landed', *History* 60, pp. 358–368, 1976; I. A. A. Thompson, 'The Invincible Armada', in *Royal Armada 400 years* (London, 1988), pp. 160–179; De Lamar Jensen, 'The Spanish Armada: The worst-kept secret in Europe', *Sixteenth Century Journal* 4, pp. 621–641, 1988; G.

211

Parker, 'David or Goliath? Philip II and his world in the 1580s', in *Spain, Europe and the Atlantic world*, R. L. Kegan and G. Parker (eds) (Cambridge, 1995).

26 The literature about the Armada is enormous, see E. L. Rasor, *The Spanish Armada of 1588: Historiography and annotated bibliography* (Westport, Conn., 1993). Among recent studies may be mentioned M. J. Rodríguez-Salgado (ed.), *Armada, 1588–1988: An international exhibition to commemorate the Spanish Armada* (London, 1988); C. Martin and G. Parker, *The Spanish Armada*; F. Fernandez-Armesto, *The Spanish Armada: The experience of war in 1588* (Oxford, 1988); M. J. Rodríguez-Salgado and S. Adams, *England, Spain and the Gran Armada* and the eight volumes with special studies about the Armada campaign published by Instituto de historia y cultura naval in 1988–90. A Spanish source publication, J. Calvar Gross et al. (eds), *La batalla del Mar Oceano: Corpus documental de las hostilidades entre Espana e Inglaterra, 1568–1604*, 5 vols in several parts (Madrid, 1988–) is in progress

27 J. L. Casado Soto, *Los barcos espanoles* has thoroughly researched the sources on Armada ships and has found or reconstructed the dimensions for nearly all units. The displacement figures are calculated by the present author from these dimensions. My figures are approximate but based on better evidence than those used in J. Glete, *Navies*, p. 149.

28 M. de Pazzis Pi Corrales, *Felipe II*, p. 301. The infantry of the Armada: M. Gracia Rivas, *Los tercios de la Gran Armada, 1587–1588* (Madrid, 1989).

29 In M. J. Rodriguez-Salgado (ed.), *The Armada, 1588–1988*, pp. 151–158 Ian Friel has revised the list with 163 private vessels usually quoted since the publication of J. Knox Laughton, *State papers relating to the defeat of the Spanish Armada*, 2 vols. Navy Records Society, nos.1–2 (London 1894–95, 1981), see vol. 2, pp. 323–331. Friel believes that the tonnage for private ships is given in 'tons burden' but, according to W. Salisbury, 'Early tonnage measurement in England', *Mariner's Mirror* 52, 1966, p. 44, tonnage for private ships hired by the navy was normally given in 'tons and tonnage' (the maximum carrying capacity of a merchantman) which usually was calculated by adding one third to the 'tons burden' (the capacity to carry commercial cargo). My displacement calculations for private English ships are based on the assumption that the tonnages in the lists are 'tons and tonnage' and that the displacement of a fully loaded wooden ship is about 50 per cent larger than its maximum cargo capacity. This assumption is partly based on the size of the crew of the private vessels in 1588 compared with the royal warships for which the dimensions are known. As long as no detailed study of tonnage measurement for English sixteenth-century merchantmen has been done, all estimates must be preliminary.

30 I. A. A. Thompson, 'Spanish Armada guns', *Mariner's Mirror* 61, pp. 355–371, 1975; C. Martin and G. Parker, *The Spanish Armada*, pp. 195–225.

31 H. J. O'Donnell y Duque de Estrada, *La fuerza de desembarco de la Gran Armada contra Inglaterra, 1588: Su origen, organizacion y vicisitudes* (Madrid, 1990); F. Riano Lozano, *Los medios navales de Alejandro Farnesio, 1587–88* (Madrid, 1989).

32 See Chapter 8. When France planned invasions of England in the early 1690s and around 1800 large forces of oared warships were built for Channel operations.

33 Summary of losses in J. L. Casado Soto, *Los barcos*, p. 245. Of 127 vessels, 92 survived but many of the lost ships were large and the losses of men were very great. Of 18,288 soldiers mustered in July, 8,723 did not return, M. Gracia Rivas, *Los tercios*, p. 208.

34 J. Glete, *Navies*, p. 149. D. Goodman, *Spanish*, is brief about the 1590s. I. A. A. Thompson, *War and government*, pp. 191–195, 303–305 gives a summary of Spain's naval rearmament after 1588.

35 C. de La Roncière, *Histoire*, vol. 4, pp. 206–254.

36 R. B. Wernham, *The return*, pp. 259–261, 319.

37 R. Gray, 'Spinola's galleys in the Narrow Seas, 1599–1603', *Mariner's Mirror* 64, pp. 71–83, 1978.

38 R. B. Wernham, *The Return*, pp. 372–387.
39 This account is mainly based on R. B. Wernham, *After* and *The return* which put English naval and military history in its diplomatic and domestic policy context. A similar study of Spain is lacking.

10 THE FIRST GLOBAL WAR AT SEA, 1600–1650

1 J. I. Israel, *The Dutch Republic and the Hispanic world* is a major study of politics and warfare in the later phase of this conflict. It is supplemented by J. I. Israel, *Empires and entrepôts* and J. I. Israel, *Conflicts of empires: Spain, the Low Countries and the struggle for world supremacy, 1585–1713* (London, 1997). Other important works on this war: J. Alcalá-Zamora, *Espana*; J. H. Elliott, *The Count-Duke of Olivares: The statesman in an age of decline* (New Haven, 1986) and M. C. 't Hart, *The making*. General about the period: R. Bonney, *The European*, pp. 188–241; R. A. Stradling, *Europe and the decline of Spain: A study of the Spanish system, 1580–1720* (London, 1981); G. Parker, *The Thirty Years' War* (London, 1984).
2 J. H. Kernkamp, *De handel op den vijand, 1572–1609*, 2 vols (Utrecht, 1931–34); J. I. Israel, *The Dutch Republic and the Hispanic world*; J. I. Israel, *Dutch primacy*; V. Enthoven, *Zeeland*; J de Vries and A. van der Woude, *The first modern economy*, pp. 350–408. Problems with Dutch trade statistics: J. T. Lindblad, 'Foreign trade of the Dutch Republic in the seventeenth century', in *The Dutch economy in the Golden Age: Nine studies*, K. Davids and L. Noordegraaf (eds), (Amsterdam, 1993), pp. 219–249.
3 J. Alcalá-Zamora, *Espana*, esp. pp. 178–186; J. I. Israel, 'Spain, the Spanish embargoes, and the struggle for mastery of world trade, 1585–1660', in J. I. Israel, *Empires and entrepôts*, pp. 189–212. The self-destructive effect of the embargoes on the Iberian economy has never been properly evaluated.
4 J. I. Israel, *Dutch primacy*, pp. 12–196.
5 Dutch, Spanish and Portuguese economy and state formation: P. W. Klein, *De Trippen*; N. Steensgaard, *The Asian trade revolution*; J. Alcalá-Zamora, *Espana*; J. C. Boyajian, *Portuguese trade*; M. C. 't Hart, *The making*; C. Lesger and L. Noordegraaf, *Entrepreneurs and entrepreneurship in early modern times: Merchants and industrialists within the orbit of the Dutch staple market* (The Hague, 1995). J. I. Israel, *The Dutch Republic and the Hispanic world* is fundamental as a comparative work in how politics and economy interacted in two states. A brief but comprehensive article: S. B. Schwartz, 'The voyage of the vassals: Royal power, noble obligations, and merchant capital before the Portuguese restoration of independence, 1624–1640', *American History Review*, 97, pp. 735–762, 1991.
6 This interpretation is inspired by C. Tilly, *Capital*.
7 This section is based on J. I. Israel, *The Dutch Republic and the Hispanic world*; C. Fernandez Duro, *Armada espanola*, vols 3–4; N. Mac Leod, De *Oost-Indische*; C. R. Boxer, 'Anglo-Portuguese rivalry in the Persian Gulf, 1615–1635', in C. R. Boxer, *Portuguese conquest and commerce in Southern Asia, 1500–1750* (Aldershot, 1985, orig. publ. 1935); C. R. Boxer, *The Dutch in Brazil*; C. C. Goslinga, *The Dutch*; S. Subrahmanyam, *The Portuguese empire*; J. C. Boyajian, *Portuguese Trade*. Pacific aspects: O. H. K. Spate, *Monopolists and Freebooters* (London, 1983). Convoys and shipping: P. and H. Chaunu, *Seville*; J. R. Bruijn, F. S. Gaastra and I. Schöffer, *Dutch-Asiatic shipping in the 17th and 18th centuries*, 3 vols (The Hague, 1979–87).

The main Portuguese work on the war in the East, A. Botelho de Sousa, *Subsidios para a história militar marítima da India, 1585–1650*, 4 vols (Lisbon, 1936–56) has not been available to me.
8 See Chapter 5.
9 M. A. P. Meilink-Roelofsz, *Asian trade*, pp. 173–294, esp. p. 182.

10 S. Subrahmanyam, *The Portuguese empire*, p. 142, 163; J. C. Boyajian, *Portuguese trade*. p. 41, 130, 203.

11 J. R. Bruijn *et al.*, *Dutch-Asiatic shipping*, vol. 1, pp. 75, 91.

12 J. C. Boyajian, *Portuguese trade*, esp. pp. 23–24, 92–93, 96–99, 106–110, 123–127, 197–198.

13 N. Mac Leod, *De Oost-Indische*, pp. 159–167, O. H. K. Spate, *Monopolists*, pp. 15–21.

14 J. C. Boyajian, *Portuguese trade*, pp. 156–157.

15 C. R. Boxer, *The great ship*, pp. 90–171.

16 W. Voorbeijtel Cannenburg, *De reis om de wereld van de Nassausche vloot, 1623–1626* (The Hague, 1964).

17 C. R. Boxer, 'Anglo-Portuguese'; N. Steensgaard, *The Asian trade revolution*, pp. 331–353.

18 E. Sluiter, 'Dutch-Spanish rivalry in the Caribbean area, 1594–1609', *Hispanic American Historical Review*, 27, pp. 165–196, 1948.

19 S. B. Schwartz, 'The voyage of the vassals', *American Historical Review* 97, pp. 735–762, 1991.

20 M. G. de Boer, *Piet Heyn en de zilveren vloot* (Amsterdam, 1946).

21 C. R. Boxer, *The Dutch in Brazil*; E. Cabral de Mello, *Olinda restaurada: Guerra e açúcar no Nordeste, 1630–1654* (Sao Paulo, 1975).

22 C. R. Boxer, 'The action between Pater and Oquendo, 12 September 1631', *Mariner's Mirror* 45, pp. 179–199, 1959.

23 K. R. Andrews, *Trade, plunder*, pp. 300–303.

24 C. R. Phillips, *Six Galleons*, pp. 181–222 is unusual in giving a logistically oriented analysis of this struggle.

25 C. R. Boxer 'The surprisal of Goa's bar', *Mariner's Mirror* 16, pp. 5–17, 1930.

26 C. R. Boxer, *The Dutch in Brazil*, pp. 204–245; W. J. van Hoboken, *Witte de With in Brazilië, 1648–1649* (Amsterdam, 1955).

27 F. Pollentier, *De Admiraliteit en de oorlog ter zee onder de Aartsherogen, 1596–1609* (Brussels, 1972); A. P. van Vliet, *Vissers*.

28 This section is based on J. I. Israel, *The Dutch Republic and the Hispanic world*; C. Fernandez Duro, *Armada espanola*, vols 3–4; J. Alcalá-Zamora, *Espana*; R. A. Stradling, *The Armada of Flanders*; E. Otero Lana, *Los corsarios espanoles durante la decadencia de los Austrias: El corso espanol del Atlántico peninsular en el siglo XVII, 1621–1697* (Madrid, 1992); A. P. van Vliet, *Vissers* and R. Baetens, 'The organisation and effects of Flemish privateering in the seventeenth century', *Acta historiae neerlandicae* 9, pp. 48–75, 1976. The operational history of the Dutch navy before 1652 is little studied, except for a number of biographies of admirals.

29 N. A. M. Rodger, *The safeguard*, pp. 347–363; H. Winkel-Rauws, *Nederlandsch-Engelsche samenwerking in de spaansche wateren, 1625–1627* (Amsterdam, 1946).

30 C. de La Roncière, *Histoire*, vol. 4, pp. 425–629; D. Parker, *La Rochelle and the French monarchy: Conflict and order in seventeenth-century France* (London, 1980), esp pp. 74–82; P. Castagnos, *Richelieu face à la mer* (Rennes, 1989); N. A. M. Rodger, *The safeguard*, pp 347–363. Size of the navies: J. Glete, *Navies*, pp. 125–133.

31 C. R. Boxer, 'War and trade in the Indian Ocean and the South China Sea, 1600–1650', *Mariner's Mirror* 70, p. 421, 1984, J. Alcalá-Zamora, *Espana*, pp. 236–242; J. C. Boyajian, *Portuguese trade*, pp. 185–201.

32 R. A. Stradling, *The Armada*, pp. 158–162.

33 When from 1662 Dunkirk became a French port the French construction of light and swift warships, *fregates*, was concentrated here into the eighteenth century. A strong local tradition of special skill and close connections with privateering must be the explanation.

34 This section is based on J. I. Israel, *The Dutch Republic and the Hispanic world*; C. Fernandez Duro, *Armada espanola*, vol. 4; C. de La Roncière, *Histoire*, vol. 5, pp.

1–178; M. G. de Boer, *Het proefjaar van Maarten Harpertsz. Tromp, 1637–1639* (Amsterdam, 1946); M. G. de Boer, *Tromp en de Duinkerkers* (Amsterdam, 1949); J. Alcalá-Zamora, *Espana;* R. A. Stradling, *The Armada;* R. C. Anderson, 'The Thirty Year's War in the Mediterranean', *Mariner's Mirror* 55, pp. 435–451, 1969, 56, pp. 41–57, 1970 compares French and Spanish accounts of battles in 1635–48.

35 R. A. Stradling, *The Armada,* pp. 102–104.

36 C. R. Boxer (ed.), *The Journal of Maarten Harpertszoon Tromp, Anno 1639* (Cambridge, 1930); M. G. de Boer, *Tromp en de Armada van 1639* (Amsterdam, 1941); J. Alcalá-Zamora, *Espana,* pp. 402–464.

37 Spanish strength: J. Alcalá-Zamora, *Espana,* pp. 429–434. Displacement calculations have been made by the present author, based on the assumption that Spanish tonnage measured in *tonelada* can be converted into displacement in tonnes by a multiplier of 1.4 to 1.5. This assumption is based on dimensions and tonnages for Spanish warships listed in C. Rahn Phillips, *Six galleons,* pp. 228–230 and D. Goodman *Spanish naval power,* pp. 269–273.

38 K. R. Andrews, *Ships, money and politics: Seafaring and naval enterprise in the reign of Charles I* (Cambridge, 1991), pp. 128–159; H. Taylor, 'Trade, neutrality, and the "English Road", 1630–1648', *Economic History Review* 2nd ser. 25, pp. 236–260.

39 J. Alcalá-Zamora, *Espana,* esp. pp. 42–44.

40 The complicated relations between the Dutch, the Spanish-Flemish forces, and the English Royalist and Parliamentarian naval forces: S. Groenveld, *Verlopend getij: De Nederlandse Republiek en de Engelse Burgeroorlog, 1640–1646* (Dieren, 1984).

41 J. R. Powell, *The navy in the English Civil War* (London, 1962); N. A. M. Rodger, *The safeguard,* pp. 411–426, R. Brenner, *Merchants;* J. Glete, *Navies,* pp. 173–252.

SELECT BIBLIOGRAPHY

This bibliography concentrates on books and articles about naval and maritime history covering the period 1500 to 1650. Works which are mentioned only once in the notes are normally omitted. Studies about a certain subject or a certain region can be found in the notes to the relevant chapter. Some old studies and works of a more general character have been included if they provide information about conflicts at sea not otherwise available.

Acerra, M. and Martinière, G. (eds) *Coligny, les protestants et la mer* (Paris, 1997)

Alcalá-Zamora y Queipo de Llano, J. *Espana, Flandes y el Mar del norte, 1618–1639* (Barcelona, 1975)

Anderson, R. C. *Naval wars in the Baltic, 1522–1850* (London, 1910, 1969)

Anderson, R. C. *Naval wars in the Levant, 1559–1853* (Liverpool, 1952)

Andrews, K. R. *The Spanish Caribbean: Trade and plunder, 1530–1630* (New Haven, 1978)

Andrews, K. R. *Trade, plunder and settlement: Maritime enterprise and the genesis of the British empire, 1480–1630* (Cambridge, 1984)

Attman, A. *The struggle for Baltic markets: Powers in conflict, 1558–1618* (Gothenburg, 1979)

Barfod, J. H. *Flådens födsel* (Copenhagen, 1990)

Barfod, J. H. *Christian 3.s flåde, 1533–1588* (Copenhagen, 1995)

Benzioni, G. (ed.) *Il Mediterraneo nella seconda metà det '500 alla luce di Lepanto* (Florence, 1974)

Boer, M. G. de *Tromp en de armada van 1639* (Amsterdam, 1941)

Bonney, R. *The European dynastic states, 1494–1660* (Oxford, 1991)

Boxer, C. R. *The Dutch in Brazil, 1624–1654* (Oxford, 1957)

Boxer, C. R. *The Great Ship from Amacon: Annals of Macao and the Old Japan trade, 1555–1640* (Lisbon, 1959)

Boxer, C. R. *The Portuguese seaborne empire, 1415–1825* (Harmondsworth, 1973)

Boxer, C. R. *Portuguese conquest and commerce in Southern Asia, 1500–1750* (Aldershot, 1985)

Boyajian, J. C. *Portuguese trade in Asia under the Habsburgs, 1580–1640* (Baltimore, 1993)

Bradford, E. *The Sultan's admiral: The life of Barbarossa* (London, 1969)

Braudel, F. *The Mediterranean and the Mediterranean world in the age of Philip II*, 2 vols (London, 1972–73)

Brenner, R. *Merchants and revolution: Commercial change, political conflict, and London over-*

seas traders, 1550–1653 (Cambridge, 1993)

Bruijn, J. R. *The Dutch navy of the seventeenth and eighteenth centuries* (Columbia, 1993)

Bruijn, J. R., Gaastra, F. S. and Schöffer, I. *Dutch-Asiatic shipping in the 17th and 18th centuries*, 3 vols (The Hague, 1979–87)

Brummett, P. *Ottoman seapower and Levantine diplomacy in the Age of Discovery* (Albany, 1994)

Buchet, C. *La lutte pour l'espace caraïbe et le façade Atlantique de l'Amerique central et du Sud, 1672–1763*, 2 vols (Paris, 1991)

Casado Soto, J. L. *Los barcos espanoles del siglo XVI y la Gran armada de 1588* (Madrid, 1988)

Cerezo Martinez, R. *Las armadas de Felipe II* (Madrid, 1988)

Chaunu, P. and Chaunu, H. *Seville et l'Atlantique, 1504–1650*, 11 vols (Paris, 1955–59)

Cipolla, C. *Guns and sails in the early phase of European expansion* (London, 1965)

Course et piraterie, 2 vols (Mimeo. Paris, 1975)

Diffie, B. W. and Winius, G. D. *Foundations of the Portuguese empire, 1415–1580* (Minneapolis, 1977)

Dollinger, P. *The German Hansa* (London, 1970)

Enthoven, V. *Zeeland en de opkomst van de Republiek: Handel en strijd in de Scheldedelta, c. 1550–1621* (Leiden, 1996)

Faroqhi, S. *et al. An economic and social history of the Ottoman empire: vol. 2, 1600–1914* (Cambridge, 1994)

Fernandez Duro, C. *Armada espanola desde la unión de los reinos de Castilla y de Aragón*, vols 1–4 (Madrid, 1895–98, 1972)

Fritze, K. and Krause, G. *Seekriege der Hanse: Das erste Kapitel deutscher Seekriegsgeschichte* (Berlin, 1997)

Gardiner, R. and Morrison, J. (eds) *The age of the galley: Mediterranean oared vessels since pre-classical times* (London, 1995)

Gardiner, R. and Unger, R. W. (eds) *Cogs, caravels and galleons: The sailing ship, 1000–1650* (London, 1994)

Glete, J. 'Svenska örlogsfartyg 1521–1560: Flottans uppbyggnad under ett tekniskt brytningsskede', *Forum Navale* 30, pp. 5–74, 1976; 31, pp. 23–119, 1977

Glete, J. *Navies and nations: Warships, navies and state building in Europe and America, 1500–1860*, 2 vols (Stockholm, 1993)

Goodman, D. *Spanish naval power, 1589–1665: Reconstruction and defeat* (Cambridge, 1997)

Goslinga, C. C. *The Dutch in the Caribbean and on the Wild Coast, 1580–1680* (Assen, 1971)

Guilmartin, Jr, J. F. *Gunpowder and galleys: Changing technology and Mediterranean warfare at sea in the sixteenth century* (Cambridge, 1974)

Guilmartin, Jr, J. F. 'The tactics of the battle of Lepanto clarified: The impact of social, economic, and political factors on sixteenth century galley warfare', in *New aspects of naval history*, Craig L. Symonds (ed.) (Annapolis, 1981), pp. 41–65

't Hart, M. C. *The making of a bourgeois state: War, politics and finance during the Dutch revolt* (Manchester, 1994)

Hebb, D. D. *Piracy and the English government, 1616–1642* (Aldershot, 1994)

Hess, A. C. 'The evolution of the Ottoman seaborne empire in the Age of the oceanic discoveries, 1453–1525', *American Historical Review* 75, pp. 1892–1919, 1970

Hess, A. C. *The forgotten frontier: A history of the sixteenth-century Ibero-African frontier* (Chicago, 1978)

217

Hoffman, P. E. *The Spanish crown and the defense of the Caribbean, 1535–1585: Precedent, patrimonialism and royal parsimony* (Baton Rouge, 1980)

Imber, C. H. 'The navy of Süleyman the Magnificent', *Archivum Ottomanicum* **6**, pp. 211–282, 1980

Inalcik, H. 'The socio-political effects of the diffusion of firearms in the Middle East'. In *War, technology and society in the Middle East*, V. J. Parry and M. E. Yapp (eds), (Oxford, 1975)

Inalcik, H. *An economic and social history of the Ottoman Empire*, vol. 1, *1300–1600* (Cambridge, 1994)

Israel, J. I. *The Dutch Republic and the Hispanic world, 1606–1661* (Oxford, 1982)

Israel, J. I. *Dutch primacy in world trade* (Oxford, 1989)

Israel, J. I. *Empires and entrepôts: The Dutch, the Spanish monarchy and the Jews, 1585–1713* (London, 1990)

Kirk, T. A. *Genoa and the sea: Ships and power in the early modern Mediterranean, 1559–1680* (PhD thesis, European University Institute, Florence, 1996)

Klein, P. W. *De Trippen in de 17e eeuw: Een studie over het ondernemergedrag op de hollandse stapelmarkt* (Assen, 1965)

La Roncière, C. de *Histoire de la marine francaise*, vols 2–5 (Paris, 1900–20)

Lane, F. C. *Navires et constructeurs á Venise pendant la Renaissance* (Paris, 1965)

Lane, F. C. *Venice: A maritime republic* (Baltimore, 1973)

Lane, F. C. *Profits from power: Readings in protection rent and violence-controlling enterprise* (Albany, 1979)

Lavery, B. *The ship of the line*, 2 vols (London, 1983–84)

Lavery, B. *The arming and fitting of English ships of war, 1600–1815* (London, 1987)

Mac Leod, N. *De Oost-Indische Compagnie als zeemogeenheid in Azië, 1602–1650*, 2 vols (Rijswijk, 1927)

Magalhaes Godinho, V. *Os descobrimentos e a economia mundial*, 4 vols (2nd edn, Lisbon, 1981–83)

Manfroni, C. *Storia della marina italiana dalla caduta di Constantinopoli alla battaglia di Lepanto* (Milano, 1897, 1970)

Maritieme geschiedenis der Nederlanden, vols 1–2 (Bussum, 1976–77)

Martin, C. *Full fathom five: Wrecks of the Spanish armada* (London, 1975)

Martin, C. and Parker, G. *The Spanish armada* (London, 1988)

Masson, Ph. and Vergé-Franceschi, M. *La France et la mer au siècle des grandes découvertes* (Paris, 1993)

Mauro, F. *Le Portugal et l'Atlantique au XVIIe siècle, 1570–1670* (Paris, 1960)

McNeill, W. H. *The pursuit of power: Technology, armed force and society since A.D. 1000* (Oxford, 1983)

Meilink-Roelofsz, M. A. P. *Asian trade and European influence in the Indonesian archipelago between 1500 and about 1630* (The Hague, 1962)

Mortensen, M. H. *Dansk Artilleri indtil 1600* (Copenhagen, 1999)

Nani Mocenigo, M. *Storia della marina veneziana de Lepanto alla caduta della Repubblica* (Rome, 1935)

Olesa Munido, F.-F. *La organizacion naval de los estados Mediterraneos y en especial de Espana durante los siglos XVI y XVII*, 2 vols (Madrid, 1968)

Padfield, P. *Guns at sea* (London, 1973)

Padfield, P. *Tide of Empires: Decisive naval campaigns in the rise of the West*, vol. 1: *1481–1654* (London, 1979)

Park, Yune-hee *Admiral Yi Sun-shin and his turtleboat armada: A comprehensive account of the resistance of Korea to the 16th century Japanese invasion* (Seoul, 1973)

Parker, G. *The Military Revolution: Military innovation and the rise of the West, 1500–1800* (Cambridge, 1988)

Pazzis Pi Corrales, M. de *Felipe II y la lucha por el dominio del mar* (Madrid, 1989)

Pearson, M. N. *The Portuguese in India* (Cambridge, 1987)

Pérez-Mallaína, P. E. *Spain's men of the sea: Daily life on the Indies fleets in the sixteenth century* (Baltimore, 1998)

Pierson, P. *Commander of the Armada: The seventh duke of Medina Sidonia* (New Haven, 1989)

Pimentel Barrata, J. da Gama *Estudos de arqueologia naval,* 2 vols (Lisbon, 1989)

Probst, N. M. *Christian 4.s flåde, 1588–1660* (Copenhagen, 1996)

Ragosta, R. (ed.) *Le genti del mare Mediterraneo,* 2 vols (Naples, 1981)

Rahn Phillips, C. *Six galleons for the King of Spain: Imperial defense in the early seventeenth century* (Baltimore, 1986)

Rodger, N. A. M. 'The development of broadside gunnery, 1450–1650', *Mariner's Mirror* 82, pp. 301–324, 1996

Rodger, N. A. M. *The safeguard of the sea: A naval history of Britain: vol. 1, 660–1649* (London, 1997)

Rodríguez-Salgado, M. J. and Adams, S. (eds) *England, Spain and the Gran Armada, 1585–1604* (Edinburgh, 1991)

Rodríguez-Salgado, M. J. (ed.) *Armada, 1588–1988: An international exhibition to commemorate the Spanish Armada* (London, 1988)

Scammell, G. V. *The world encompassed: The first European maritime empires, c. 800–1650* (London, 1981)

Sicking, L. *Zeemacht en onmacht: Maritieme politiek in de Nederlanden, 1488–1558* (Amsterdam, 1998)

Spate, O. H. K. *The Spanish lake* (Minneapolis, 1979)

Spate, O. H. K. *Monopolists and freebooters* (London, 1983)

Steensgaard, N. *The Asian trade revolution of the seventeenth century* (Chicago, 1974)

Stradling, R. A. *The Armada of Flanders: Spanish maritime policy and European war, 1568–1665* (Cambridge, 1992)

Subrahmanyam, S. *The Portuguese empire in Asia, 1500–1700: A political and economic history* (London, 1993)

Svenska flottans historia, vol. 1, 1521–1679 (Malmö, 1942)

Sveriges Krig, 1611–1632: Bilagsband I, Sveriges Sjökrig, 1611–1632 (Stockholm, 1937)

Teitler, G. *The genesis of the modern officer corps* (London, 1977)

Tenenti, A. *Cristoforo Da Canal: La marine Vénitienne avant Lepante* (Paris, 1962)

Tenenti, A. *Piracy and the decline of Venice, 1580–1615* (Berkeley, 1967)

Thompson, I. A. A. *War and government in Habsburg Spain, 1560–1620* (London, 1976)

Tilly, C. *Coercion, capital, and European states, AD 990–1990* (Oxford, 1990)

Tracy. J. D. (ed.) *The rise of merchant empires: Long-distance trade in the early modern world, 1350–1750* (Cambridge, 1990)

Tracy. J. D. (ed.) *The political economy of merchant empires* (Cambridge, 1991)

Unger, R. W. *The ship in the medieval economy, 600–1600* (London, 1980)

Wallerstein, I. *The modern world-system, vols 1–2* (New York, 1974–80)

Weber, R. E. J. 'Met smakzeilen en spiegelschepen tegen den Spanjaard', in J. Romein et al., *De Tachtigjarige oorlog* (Amsterdam, 1941), pp. 132–158

Vergé-Francheschi, M. *Marine et education sous l'ancien régime* (Paris, 1991)

Wernham, R. B. *After the armada: Elizabethan England and the struggle for Western Europe, 1588–1595* (Oxford, 1984)

Wernham, R. B. *The return of the armadas: The last years of the Elizabethan war against Spain, 1595–1603* (Oxford, 1994)

Vliet, A. P. van *Vissers en kapers: De zeevisserij vanuit het Maasmondgebied en de Duinkerker kapers (c. 1570–1648)* (The Hague, 1994)

Vries, J. de and Woude, A. van der *The first modern economy: Success, failure and perseverance of the Dutch economy, 1500–1815* (Cambridge, 1997)

Zettersten, A. *Svenska flottans historia, 1522–1680*, 2 vols (Stockholm and Norrtälje, 1890–1903)

INDEX

Printed in the United Kingdom
by Lightning Source UK Ltd.
131636UK00003B/41/A

9 780415 214551